P9-CRS-505

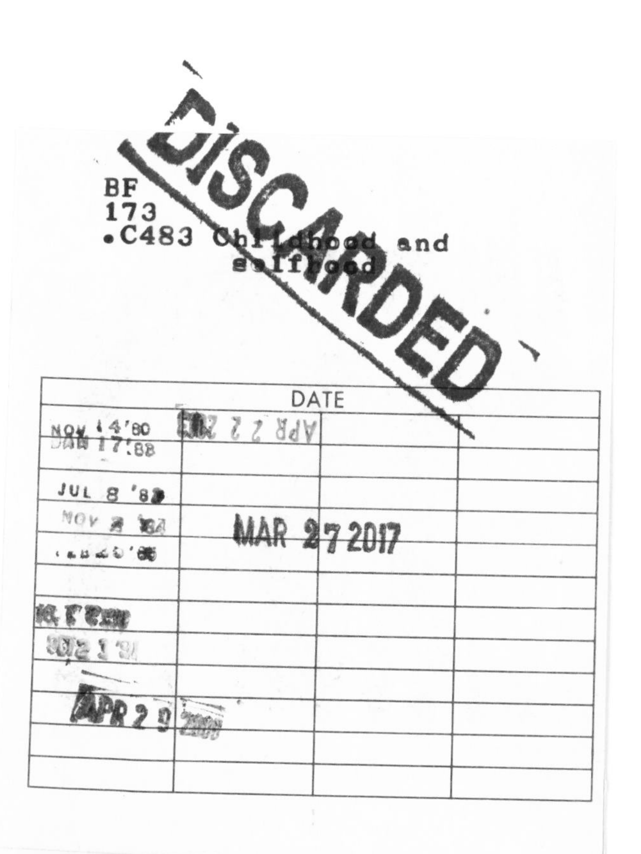
BF
173
.C483 Childhood and
selfhood
DISCARDED
DATE
MAR 27 2017

Childhood and Selfhood

ESSAYS ON
TRADITION, RELIGION, AND MODERNITY
IN THE PSYCHOLOGY OF
ERIK H. ERIKSON

Also by PETER HOMANS:

The Dialogue between Theology and Psychology (editor and contributor)
Theology after Freud: An Interpretive Inquiry

Childhood and Selfhood

ESSAYS ON TRADITION,
RELIGION, AND MODERNITY
IN THE PSYCHOLOGY OF
ERIK H. ERIKSON

Edited with an Introduction by Peter Homans

Lewisburg
Bucknell University Press
London: Associated University Presses

Associated University Presses, Inc.
Cranbury, New Jersey 08512

Associated University Presses
Magdalen House
136–148 Tooley Street
London SE1 2TT, England

Library of Congress Cataloging in Publication Data
Main entry under title:

Childhood and selfhood.

Includes bibliographical references.
CONTENTS: Homans, P. Introduction.—pt. 1. Erikson's psychology and religion. Bornkamm, H., translated by C. Stauder. Luther and his father. Edwards, M. U., Jr. Erikson, experimental psychology, and Luther's identity. Appadurai, A. Understanding Gandhi.—pt. 2. Erikson's psychology and methodology. Kracke, W. H. A psychoanalyst in the field. Capps, D. Psychohistory and historical genres.—pt. 3. Erikson's psychology and modernity. Homans, P. The significance of Erikson's psychology for modern understandings of religion. Browning, D. Erikson and the search for a normative image of man.
1. Psychoanalysis. 2. Erikson, Erik Homburger, 1902– 3. Psychohistory. 4. Psychology, Religious. I. Homans, Peter.
BF173.C483 150'.19'52 77-74406
ISBN 0-8387-2093-5

PRINTED IN THE UNITED STATES OF AMERICA

Contents

Preface

At the present time the theory of psychoanalysis is roughly three-quarters of a century old. Since its appearance at the beginning of this century, it has developed in an increasingly rich, complex, and diversified way. However, while its foundations in clinical theory and practice have never been doubted, it has also engaged in the nonclinical interpretation of such cultural phenomena as art, religion, and historical movements. The truly creative figures in the psychoanalytic movement have always felt it necessary, and fully consistent with their calling, to interpret culture as well as clinical processes. As a result, humanists, the rightful occupants of the cultural disciplines, have entered more and more into discussion of the claims and interpretations of psychoanalysis. So there now exists, alongside the literature of psychoanalytic interpretation of culture, a literature of *cultural reflection on psychoanalysis.*

The work of Erik H. Erikson testifies to the creativity of interpretation inherent within the evolving tradition of psychoanalytic inquiry. Erikson has not only devoted his life to the elucidation of clinical concepts and processes, but he has also continually sought to explain broader, transclinical, cultural questions—questions of value and meaning not so readily apparent in the immediacies of clinical involvement. But in this he has not merely followed in the footsteps of Freud, himself, and of other innovative figures in the psychoanalytic movement. It is more correct to say that Erikson has broadened and extended this path into those preserves traditionally guarded and ruled by the humanities.

The purpose of this volume is to describe and assess Erikson's contribution to the nonclinical and more humanistic disciplines from the perspective of these disciplines—hence the first part of its title: childhood (the goal of the clinical thrust of psychoanalysis) and selfhood (those wider aspects of personal meaning, value, and significance usually associated with the humanities). My procedure in designing this volume was to locate individual scholars whose spheres of expertise encompassed those areas of humanistic study engaged by Erikson's transclinical work. I asked each scholar to write a paper that would describe and assess in as definitive a way as possible the significance of Erikson's thought for his academic specialty. Thus this volume belongs to that emerging body of literature that I have called cultural reflection on psychoanalysis.

Erikson's now-famous book on Luther is analyzed and evaluated both by a Protestant Reformation historian and by a secular Reformation historian. A scholar of Indian civilization discusses the study of Gandhi. A psychoanalytically trained anthropologist evaluates Erikson's contribution to the field of cultural anthropology. A psychohistorian assesses Erikson's significance for his discipline. And two scholars of religion review and evaluate the relevance of Erikson's total work for contemporary religious studies and for ethics. As might be expected, some of the essays are critical, and several center on particular problems within their discipline, but all strive for comprehensiveness. No existing publication on Erikson's thought attempts to review it thoroughly from the point of view of relevant, different disciplines.

While the contents of this volume are determined entirely by the various ways in which Erikson has addressed himself to problems of a transclinical nature, the arrangement of the essays within the volume as a whole derives from a very different principle. As is illustrated in the first section of the Introduction, which draws upon two major figures in the cultural reflection upon psychoanalysis, Philip Rieff and Paul Ricoeur, psychoanalysis is not only a clinical theory and a theory of culture but also a theory of modernity. While this judgment has been applied most compellingly to Freud's thought, it is even more applicable to the work of Erikson. For Erikson has been less reticent than Freud and his early followers in arguing that psychoanalysis is an important ingredient in modern man's self-understanding. Furthermore, Erikson has turned more forthrightly than did Freud to tradition and religion for his conception of the polar opposite of modernity. Hence, the essays in this volume are arranged in light of the theme of the tension between tradition and its most persistent form, religion, on the one hand, and modernity, on the other hand.

In addition to discussing the centrality of the problem of tradition and modernity in the psychoanalytic theory of culture both in the literature of cultural reflection on psychoanalysis and in Erikson's work, the Introduction also summarizes the contents of each essay and briefly notes the bearing of each on the tradition-modernity question. Accordingly, these essays are to be read not only as individual and self-contained studies analyzing Erikson's contributions to specific disciplines, but also as instances of the more general problem of tradition and modernity, as it bears upon Erikson's thought.

Acknowledgments

In the early stages of preparing this volume, I was greatly aided by the generous advice of several colleagues in my search for contributors, and I wish to thank them: Professor Robert Levine, now at Harvard University but at the time at the University of Chicago; Professor Benjamin Nelson of the New School for Social Research; Professor Lewis Spitz of Stanford University; and Professor Victor Turner of the University of Chicago. I am indebted to my colleague Professor Brian Gerrish of the University of Chicago for his helpful evaluation of translations of the article by Heinrich Bornkamm, and for securing its translator, Christoph Stauder. Some time after the preparations for this volume were underway, my colleague Professor Don Browning invited Erik Erikson to the University of Chicago for a two-day conference on Erikson's thought and suggested that several of the papers planned for this volume be presented at the conference for discussion. On behalf of their authors—Appadurai, Browning, Edwards, and Homans—I wish to thank Prof. Erikson for his generous commentary on these papers.

I also wish to thank the following publishers for permission to quote from published works:

Faber and Faber, Ltd., for permission to quote from

Erik H. Erikson, *Gandhi's Truth: On the Origins of Militant Nonviolence*, 1969.

Harper & Row, Publishers, for permission to quote from Theodore K. Rabb and Robert I. Rotberg, eds., *The Family in History*, 1971.

J. C. B. Mohr (Paul Sieback), for permission to reprint Heinrich Bornkamm, "Luther and His Father: Observations on Erik H. Erikson's *Young Man Luther: A Study in Psychoanalysis and History*," which first appeared in German as "Luther und sein Vater: Bemerkungen zu Erik Erikson," in *Zeitschrift fur Theologie und Kirche* 66 (1969), 1: 38–61. It appears here in English translation for the first time. Reprinted also by permission of Professor Bornkamm.

W. W. Norton & Company, Inc., for permission to quote from Erik H. Erikson, *Childhood and Society*, 2d ed., 1963.

W. W. Norton & Company, Inc., for permission to quote from Erik H. Erikson, *Gandhi's Truth: On the Origins of Militant Nonviolence*, 1969.

Introduction

I

Since its inception at the turn of the century, psychoanalysis has come to be increasingly well known and accepted throughout western Europe and the United States, especially. Once a nucleus of innovative ideas, it has unfolded into a variety of revisions, transformations, and even alternatives to itself. Once a controversial theory of the mind and its abnormalities, it offers to the contemporary person a series of principle ideas that range in content and import all the way from a cure for neurosis to a charismatically informed orientation toward the modern world. And, once the sole property of a small group of gifted men, it has made its way into such areas as entertainment, the press, and politics, and in doing so has become part of the fabric of everyday existence, a series of vague and unorganized assumptions about contemporary social life.

It is difficult to recognize clarity and continuity in the midst of this proliferation of schools, orientations, and attitudes. And it is hardly surprising that the intellectual status of psychoanalytic ideas remains undetermined. Many disciplines have made serious efforts to clarify the character of psychoanalytic thought. Philosophers have studied the scientific and epistemological claims of psychoanalysis; some historians and theologians have claimed that it is an ideology or secular belief system; and sociologists have examined the social forces that underlie the formation of its ideas and institutions. But these discussions incorporate much of the amorphous quality that characterizes the phenomenon that such people are attempting to analyze and order.

Those who wish to explore such a situation had better be cautious, and are well-advised to restrict their reflection to whatever points of clarity may already exist. It is quite evident that, despite the plurality of psychodynamic orientations at play in our society today, the psychoanalytic psychologies, conceived broadly, constitute a substantial, single group. The literature on these psychologies falls into two easily definable categories: the scientific-clinical discussion and the nonclinical or transclinical—what I prefer to call the humanistic or cultural—discussion. The first attempts to analyze personality, therapy, and culture from a perspective within the psychoanalytic psychology itself. The second attempts to assess the cultural significance of the psychoanalytic psychology.

The essays in this volume are addressed to the second issue—the cultural or humanistic dimensions of psychoanalysis. They explore the various ways in which we can understand the significance of the psychoanalytic psychology as a phenomenon expressive of modern life. While such is the general intention of these essays—the cultural significance of psychoanalysis provides their context, so to speak—their specific and particular goal is an examination of this issue through the writings of one of the most prominent and articulate men in psychoanalysis today, Erik H. Erikson.

There are several reasons why Erikson's work is especially congenial to this task. Erikson is deeply committed to classical psychoanalysis. Again and again he recurs to the Freudian texts, drawing upon them almost exclusively, with little debt to any other originative figures in the psychoanalytic movement. Thus, an assessment of Erikson's work is, from the beginning, a reflection upon the current status of the original themes of psychoanalytic thought. But Erikson also possesses outstanding qualifications as a "bridge figure" in the psychoanalytic movement. Much of the excitement and appeal of his work lies in its ability to relate classical psychoanalysis to nonpsychological or cultural questions; questions of history, religion, and ethics all fall within the purview of his synthesizing perceptions. Writers in these fields who are interested in psychoanalysis are naturally attracted to Erikson, who has opened his discipline to their questions. Through Erikson the interdisciplinary potential of psychoanalysis is made especially evident.

Erikson not only applies psychoanalysis to other, nonpsychological areas of inquiry and understanding, but also reflects upon the cultural significance of psychoanalysis. The fact that he was at first an artist and later a psychoanalyst makes it seem only natural that Erikson should share with the originators of psychoanalysis a strong interest in its "applications." But Erikson joins this feature of early psychoanalysis with recent efforts of some in the humanities to analyze the significance of psychoanalysis for modernity as a whole. Erikson not only applies psychoanalysis, arousing interdisciplinary inquiry, but also reflects upon his applications from the perspective of what is distinctively transpsychological about his science. In this he makes humanistic reflection on psychoanalysis more possible—and more necessary.

But Erikson is not a revisionist; he is not a "neo-Freudian." Despite his loyalty to Freud, he stands out not as a mere corrective to Freud, but as a truly innovative figure. He has accomplished a transformation of Freud's thought, while at the same time informing the lay public about an otherwise technical and abstruse terminology, the conceptual legacy of psychoanalysis. Therefore, in addition to his work in carrying forward psychoanalytic theory, Erikson has established himself as a contemporary thinker of independence and originality. There exists as yet no substantial discussion of the wider, nonclinical, and cultural significance of Erikson's work.

But how does one render manageable a discussion of so

broad an issue as the cultural significance of psychoanalysis, and in particular, of Erikson's work? Two major trends, briefly alluded to already, form the basis of such a discussion: the formation of the psychoanalytic psychology of culture, and the accompanying emergence of cultural reflection upon psychoanalysis. Uniting these two trends are several major themes—themes that originate in Freud's thought, which stands at the beginning of this discussion, and that culminate in Erikson's thought, which stands, so to speak, at the end of the discussion. In other words, the purpose of this introduction is to identify several major trends in Freud's "application" of psychoanalysis to culture, to show how these trends are taken up by the literature of cultural reflection on psychoanalysis, and then to relate both to Erikson's thought. Such a discussion provides the context for the essays that follow. Lest the reader think that such an analysis is less than substantive, I can only offer the sober reminder that psychoanalysis has yet to find a thoroughly congenial "home" for itself, either in contemporary traditions of inquiry or in contemporary institutional life.

It is generally accepted that a specific cluster of concepts lies at the heart of Freud's psychoanalysis: the *unconscious, repression, transference,* the *Oedipus complex,* and the like. Ernest Jones points out that Freud juxtaposed these "primary" processes to the "secondary" processes of ordinary thinking.[1] The mind constantly arbitrates a debate between these two psychic modalities as it attempts to cope with the routine demands of everyday life.[2] A discussion of the cultural or humanistic significance of psychoanalysis requires that these processes, so central to psychoanalysis, be situated in a context that also relates them to the personal, to the distinctly human, to the self. If we view society as the locus of everyday valuing, and if we then take the notion of the human self to refer to these wider ranges of meaning, which include history, art, and religion, then it is correct to say that Freud's thought betrays a preoccupation not only with the tensions between childhood and society, but also with the interface between childhood and selfhood. In his clinical investigations, Freud, in effect, developed a methodology that allowed him to discover and describe the elaborate mechanisms whereby childhood wishes and fears persisted unnoticed—not only into society, but also into the life of the adult self, engaged as it was in construing in a total way the nature of both value and meaning.

Whenever Freud turned to the analysis of culture, he searched for evidence of the persistence of childhood into selfhood—whether it was the child of the artist, the child of the collective, or the child of an entire civilization. But he did not choose to cast these investigations in so simple a way. The theme of childhood, while ever-present, took the form of different ideas or types of questions. I have chosen to conceptualize Freud's writings on culture in terms of three issues, or themes or polarities. While Freud did not literally speak of these themes, they are nevertheless implicit in his work and, when recognized, give coherence to his cultural writings as a whole. This is true both of his shorter papers on art and religion as well as of his longer monographs addressed to the problem of the meaning of civilization and modernity. The validity of this choice of themes is given further support by the fact that they have been taken up by the cultural reflection upon the meaning of psychoanalysis for modernity, and also by the fact that they reappear with even greater visibility in the writings of Erikson himself. Finally, it is possible to claim that these three themes in turn combine to give expression to a single, privileged theme that captures the essence of psychoanalytic reflection upon culture, the theme of the tension between religion and modernity.

Freud's writings indicate three major preoccupations: (1) the theme of tension between the demands of tradition and the necessities of modernity; (2) the theme of tension between personal fulfillment and an oppressive social order; and (3) the theme of the inevitability of tension between religion and science—psychoanalytic science, in particular. Each theme is grounded in the prior, clinically derived tension between childhood and selfhood, and in turn combines into the very comprehensive, privileged theme of tension between religion and modernity. How do these themes work out in Freud's thought, in the cultural reflection on psychoanalysis, and in Erikson's work?

Freud's psychology was at once a clinical psychology and a psychology of culture. It has become customary to divide his psychological writings into three major periods: the early and formative period of 1890 to 1900; the middle or metapsychological period of 1910 to 1923; and the later, cultural period, consisting of a more persistent concern with historical issues and extending from the early 1920s to the end of his life. While it is important to note that Freud wrote throughout his career about both clinical problems and culture, it is even more important to recognize that the last period produced the great monographs commonly referred to as the "cultural texts."

Of these writings three stand out: *Moses and Monotheism* (1939),[3] *Civilization and Its Discontents* (1930),[4] and *The Future of an Illusion* (1927).[5] To these some choose to add the essay "A Philosophy of Life" (in *New Introductory Lectures* [1933]),[6] the early anthropological effort, *Totem and Taboo* (1912),[7] the speculative *Beyond the Pleasure Principle* (1920),[8] and the partly cultural, partly metapsychological *Group Psychology and the Analysis of the Ego* (1921).[9] But the three outstanding texts engage the question of culture and civilization most directly and comprehensively, casting the specificities of the other texts in a broader framework. Each of these three books embodies all three themes, but each book also gives preeminence to one of these themes. Together they provide the main guidelines for Freud's assessment of culture. I will briefly note these themes and their texts, but not in chronological order of appearance, since nothing is gained by attempting to demonstrate that one theme may or may not have antedated another.

In *Moses and Monotheism* Freud is clearly and centrally preoccupied with the power of tradition in Hebrew-Christian culture. Through this book he expresses fascination with the way in which a tradition can emerge, become autonomous of its circumstances of emergence—transcending, so to speak, its origins—and finally turn back upon the people who created it, exerting power over them and coercing them to think and behave in certain ways. Equally clear is the fact that, in Freud's mind, the most interesting and imaginatively compelling tradition was the Hebraic tradition of monotheism and its transformation into the Christian tradition in the hands of St. Paul.

But Freud viewed tradition from the perspective of that which is nontraditional, that is, from the perspective of modernity. It is modernity that "sees through" the power and claims of the cultural forms of tradition. And the key instrument or tool for seeing through the power of the past is not simply science, but specifically the new science of psychoanalysis. So it is that such concepts as the *primal horde, latency,* and the *return of the repressed* advance the claims of modernity over those of tradition, for by means of them the psychoanalytic psychology seeks to free the modern mind from the claims of the ancient past.

Civilization and Its Discontents gives the theme of tradition and modernity a contemporary and sociological cast. Here Freud indulges his second great preoccupation, the tension between personal self-fulfillment and the coercive power of an oppressive social order. Through its institutions, role models, and ethical imperatives, society gains power over the individual, forcing him to give up satisfactions that, according to Freud at least, are rightfully his. Only science in the form of the psychoanalytic psychology can give the beleaguered individual the necessary distance from the social order that facilitates his capacity to resist successfully its oppressive efforts. Here Freud creates an analysis of the dynamics of the harsh, cultural superego in order to free the individual from the blind, excessively coercive power of society.

These historical and sociological tensions were paralleled in Freud's mind by an epistemological tension. Psychoanalysis is not only a perspective upon the past and upon the contemporary social order, but also a particular type of scientific thinking about the nature of the world. As such, it exists in an unalterable, inverse relation to religion. Religion, too, is a way of knowing the world, but its ways are diametrically opposed to those of science. Thus, insofar as science can win the day, it does so at the expense of religion—and vice versa. In behalf of the psychoanalytic view of the world, Freud adduced the reality principle and linked it to normal thinking and normal development, thereby juxtaposing it to the neurotic thinking and neurotic development of religion. This epistemological tension is the burden of *The Future of an Illusion*. In that text the theme of the tension between religion and science receives its fullest statement, despite the fact that it appears in many other places in Freud's work.

It is important to recognize that these three themes or tensions are of a similar order of significance in Freud's work and, further, that all three combine to create an even more fundamental tension—the tension between religion and modernity. For tradition acquires its power to influence whole peoples from religion, and it is religion that energizes and gives form to the oppressive social order. On the other hand, psychoanalysis is a psychological form of modernization. As such, it is a technique for freeing the modern person not only from the power of tradition, but also from all religion-oriented social constraint, and also from religiously inspired epistemologies. And in all three cases Freud grounds his criticism of religion and his affirmation of modernity in his analysis of the dynamics of childhood. Modern man is the man free from religion—free from the childhood that binds him to the power of the past, to an oppressive social order, and to a warped epistemology. The theme of religion and modernity is the central, overarching theme of Freud's cultural texts. Through these texts Freud not only articulates the psychoanalytic theory of culture; he also gives precedent to a second type of discussion—cultural reflection upon the significance of psychoanalysis.

Erikson's thought articulates these themes directly, although in his hands they undergo considerable modification. In such modification lies the essence of Erikson's creative transformation of Freud's thought and, in particular, of his diagnosis of modernity. But Erikson's thought cannot be fully understood by means of a comparison with Freud alone; rather, it must be set in the context of the development of psychoanalytic thought as a whole. This development, as already noted, has occurred at two levels: an evolution within psychoanalytic thought itself regarding the nature of culture, and the evolution, without the psychoanalytic theory of culture, of cultural reflection upon the significance of psychoanalysis. Erikson's thought participates in both of these developments. Indeed, it does much to unite them. His first major work, *Childhood and Society* (1950),[10] belongs to the psychoanalytic theory of culture, while his second work of significance, *Young Man Luther* (1958),[11] belongs in part to the category of cultural reflection on psychoanalysis. As Erikson's work develops, the overall theme of religion and modernity becomes increasingly more visible and culminates in *Gandhi's Truth* (1969).[12] Still, even in Erikson's thought, in which psychoanalysis becomes increasingly self-reflective, this privileged theme cannot be identified apart from the others.

It is customary to think of psychoanalytic theory as moving through several stages, and at each of these stages the themes already identified in Freud's writings are at work. To the first generation of writers belong such figures as Jung, Adler, Rank, Ferenczi, Abraham, and Jones. Their interest in culture follows very much the pattern of Freud's own work. While a study of the interplay of the several themes in their work would be instructive, it is sufficient to note, in passing, that they accentuate very heavily the tension between tradition and modernity. Like Freud, they argue that psychoanalysis is an inevitable alternative to traditional ways of understanding. The tension between personal fulfillment and a coercive social order is less evident (except in the case of Jung), and the conflict between religion and science is a particularly potent assumption in almost every case.

The balance of emphasis among the three themes shifts considerably in the case of the neo-Freudian school of psychoanalytic thinkers. Horney[13] and Sullivan[14] were for the most part quite unconcerned with either the problem of tradition and modernity or with the debate between religion and science. Instead, Horney built her revision of Freud on the role of societal and socially toned cultural forces in fostering self-deception in her patients' struggles to come to know themselves without distortion. Whereas Horney stressed the self's need to transcend cultural restraint, Sullivan took up the same theme, but came to very different conclusions regarding it. His interpersonal behavorism portrayed dramatically the power of social forces over the self, and lent credence to his almost cynical conclusion that personal individuality is often a fond illusion. Both writers in effect supported—although in very different concepts and language—Freud's sense of the power of the superego to limit personal fulfillment.

Erich Fromm's writings do much to restore to the neo-Freudian orientation the interplay of all three themes. His association with the Frankfürt School and his subsequent reinterpretation of its emphasis on the social determination of personality link him to Horney and Sullivan. But Fromm's efforts to interpret the Reformation (*Escape from Freedom* [1941])[15] and early Christianity (*The Dogma of Christ* [1930])[16] reopened the problem of tradition and modernity for psychoanalysis, and his interest both in the general nature of religion (*Psychoanalysis and Religion* [1950])[17] and even in specific religious phenomena (*Zen Buddhism and Psychoanalysis* [1963])[18]—despite the relaxed atmosphere of easy compromise—harken back to Freud's own epistemological concerns. For these reasons

Fromm has probably more right to the title "neo-Freudian" than do either Horney or Sullivan.

Whether or not existential psychology is a bona fide development of psychoanalysis is one root question with which the movement as a whole has been preoccupied. Different figures have tried to come to terms with this issue, each struggling with Freud's legacy in his own particular fashion. Medard Boss has found Heidegger's analysis of Dasein "secretly" present in the otherwise mechanistic formulations and procedures of Freud.[19] Binswanger on the other hand has argued that Freud's naturalism prevented him from understanding the essence of existential self-understanding.[20] In America Rollo May steered a middle path between these two positions, believing that much of Freud was compatible with Paul Tillich's ontology.[21] This movement has reinterpreted the Freudian theme of the tension between self-fulfillment and an oppressive social order by means of the existentialist concern with the struggle for personal uniqueness and authenticity in the face of an alien natural and social order. These figures have worked out what Freud believed to be the tension between religion and science through their epistemological and ontological concerns, which are for them inseparable from the problem of social alienation. But because estrangement is for the most part interpreted within the framework of Western philosophical categories, these philosophical psychologies are far more indebted to traditional modes of thought than was Freud, and strongly repudiate his defense of modernity.

Ego psychology represents still another permutation on the legacy of Freud, and Erikson's work is most often associated with it. But while it is undoubtedly true that his work belongs more to ego psychology than to any other school, orientation, or movement in psychoanalysis, it is also a mistake to see Erikson as simply one more ego psychologist. In certain important ways he stands sharply outside the ego-psychology orientation. Erikson shares with this orientation, through his concept of identity, the positive value it assigns to the autonomy of the ego in relation to the social order. For this reason we must situate *Childhood and Society* and *Identity and the Life Cycle* (1959)[22] with the ego-psychology movement, and link both with modernity. However, in *Young Man Luther* Erikson returns to the reverse side of this central preoccupation of psychoanalysis, the concern with tradition, and to the source of the power of tradition, religion. Erikson both is and is not an ego psychologist.

The work of ego psychologists such as Hartmann, Kris, Schafer, and Rapaport centers upon and thoroughly modifies the theme of the tension between self and society. These writers persistently concern themselves with the adaptive potential of the ego in relation to the material and social environment. For those thinkers who lived prior to the appearance of ego psychology, the relation between self and society was a conflictual one, characterized by inevitable alienation, struggle, and compromise. However, the ego psychologists do not center their analysis upon a struggle between self and society, but rather upon the internal aspect of this relation, and upon the positive, adaptive capacities of the ego. Herein lies the meaning of such key terms as *conflict-free ego sphere* (Hartmann),[23] *regression in the service of the ego* (Kris)[24] and *loving superego* (Schafer).[25] Through their discovery of a new level of functioning in the ego, the ego psychologists have created a new estimate of the social order: it is neither "against" the ego, in the earlier conflictual sense, nor is it "for" the ego, in any simplistic, conformist sense. Instead, the social order is a neutral source of reality-demands and of ideals that, under appropriate circumstances, can be the object of successful, although complex, adaptive processes.

In their efforts to comprehend the inner, complex structure of the ego, to the exclusion of any inevitable and implacable alienation from the social order, the ego psychologists have given primacy to the view of psychoanalysis as a fundamental instrument of modernization—that means whereby the ego within the individual person becomes autonomous not only in relation to the social order, but also in relation to the power of tradition and, more fully, to the power of religion. It is important to note that the ego psychologists treat religion as a positive, albeit residual category.[26] Tradition, religion, society—these are no longer a source of oppression. In ego psychology psychoanalysis comes of age as a truly modern trend.

Childhood and Society and *Identity and the Life Cycle* articulate the orientation of ego psychology, although they contain departures from it as well. Erikson's key psychological concept, the now-famous notion of *identity,* provides the proper point of contrast. For the ego psychologists, the structure of the ego is not limited to its conflicts—either individual or cultural—with the superego. The ego is capable of autonomy, which is to say that it is structurally capable of integrating tensions between it and the encroachments of the social order. Following this line of thinking, Erikson makes it quite clear that through the formation of identity a person is capable of experiencing himself from time to time as beyond the conflict-inducing limitations of the superego. Identity formation is associated with the fifth developmental stage, while formation of the superego is associated with the third developmental stage, the stage of initiative versus guilt, in which the Oedipal conflict is central. Identity is really a second major phase in the formation of the individual's concept of himself. For this reason identity is "conflict-free"—that is, free from the conflicts of the first stage of socialization.

But Erikson parts company with the ego psychologists on several important points. His psychology of identity is not written in the metapsychological mode of Freud and the ego psychologists. He does not wish to discover and describe elaborate psychological structures, agencies, and institutions in the mind. He does not worry, for example, about which of the two topographies is the more accurate, nor is he concerned to revise the libido theory. And Erikson's analysis of identity is motivational, moral, and literary. It is this approach, with its clarity of description of experiential states of mind, as these are determined by social forces and by forces close to consciousness, that constitute Erikson's style and that makes his work so compelling.

To speak of the motivational effects of social forces is to speak, in Erikson's case, not of the "social environment" but of influences deeply embedded in the character of nations and communities. These evoke questions about history, ideology, and the relativities of historical change, concerns that also separate Erikson's work from ego psychology. With them in mind, he returns, paradoxically, to the classical Freudian preoccupation with problems of tradition and religion. But he makes this return with his work on identity well in hand. His theory of identity and his concern with history merge in *Young Man Luther,* his second major book —a book that belongs in part to the application of psychoanalytic theory to culture, but also to cultural reflection upon psychoanalysis.

The development of cultural reflection upon psychoanalysis has taken place in several phases, each giving preference to one of the three themes, but each including aspects of the other. The first posed questions to psychoanalysis that were primarily epistemological and ethical in character. The second shifted this emphasis rather drastically by questioning the relationship of psychoanalysis to Western history, tradition, and religion. The third, which is extremely promising but which is only now making its appearance, approaches psychoanalysis from the point of view of the sociology of knowledge, emphasizing the decline of religion as a cultural force and the role of social conditions in the formation of psychological ideas. Each phase has taken up one of the themes of classic psychoanalysis but has transformed that theme into a perspective outside of psychoanalytic concerns. If we recall that Freud identified religion and philosophy, then the first phase reflected upon the classic psychoanalysts' preoccupation with the epistemological status of psychoanalysis—the tension between religion and science; the second or historical phase took up the theme of tradition and modernity; and the third or sociological phase takes up and transforms the problem of self and society. Each in its own way has provided reflection upon the very broad and inclusive theme of the problem of religion and modernity, although the central perception of all psychoanalytic theory, the complex relation that exists between childhood and selfhood, while never lost in these dimensions, is often only indirectly present.

The first group of writers to sense the cultural significance of psychoanalysis were philosophers and theologians. They fall roughly into three groups: (1) existentialists such as the early Sartre, Tillich, and Buber;[27] (2) philosophers of language such as Wisdom and Flew;[28] and (3) phenomenologists such as Merleau-Ponty and the early Ricoeur.[29] Despite the truly extraordinary diversity of epistemological and ontological commitment that these figures represent, they were all concerned with a remarkably similar matter: the claim of psychoanalysis to have created a new vision of the human self and, in particular, a new vision of the self's way of both deceiving and knowing itself.

The existentialists were concerned about restating a vision of human authenticity and personal uniqueness and clarifying the mechanisms of self-deception whereby this authenticity was surrendered to the conditions of modern life. The philosophers of language focused upon the integrity of the claims of psychoanalysis to be a genuinely new science of human behavior, and the phenomenologists questioned whether psychoanalysis was a genuinely new method by which the nature of consciousness could be derived. And all were convinced, again on very different grounds, that in each case Freud's version of self-understanding was fundamentally reductive. His concepts of superego and repression reduced self-knowledge and self-deception to a function of society; the psychoanalytic method of inquiry could not be falsified and therefore could not be verified; psychoanalytic theory at best reflected only the distortions of human consciousness, not its possibilities.

But the style of these discussions is just as important as their contents, a point that is often overlooked. These evaluations of psychoanalysis viewed it entirely from the perspective of their own disciplines and orientations. They dealt with it only insofar as they could see reflected in it their own questions and problems.[30] Consequently, these critics did not engage the total body of insights, tenets, and texts that make up Freud's thought. They read him in a highly selective manner and made no effort to comprehend psychoanalysis as a system of texts that, while often confusing and contradictory, nevertheless comprise a single whole.

The first phase of cultural reflection on psychoanalysis began shortly after Freud's thought became known—that is, well within his lifetime—and extended into the post–World War II years. Then in the late 1950s and early 1960s a very different type of discussion of psychoanalysis appeared. The writings of Philip Rieff, Norman O. Brown, Herbert Marcuse, and, later, of Paul Ricoeur created a totally fresh mood of assessment of psychoanalysis—a mood produced as much by the style of these works as it was by their contents.[31]

The second group of interpretations of Freud came not only from philosophy and theology but also from history and sociology.[32] Rather than looking at Freud selectively, through the lenses of their own disciplines, they submitted their disciplines to an extraordinary extent to the full impact of Freud's thought upon them. This procedure in turn forced them to take into account the full range of the Freudian texts, and by viewing Freud's work as a whole, they found themselves searching it for the deepest strands of meaning and commitment. Under their auspices the problem of the knowledge-claims of psychoanalysis—the epistemological problem, gave way to the problem of tradition and modernity, and, with the exception of Marcuse, they readily concurred with Freud's judgment that, at least as far as psychoanalytic thought was concerned, the problem of tradition was at bottom the problem of religion. In these writers the tension between religion and modernity asserted itself as the central problem, although, of course, the other themes were by no means absent.

These new discussions, otherwise so complex, far-reach-ing, and multifaceted, nevertheless dissolve into a debate over a single question: Does the psychoanalytic theory cut modern man off from the power that the past possesses to influence his behavior and loyalties, or has Freud, while having broken with the past, provided a subtle, perhaps even devious means for the retrieval of that same past? Did Freud erect insuperable barriers between traditional religion and modernity, or did he, paradoxically, provide modernity with a detour around these barriers? Philip Rieff powerfully and convincingly supported the first alternative. His analysis of Freud's creation of "psychological man" and of the absolute incompatibility between this new type of character and the image of person and society created by Christian tradition has earned a permanent place in the literature of Freudian criticism.[33] Paul Ricoeur took the second view. Freud's psychology provides modern thought with a hermeneutic of consciousness that encourages the retrieval of traditional symbols in the very midst of modernity's antimythological skepticism.[34] Midway between these two extremes lies the work of Norman Brown and Herbert Marcuse, as well as some of the more recent theological writing on fantasy[35] and some of the even more recent theological writing on narrative and story.

Young Man Luther must be understood in the context of this debate about the cultural significance of psychoanalysis, and, in particular, it belongs to this second trend—the attempt to interpret psychoanalysis as an instance of the debate between tradition and modernity. *Young Man Luther* resembles the writings of Rieff, Ricoeur, and Brown every bit as much as it does the work of the ego psychologists. More to the point, Erikson's work brings together the two levels of development of psychoanalytic thought: the application of psychoanalysis to problems of culture and cultural reflection on the nature of psychoanalysis. Yet Erikson does not simply fuse these two types of reflection; in each case he brings to them his own unique orientation. Erikson is explicitly more Freudian than any of the revisionists or ego psychologists. And he goes beyond generalizing about psychoanalysis, tradition, and religion by investigating a particular religious figure, only then reflecting upon the significance of his analysis for modernity.

Erikson's book on Luther unites the orientations of Rieff and Ricoeur. Like both, he finds in religion the key to the cultural meaning of psychoanalysis. In a way that Rieff would expect, Erikson sees a developmental basis to Luther's experience of justification by faith. At this point he subverts the religious tradition by exposing its psychological infrastructure, which remains hidden from the eyes of the religious tradition itself by the language of that tradition. But, following upon this reductive effort, Erikson then takes up a strategy of recovery similar to Ricoeur's. He concludes that something of positive value must be retrieved from Luther's experience and appropriated by the modern mind.

But Erikson differs from the Rieff-Ricoeur debate about the cultural significance of psychoanalysis, not simply because his work fuses these two orientations, but also because he introduces new psychological concepts to the discussion. When Erikson proposed his inquiry into the psychological significance of Luther's life and thought, he advanced that inquiry by means of the hard-won concept of identity. This in turn permitted him to construct the sociohistorical counterpart of identity—a positively valued understanding of ideology. With these two concepts in hand, Erikson could mediate the central dilemma of psychoanalysis—namely, that it leads to a rejection of the past because it discloses the psychological beneath the theological. (Justification by faith is ideological.) But it also leads to a retrieval of the past. (Ideology is necessary for psychological well-being.) Erikson recovered dimensions of Luther's life and thought by casting these in terms that transformed Freudian theory —as used by Rieff and Ricoeur—and that were of positive value. In this way, Erikson has made a unique contribution to the cultural problem of religion and modernity.

For these reasons *Young Man Luther* must not be understood as simply "another psychoanalytic study of religion."

For that matter, no psychoanalytic study of religion is ever simply that. All such studies—from *Totem and Taboo* to *Moses and Monotheism* to *Young Man Luther*—are attempts to reflect on the tension between traditional religion and modernity. This may hold equally well for nonpsychoanalytic psychological studies of religion. Whether or not Erikson's concepts of identity and ideology contain an implicit religious element is of course a key question, and receives debate in many of the following essays.

By now it should be clear that Erikson's thought does indeed articulate themes that comprise both the application of psychoanalytic concepts to culture and cultural reflection on psychoanalysis. Each of these two types of reflection gives attention in varying degrees to the several themes that constitute them. *Childhood and Society* and *Identity and the Life Cycle* engage directly the theme of tension between personal fulfillment and an oppressive social order, as this theme is found in the psychoanalytic literature on culture. *Young Man Luther* articulates that portion of cultural reflection on psychoanalysis wherein the theme of tension between tradition and modernity is central.[36] Neither study belongs entirely to one or the other type of literature, but the first is obviously more of a clinical book, while the second is more of a cultural and historical study.

But what of the third theme that goes to make up the cultural legacy of psychoanalysis, the theme of tension between religion and science? Freud believed that this issue was integral to an understanding of psychoanalysis. For Freud religion was "the other" on which psychoanalysis works out its own self-definition, the means by which it discovers its own historical uniqueness, the meaning of its own destiny, or, as others have put it, its own "modernity." Does the tension between religion and science appear, per se, in Erikson's thought? And, if so, does it occupy as prominent a position as it did in Freud's?

The answer to these questions is yes, but with all the qualifications necessary to a comparison and a contrasting of Erikson and Freud. Erikson does carry forward this theme, which is found both in classic psychoanalysis and in the cultural reflection on psychoanalysis. But he casts it in a very different form, one that fuses both clinical considerations and cultural reflection. Erikson does not make this theme an epistemological question, as did Freud—in *The Future of an Illusion*, for example—and as does philosophical commentary on psychoanalysis, which has been concerned to work out the relation, or lack of relation, between Western metaphysics and emerging psychoanalysis. Instead, Erikson transforms psychoanalysis by casting this theme not in epistemological terms, but in terms of a variation upon the theme, already discussed, of tension between tradition and modernity; he gives it the form of *psychohistory*.

Young Man Luther is subtitled *A Study in Psychoanalysis and History*. In it Erikson conceives of psychoanalysis as a body of principles with its own particular type of subject matter and rules of interpretation. Rather than setting forth psychoanalysis as a science in Freud's positivistic and totalistic way, Erikson instead thinks of it as a method of inference. As such, it has the power to disclose the developmental basis of an event in the life history of a leader. In this, psychohistory remains an innovative transformation within the psychoanalytic interpretation of culture. But it is hardly coincidental that Erikson should, like Freud, select religion as the privileged object of psychohistorical study. In *Young Man Luther* the modern science of psychoanalytic history plays itself out against religious tradition. In such interplay is found a fresh edition of the Freudian debate between science and religion.

But Erikson's psychohistorical study of religion must also be distinguished from Freud's "science" of religion, for the former also includes cultural reflection upon the meaning of psychoanalysis. By including within his definition of psychology such higher processes as identity and ideology, Erikson is able not only to interpret portions of the past reductively, but also to reinterpret portions of the past, thereby appropriating them into a vision of the present.

Evident at this point is Erikson's recognition—far clearer

than Freud's—that psychoanalysis is a system of meaning that is especially sensitive to the needs of modern man, and his further recognition that, in fact, without psychoanalysis modern man becomes a victim of those forces of change that have intervened between the religious past and the not-so-religious present. Thus *Young Man Luther* illustrates a viewpoint that Erikson has in other places made more explicit—namely, that psychoanalysis is entrusted with the special mission of providing modern man with the absolutely necessary tools of self-understanding.[37]

The tension between religious tradition and psychohistorical method—Erikson's revision of Freud's sense of the irreconcilability of religion and science—is perhaps the most advanced rendition of what is meant by the tension between religion and modernity. Psychoanalysis is an epoch-specific orientation and set of tools by means of which modern man can cope with the present through interpretation of the religious past. This tension, which is for the most part implicit throughout *Young Man Luther,* becomes explicit in Erikson's third major book, *Gandhi's Truth.*

Throughout *Childhood and Society* and *Young Man Luther* Erikson worked creatively with the legacy of Freud, drawing its various implicit themes together and giving them more depth, breadth, and complexity. His efforts were extremely successful. In *Gandhi's Truth* the task of mediation becomes so complex that the firm sense of opposites and tensions characteristic of Erikson's earlier works threatens to vanish altogether. Religion is no longer Judaism or Christianity, or simply Protestantism. It becomes "The East," the past, all of tradition—in a cosmic rather than a historical sense. And psychohistory, in turn, loses its specificity. It is no longer a "helping hand" to historical investigation, but becomes a general hermeneutic for appreciating and appropriating the past in order to enrich the present.

As a result of such loss of specificity, the sharp tension between religion and modernity itself becomes diffuse. It is difficult to tell whether the "homo religiosus" of *Gandhi's*

Truth is an imago embedded in the past, or whether it springs from a contemporary psychoanalytic psychology that has become infused—deliberately or inadvertently—with the forms of the past. Some argue that this diffuseness in Erikson's later work is a result of a general forfeiture on his part of the analytic legacy of psychoanalysis. But it could also stem from a deeper perception that psychoanalysis, that peculiarly modern discipline, is neither so modern, nor so scientific, as it has claimed.

Each of the essays in this volume is addressed to a specific feature, issue, or problem in Erikson's thought. The authors are scholars who represent those cultural and humanistic disciplines for which Erikson's work is of special relevance, and who have themselves found Erikson's thought of value for their own reflection upon their own work. Of course, none of the essays directly addresses the several themes of psychoanalysis that have been the subject of this introduction thus far. However, each essay does in its own way treat and clarify aspects of these themes. All but two of the essays fall into one of two groups, based on what has been set forth as the privileged theme of psychoanalytic thought: the first three deal with Erikson's treatment of religion, and the last two focus on the relation of his thought to modernity. Two additional essays also deal with aspects of this theme and, like the others, concern themselves with the cultural and humanistic aspects of Erikson's thought. But they do so in a very special way and, accordingly, are grouped together. Erikson's work has been a major stimulus to the rise of psychohistory—hence an essay is included on this subject. Anthropology is, of course, a social science rather than a humanistic discipline. But anthropology in the case of Erikson's work also provides the context for the most direct access to his understanding of the phenomenon of culture, and his treatment of culture is easily as humanistic as it is scientific—culture provides the setting in which the modern self must find meaning and value for itself. Because Erikson's discussions of psychohistory and his psychology of culture are heavily methodological, these two essays are grouped together under the rubric of methodology, although it should be kept in mind that this issue is only a particular instance of the larger question of religion and modernity.

The remainder of this introduction briefly summarizes the argument of each paper, in order that the reader may have in advance an overview of the contents of the volume as a whole, and then suggests how each paper bears upon the major themes found in Erikson's thought.

II

The first three essays in this volume examine Erikson's principal historical investigations, which have dwelt on two major religious figures, from the point of view of those fields of scholarly work to which he has addressed himself. The first, by Bornkamm, represents well the criticisms of Erikson's *Young Man Luther,* which came initially from within the Protestant theological community. Following Bornkamm's essay, and contrasting sharply with it, is a second discussion of Erikson's study of Luther, also by a Reformation historian, but one who brackets theological questions, and who is also committed to a psychological methodology very different from psychoanalysis. In the third essay a scholar of contemporary Indian civilization analyzes, assesses, and criticizes Erikson's *Gandhi's Truth* from the perspective of his special knowledge.

Heinrich Bornkamm is a Protestant Reformation historian and life-long Luther scholar. His paper appears in this volume in order to set forth and make available to the reader in the most direct manner possible those issues which initially emerged when *Young Man Luther* was first published. Some of the earliest responses to the book came from the Protestant community and consisted of a debate between the theological assumptions of the church historian, who has been a primary caretaker of Luther scholarship and interpretation, and the very different assumptions of the psychoanalytically oriented psychologist. The essay comes at the beginning of the volume, not because it is superior to the others, or because the issues it takes up are more important than those discussed by the other papers, but because the arrangement of these essays—in addition to being based on the major themes of psychoanalysis—is intended to reflect something of the progression of commentary made upon Erikson's work by scholars in the humanities and in religious studies. It has been almost twenty years since the appearance of *Young Man Luther*, and since then some scholars in religious studies have shifted their attention away from a debate between the claims of theology and psychoanalysis and in the direction of other issues, such as the nature of psychohistorical inquiry and the view of modernity that psychoanalysis assumes. Several of the essays in this volume represent this trend.

Bornkamm's paper is an extended series of criticisms of Erikson's study, all arguing in effect that *Young Man Luther* contains many inaccurate interpretations of Luther's personal struggle. Bornkamm believes, for example, that Erikson exaggerates the oppressiveness of Luther's early family life and that his portrait of Hans Luder, Luther's father, is overly harsh. Luther's relation to his father was not a tragic one, but rather a story of alienation followed by final reconciliation. Bornkamm cites much evidence in support of his criticisms. But all of his objections are grounded in the single accusation that Erikson has not taken Luther "at his word." Erikson suggests that Luther transferred ambivalent feelings, derived from his paternal relation, to the Pope and, further, that he created his ideology of justification by faith in order to bring to a successful conclusion his own developmental crisis of identity formation. For Bornkamm the historian must accept Luther's account of the existence of God in his life as a "given" of historical evidence. To infer clinically that this account has a psychodynamic origin robs it of its reality as a factor independent of other forces. Bornkamm believes that Luther's faith in God was a historical factor that had perceivable effects upon both the formation of his desires and his evaluation of others and ideas, and that as such it was the decisive occasion for the creation of his personal faith and his theology.

Bornkamm's debate with Erikson restates two of the themes associated with the cultural significance of psychoanalysis. The essay reflects the tension between science and religion, and because it casts this tension in terms of science as psychohistory and religion as Protestant theology, it shows how the old debate can take a fresh form. In addition, because the debate is here cast in historiographic terminology, it also reflects how religion or faith is linked with tradition and how the psychoanalytic view comes to be associated with modernity. In his concern that the theological factor not be neglected in any estimate of Luther's life, Bornkamm is also implicitly attempting to rescue a traditional, Western view of the self, whereas Erikson's position, in arguing that Luther must be interpreted psychologically, comes to be associated with a modern, that is, a posttraditional, view.

Bornkamm's essay expresses great dignity and passion in its effort to comprehend Luther's life. Whether readers are convinced by his argument or whether they remain on the whole indifferent to it, it is important to recognize in it a unique and powerful fusion of faith and scholarly inquiry. This is the only paper in the volume written from a theological perspective.

Mark Edwards takes up the question of the origin and formation of Luther's identity from the point of view of experimental psychology—a perspective very different from that of both Bornkamm and Erikson. Because his point of view is neither theological nor psychoanalytic, it serves as a foil to Bornkamm's discussion of Erikson. It also demonstrates well that objections to the psychoanalytic study of a historical and religious figure can come from within psychology. Edwards believes that psychoanalysis and psychohistory are not scientific, and he has therefore chosen what he finds to be a far more reliable psychological-scientific framework to apply to Luther's life. Edwards's work also poses a question within historiography itself—namely, whether history is best studied by means of a methodology that, in its detachment and objectivity, emulates exact science, or whether it is best studied by means of a methodology that requires participation on the part of the investigator.

Edwards's approach to Luther differs from Erikson's in several respects. Edwards focuses more on the social environment of the adult Luther, on his interpersonal relations, and on his conscious motivations, whereas Erikson emphasizes family circumstances, intrapsychic processes, and the unconscious. Edwards uses cognitive-dissonance theory to account for the way in which Luther arrived at his concept of himself as a reformer, how he legitimated this concept, and how he discredited his opponents by interpreting his own role and the role of his opponents. When Luther emerged as a central figure in the Reformation, he came into conflict with Protestant figures who opposed him, thereby creating "dissonance" between his emerging self-concept and the concept that his opponents held of him. Luther reduced this dissonance, Edwards argues, by modeling himself upon the prophets of Scripture, and by linking his opponents to typical images of false prophets.

Edwards's paper provides an important critical observation of Erikson's psychohistorical methodology, but in doing so it also, in effect, places in a new perspective the tension between psychological science and religion that appears in almost pure form in Freud's writings and that reappears in a new edition, so to speak, in Bornkamm's debate with Erikson. Edwards believes that psychoanalysis is not an observational science and that therefore it is improper for the historian to use it. For this reason his brand of psychological history does much to neutralize the tension between religion and science. There is no inner logic to cognitive-dissonance theory that demands—as does psychoanalysis—that psychology from time to time take religion as its object. Therefore, although Edwards does not use the term, his approach implies that Erikson's psychohistory is a kind of *ideology*. But the significance of Edwards's paper lies not in this claim, which is at best made only indirectly, but in his ability to demonstrate the methodological ineffectiveness of psychoanalysis as a theory of history. Still, cognitive-dissonance theory does join psychoanalysis in its juxtaposition to religion, at one point. It, too, appears to be one more way in which modern psychology can make sense of the traditional past. Luther formed his self-concept in a manner that modern, scientific psychology is peculiarly equipped to understand, something that was not possible for Luther or the people of his time. And, paradoxically, Edwards agrees with Bornkamm on one point: psychoanalysis is an unreliable interpretive framework, for it actually creates inferences from a paucity of facts.

The essay by Arjun Appadurai continues the argumentation developed in the preceding two discussions of Erikson's work on religion, but it also introduces new questions and new criticisms. Just as Bornkamm and Edwards reflect upon Erikson's study of Luther in relation to their field of specialization, Reformation studies, Appadurai creates a critical assessment of *Gandhi's Truth* in terms of his special field, the study of Indian civilization. Like the two Reformation scholars, Appadurai is concerned with the status of the psychoanalytic framework of interpretation, especially with its potential claims to historical accuracy and its potentially ideological character. However, Appadurai approaches the relativity of psychoanalysis not on historical or scientific grounds, but on the basis of cultural presuppositions. His major point of investigation is whether psychoanalysis, rooted as it is in the Western cultural tradition, can be an effective framework for interpreting Gandhi's moral and religious life.

Appadurai is appreciative of Erikson's sensitive and insightful treatment of Gandhi from the psychoanalytic point of view, but he is fundamentally critical of what he believes to be Erikson's culturally determined assumptions. Erikson's psychology, he argues, is fundamentally based on Freud's, and Freud's psychoanalysis has deep roots in the

Judeo-Christian past. It is in fact a transformation of the Judeo-Christian past, and its basic interpretive categories repeat those of its past. Two such categories are the Christian conception of time, which locates meaning in a supreme past event, and a division of human life into such dualities as mind and flesh, intellect and instinct, love and death. These dualisms are reflected in Freud's thought, derive from the social and intellectual heritage of Western religious tradition, and provide the cultural matrix for psychoanalytic theory. While Erikson is far more sensitive to the cultural factors influencing his framework than was Freud, he nevertheless inadvertently applies these culturally determined themes to Gandhi's life and work.

According to Appadurai, the Hindu cultural heritage shaped Gandhi's life and work. One assumption central to this heritage is the view that morality and nature are but two aspects of a single order. This unity organizes the Hindu understanding of such specific cultural phenomena as sexuality, authority, parent-child relations, and duty. Consequently, Erikson's work, grounded as it is in the dualities of Freud's thought and the Judeo-Christian tradition, is destined to distort not only the meaning of specific cultural events in the life of Gandhi, but also the meanings of the political innovations he instituted. Appadurai's paper spells out the differences between the cultural presuppositions of Erikson's framework and the world in which Gandhi lived.

This essay makes an important contribution to the literature of cultural reflection upon the significance of psychoanalysis. According to many writers who have taken up this theme, including to some extent Erikson himself, psychoanalysis is an interpretation of modernity and, as such, must be distinguished from alternative systems of meaning in Western religious tradition. But Appadurai's argument collapses this distinction. For him the cultural significance of psychoanalysis lies in its unwitting repetition of traditional religious themes. Still, it can also be said that Appadurai does not altogether abandon the distinction between Western religion and modernity, for in arguing that psychoanalysis is a transformation of the Judeo-Christian heritage, he also gives reason to think about a view that receives discussion in later essays—namely, that psychoanalysis is intended to retrieve certain meanings from the Western past, as well as offer an interpretive perspective upon them.

The first three essays in this volume discuss Erikson's work from the perspective of the author's expertise in humanistic, historical questions. Each writer challenges, directly or indirectly, the validity of Erikson's analyses of Luther and Gandhi and, in so doing, questions the method of psychoanalytic inquiry in relation to the assumptive world of its cultural context. A detailed exploration of the cultural relativity of psychoanalysis, while beyond the scope of these three essays, is nonetheless called for by them. Such an exploration requires not so much a detailed and technical understanding of the origins of psychoanalytic method as a general conception of the way in which the phenomenon of culture is understood. The psychological investigation of cultural forms is not simply a series of rules drawn from clinical work; rather, it is, in a more fundamental sense, a particular kind of sensitivity characterized as "empathic." We can best explore the problem of cultural relativity in Erikson's thought by inquiring into the nature of empathic communication. This question shifts our focus away from tradition, religion, and history to a dimension of experience that, in Erikson's mind, underlies them all—the experience of childhood. For empathy is directed toward understanding the universal cultural factor, childhood itself, and through such understanding the problem of relativity is resolved.

Waud H. Kracke is an anthropologist with additional, advanced training in psychoanalysis. He brings to bear his knowledge of the earlier work in culture and personality and the more current investigations in psychological anthropology. He approaches Erikson's writings through the category of *culture* rather than that of *history,* and this is essential, for Erikson derives his method for historical analysis from the person-culture relation. Kracke's essay raises and answers two questions central to this aspect of Erikson's work: Can a member of one culture truly understand a different culture? And how can one integrate the psychoanalytic view that the person is shaped primarily by internal patternings with the view that the person is a product of his culture? The second question is a microcosm of the first.

Erikson answers the first question in the affirmative, according to Kracke: it is possible for a member of one culture to break through the barrier of cultural patterns in another culture and to achieve empathic understanding of members of that other culture. But the basis of such understanding lies in the child that is in everyone—whether one is a middle-class American, a Sioux, a Hindu, or a Protestant reformer. More precisely, this basis is empathic communication with childhood, the universal in all persons that makes deep and genuine understanding possible. Erikson's answer to the first question determines his answer to the second—the problem of the relation between person and culture, within a homogeneous culture. It is possible for personal uniqueness to combine with cultural form, within the individual's own cultural situation, for the tension between person and culture can be mediated successfully through the phenomenon of identity. Identity supercedes childhood but remains forever in touch with it, and identity links the person to his cultural surroundings in a homogeneous way.

Empathic communication mediated through the universality of childhood experience—this is Erikson's answer to the question of cultural relativism. And identity formation resolves the tension between private experience and cultural form. In these two convictions lies Erikson's response to two main themes in the psychoanalytic tradition. Identity formation resolves the dilemma of the tension between personal fulfillment and an oppressive social order. And in the notion of empathic communication through a shared childhood Erikson gives a new shade of meaning to the problem of tradition and modernity. Luther and Gandhi were steeped in the past, and, consequently, their motives and thoughts strike the modern consciousness as alien and different. What makes them familiar—what renders the barrier between tradition and modernity less than total—is the archaism of childhood common to both the ancient and the new, to both the investigator and his object. Erikson's answer to the problem of cultural relativism lies in the subtleties of his analysis of the "cog-wheeling" of childhood patterns (the universal in all men) with the uniqueness of cultural configurations (the source of particularity).

The essays in this volume by the three historians deal with the accuracy of Erikson's analyses of two religious leaders. The authors are able to remark in only a cursory way about the assumptions underlying these analyses, but each in his own way believes that Erikson's interpretations are grounded in questionable assumptions. For this reason, they raise questions about Erikson's methodology. Kracke's essay, subsequently, addresses one aspect of methodology—that aspect that states that the key to psychoanalytic inquiry lies in its capacity to produce an empathic linkage between the investigator and patterns of childhood in his own and in other cultures. His essay discloses a debate between Erikson and his historically minded critics, the critics arguing that childhood is different in different cultures, and Erikson arguing, in the eyes of anthrolopogist Kracke, that the method is all important: if one is empathic enough and listens carefully enough, the universal elements in childhood are there for all to see, despite the autonomy of very different cultural configurations.

For the past twenty years a new type of inquiry called psychohistory has been emerging, due largely to the stimulus of Erikson's writings. All of the above-mentioned essays, insofar as they address the question of method, do so from outside the sphere of psychohistory itself; thus they point to the need for a discussion of Erikson's psychology from within the perspective of psychohistory. The paper by Donald Capps places Erikson's psychology within the new burgeoning literature of psychohistory, just as Kracke's paper relates Erikson's work to the growing tradition of psychological anthropology. Capps thus introduces new concepts and advances new conclusions regarding the precise nature of psychohistorical inquiry. Eriksonian psychohistory, he argues, must not be classified as a subdivision of historical studies, nor should it be labeled as simply a form of applied psychology. Erikson's studies of historical figures have created a type or genre of inquiry that is similar in some ways to these approaches, but that is actually quite different. The key to this difference lies in the phenomenon of narrative, for while narrative is an element that can be found in all three methods, it is, nevertheless, handled differently in psychohistory. Although several of the essays in this volume allude to psychohistory, none mentions the phenomenon of narrative, a fact that suggests that the concept may be esoteric, perhaps even irrelevant. Capps's essay decisively removes any such doubt and, in so doing, gives further concrete testimony to the incredibly broad range of implication inherent in Erikson's total work.

Capps argues that a correct interpretation of the method of Eriksonian psychohistory does not dwell primarily upon its handling of historical materials, nor upon the adequacy of its psychological framework, but rather upon the question of the genre or type of inquiry it represents. Capps summarizes several such types of historical inquiry and shows how psychohistory does and does not belong to these genres. From this he concludes that understanding the function of narrative is the key to Erikson's work. Erikson uses psychological categories—such as *intimacy versus isolation*—to interpret life histories. These categories have the power to generate a story line or narrative line. The psychological construct makes it possible for the historian to integrate many otherwise disparate events in the life of his subject. To this Capps adds the observation that there is "something religious" about Erikson's use of narrative that cannot be accounted for simply by the fact that he has studied religious figures. Capps notes that Erikson himself recognized that a "mythological trend" could be found in his psychological framework of the life cycle. The presence of such a mythological trend prompts Capps to conclude that Erikson's psychohistory is really an inadvertent form of religious biography. His thesis is carefully argued and is totally lacking in polemical or apologetic intent.

Capps's conclusion provides one possible answer to the debate with Erikson begun by the first three papers. Like Bornkamm and Edwards, Capps believes that there are assumptions in Erikson's interpretive framework that make it more than scientific psychohistory. And, like Appadurai, he believes that these assumptions resemble the theological tradition into which psychoanalysis was born. Unlike these three authors, however, Capp believes that these assumptions are not mere ideology but legitimate and necessary, although inadvertent, ingredients to Erikson's psychohistorical perspective. Such a conclusion is yet another variant of what has been identified as an extremely pervasive theme in psychoanalytic thought—the tension between religion and modernity. In one sense, psychohistory is "modern," and, as such, it studies "tradition." Yet psychohistory, according to Capps, incorporates into its own analytic framework aspects of that very tradition that it seeks to interpret. Eriksonian psychohistory is in part composed of religious biography or hagiography.

The remaining two essays in this volume address themselves directly to the problem of modernity in Erikson's work. They are not primarily concerned with assessing his studies of historical religious figures from the point of view of special knowledge, nor are they concerned with clarifying his methodological writings, whether these involve the role of empathic communication or questions of formal criteria internal to the work of the psychohistorian as a new type of modern investigator into the past. Instead, they focus upon the place of Erikson's work in relation to the problem of modernity itself, as this problem has been discussed by various analysts of modernity, both religious and secular. The paper by Homans assesses Erikson's theory of religion in relation to various diagnoses of modernity in the contemporary study of religion, while Browning's essay clarifies Erikson's vision of the normative image of man in relation to selected social critics and from the point of view of what could be called psychological ethics. Because both essays center on the question of modernity, they carry forward still further reflection upon issues central to this volume—the major questions and dilemmas of the cultural significance of psychoanalysis.

While Erikson has written a good deal about religion, and while many of the essays in this volume discuss his interpretations of religious figures, none that has been mentioned thus far explores in depth and in detail the various elements that compose his theory of religion. Homans's paper takes this question as its theme and attempts to handle it critically by relating it to other, current discussions of how religion is to be understood in the context of contemporary life. Since Erikson's thought is at every point a transformation of Freud's, Homans begins by describing the ways in which both Erikson's psychology and his psychology of religion differ from Freud and notes that the two views of religion are determined a priori by different assumptions about psychology. He then goes on to spell out in descriptive fashion the various ways in which Erikson speaks of religion. These discussions serve as preparation for the major issue of the paper—the relation between Erikson's theory of religion and the variety of theories of religion in contemporary thought. Homans shows how Erikson's work synthesizes elements of different strands of contemporary thought and argues that it is this synthesizing capacity that accounts for the appeal of Erikson to many students of religion. Homans concludes that Erikson's thought is both a departure from and an advance over the Western, Christian past, but that it is also an attempt to incorporate into his theory, in psychological form, theological elements of the past. In so concluding, he in effect gives an account of a point made by other essays in this volume, primarily those of Appadurai and Capps—namely, that Erikson's thought actually repeats at one level certain features of the very same past that at another level it seeks to interpret.

Browning is also concerned with Erikson's treatment of modernity, but his paper addresses the contents of Erikson's vision of modernity, rather than the question of its sources and its possible double relation to the past. Browning discusses what he calls Erikson's "normative vision of man." Browning notes that a great deal of contemporary social science has engaged the question "What kind of people are we becoming?" which is a descriptive question, and while he does not ignore this question, he is decidedly more interested in Erikson's answer to a second, related question—"What kind of people ought we to be?" Browning's concern is, in other words, normative rather than descriptive.

Browning first situates Erikson in a particular tradition of social-science inquiry and then spells out Erikson's diagnosis of modernity. Modernity takes its peculiar shape from rapid social change because such change, in turn, has created such phenomena as vocational pluralization, generational distance, the impersonalism of technological knowledge, and the psychological effects of the mass media. In all this Erikson sees the groundwork for pervasive identity confusion and a widening gap between the generations. But Browning is concerned with Erikson's diagnosis for modernity largely in terms of his implicit "therapy" for it. This therapy or "cure" for modernity Browning calls Erikson's normative image of man, his conception of the kind of people we ought to be, the key concepts of which are identity and ideology. According to Erikson, modern man needs a firm sense of identity, but the key to this identity lies in one's capacity to commit oneself to a vivid and convincing ideology, a vision of commanding ideas and ideals that will bring cohesiveness to the modern self and heal the fragmentation of generations. Browning notes such elements in the structure of Erikson's vision as identity, the capacity for generativity, and care. He also notes the sources of Erikson's vision in ethology and developmental psychology and describes the parallels and differences between this vision and that of man contained in Max Weber's concept of the Protestant ethic. He summarizes Erikson's vision as a synthesis of evolutionary perspectives and perspectives drawn from the reinterpretation of the cultural traditions of the West.

Browning's paper engages diverse aspects of the central theme that runs through all of the papers—the tension between tradition, religion, and modernity. But Browning also provides fresh discussion of a very specific issue that this theme provokes and that many of the preceding papers touch upon—the concept of ideology. Browning is not so much concerned with whether or not Erikson's psychology embodies an ideology—what he calls a vision or normative image—as he is with delineating the contents of that vision or ideology. He differs in this respect from Appadurai, who is more concerned with the hidden character of this ideology, and from Capps and Homans, who are concerned primarily with the sources of this ideology in both the orientations of Christian tradition and of modern psychoanalysis. On the other hand, Browning does believe that Erikson's vision itself resembles in certain respects the Judeo-Christian tradition. Thus, Browning's paper adds further clarity to the assumptive character of Erikson's psychological work.

The essays in this volume represent the sustained and disciplined commentary of scholars working in very different fields of study upon the cultural significance of Erikson's writings. While all of the essays seek to bring further clarity to Erikson's work, many are also critical of it, and some have gone beyond even this point to make interpretations. Taken together, they testify to the incredible range of subject matter that Erikson's writings encompass, and to the equally impressive "synthesizing capacities" of his mind. Erikson is truly an interdisciplinary thinker, for he has provoked searching reflection on substantive issues in many areas.

It is natural to wonder whether in the midst of the diversity of commentary that is the substance of these essays there is some underlying unity. It has, of course, been the purpose of this introduction to offer the following broad generalization in reply: the enigmatic and paradoxical presence of childhood, always in tension with the mature, conscious, and self-reflective aspects of adult selfhood, creates and throws into motion those tensions or themes that unite psychoanalytic thought and cultural reflection upon it. The "debate" between childhood and selfhood in the modern mind both separates and unites modern man in relation to himself, his immediate cultural surroundings, other cultures, traditions, and a past common to all. This separation is both sociological and epistemological. Erikson has created his own special synthesis between the Freudian tradition and cultural reflection upon Freud, and, in so doing, has established himself not only as a clinical investigator, but also as a social critic, a moralist, and a particularly persuasive theorist regarding the nature of modernity.

In addition to those themes already discussed, a new theme can also be detected in these essays. While for the most part appearing only indirectly, it nevertheless recurs at a number of different points and suggests an area of future work for those interested in further reflection on the cultural significance of both classic and Eriksonian psychoanalysis. Many of the essays in this volume explore the question of the precise objectives of Erikson's psychoanalytic psychology: does he seek to comprehend the dynamics of an individual personality, or the historical process itself, or the attitudes, values, and beliefs that people hold about life and the world? Several of the essays also probe in one way or another the question of the subjective assumptions that underlie Erikson's psychology. Common to both of these questions is the problem of ideology. It is perhaps somewhat ironic that a man who has actively pleaded that more self-conscious attention should be given to the study of ideology should himself be queried further not only as to the precise nature of ideology as an object of psychological study, but also as to how that very process affects the sources of his own thought.

Erikson himself has used the term *ideology* with some

regularity. In fact, his work might well be considered, in its more sociological aspects, as a psychology of ideology, a sort of psychology of knowledge modeling itself after the sociology of knowledge. By exploring ideology as an object of psychological study, further light could be shed upon Erikson's view of historical leadership, his notion of the role of society in the formation of the person, and his estimate of what is psychologically effective in the great religions. For Erikson does not see ideology as a distortion of the truth; rather, he considers it a necessary, valuable, and therefore implicitly true aspect of a person's world. Second, Erikson insists also that psychoanalysis, like science and like religion and politics, functions within an ideological context. Still, Erikson has far more to say about the functions of ideology than he does about its exact nature, and he has little to say about how the term might apply to psychoanalysis itself as a new form of thinking and valuing in the modern, postindustrial West.

The fact that Erikson has largely ignored a more detailed explication of the notion of ideology in both these senses is perhaps to be accounted for by the unavoidably simplistic and pejorative connotations of the word *ideology*; it is at best a poor choice. On the one hand, the beliefs and values of a person tend to be reduced in meaning and significance when the term *ideology* is applied to them. On the other hand, psychoanalysis loses not only its epistemological status, but also its clinical claims, when it is labeled *ideology*. Clearly, psychoanalysis is not just another experimental science, although it has a legitimate claim to science of some sort, nor is it a "crypto-religion," as some have argued, although in certain respects it may resemble religious systems (in its adoption of moral attitudes, for instance). For these reasons the term *ideology*, if it is to be used at all, needs to be reformulated.

Erikson points the way to an understanding both of the past, by explaining it psychologically, and of the present, by demonstrating the relevance of psychoanalysis for modernity. By his own avowal, ideology is an important key to both. It is crucial, therefore, that more be learned about ideology. Ideology is a "frontier" of the ego that, when explored further, will shed light not only on that which psychoanalysis studies, but also on the precise nature of psychoanalysis itself.

NOTES

1. Ernest Jones, *The Life and Work of Sigmund Freud*, vol. 2, *Years of Maturity, 1901–1919* (New York: Basic Books, 1955), p. 313.
2. The text most often used to document this point is Sigmund Freud, "Formulations Regarding the Two Principles of Mental Functioning," in *The Collected Papers of Sigmund Freud*, ed. Ernest Jones, trans. Joan Rivière, 5 vols. (1911; New York: Basic Books, 1959), 4:13–21.
3. Sigmund Freud, *Moses and Monotheism*, trans. Katherine Jones (1939; New York: Vintage Books, 1955).
4. Sigmund Freud, *Civilization and Its Discontents*, trans. Joan Rivière (1930; New York: Doubleday Anchor, 1958).
5. Sigmund Freud, *The Future of an Illusion*, trans. W. D. Robson-Scott (1927; New York: Doubleday Anchor, 1957).
6. Sigmund Freud, *New Introductory Lectures on Psychoanalysis*, trans. W. J. H. Sprott (New York: W. W. Norton & Co., 1933).
7. Sigmund Freud, *Totem and Taboo*, trans. James Strachey (1912; New York: W. W. Norton & Co., 1950).
8. Sigmund Freud, *Beyond the Pleasure Principle*, trans. James Strachey (1920; New York: Bantam Books, 1959).
9. Sigmund Freud, *Group Psychology and the Analysis of the Ego*, trans. James Strachey (New York: Bantam Books, 1960).
10. Erik H. Erikson, *Childhood and Society*, 2d ed. (New York: W. W. Norton & Co., 1963).
11. Erik H. Erikson, *Young Man Luther: A Study in Psychoanalysis and History* (New York: W. W. Norton & Co., 1958).
12. Erik H. Erikson, *Gandhi's Truth: On the Origins of Militant Nonviolence* (New York: W. W. Norton & Co., 1969).
13. Karen Horney, *The Neurotic Personality of Our Time* (New York: W. W. Norton & Co., 1937).
14. Harry Stack Sullivan, *The Interpersonal Theory of Psychiatry* (New York: W. W. Norton & Co., 1953).
15. Erich Fromm, *Escape from Freedom* (New York: Rinehart & Co., 1941).
16. Erich Fromm, *"The Dogma of Christ" and Other Essays on Religion, Psychology, and Culture* (1930; London: Routledge and Kegan Paul, 1963).

17. Erich Fromm, *Psychoanalysis and Religion* (New Haven: Yale University Press, 1950).

18. Erich Fromm, ed., *Zen Buddhism and Psychoanalysis* (New York: Grove Press, 1963).

19. Medard Boss, *Psychoanalysis and Daseinsanalysis*, trans. Ludwig B. Le Febre (1957; New York: Basic Books, 1963).

20. Ludwig Binswanger, *Being-in-the-World*, trans. Jacob Needleman (New York: Basic Books, 1963). This volume contains essays published between 1936 and 1957.

21. May's debt to Tillich is made most explicit in a lesser-known essay, Rollo May, "On the Phenomenological Bases of Psychotherapy," in *Phenomenology: Pure and Applied*, ed. Erwin W. Strauss (Pittsburgh: Duquesne University Press, 1964).

22. Erik H. Erikson, *Identity and the Life Cycle: Selected Papers*, Psychological Issues, vol. 1, no. 1 (New York: International Universities Press, 1959).

23. Heinz Hartmann, *Ego Psychology and the Problem of Adapatation*, trans. David Rapaport (New York: International Universities Press, 1958).

24. Ernst Kris, *Psychoanalytic Explorations in Art* (1950; New York: Schocken Books, 1964). See esp. the essay entitled "On Preconscious Mental Processes," pp. 301–21.

25. Roy Schafer, "The Loving and Beloved Superego in Freud's Structural Theory," in *The Psychoanalytic Study of the Child*, vol. 15 (New York: International Universities Press, 1960).

26. See, for example, Hartmann, *Ego Psychology*, pp. 74–79.

27. Jean-Paul Sartre, *Being and Nothingness*, trans. Hazel E. Barnes (1946; New York: Philosophical Library, 1956); Paul Tillich, "The Theological Significance of Existentialism and Psychoanalysis," in *Theology of Culture*, ed. Robert C. Kimball (1955; New York: Oxford University Press, 1959); and Martin Buber, "Guilt and Guilt Feelings," in *The Knowledge of Man*, ed. and trans. Maurice Friedman (1957; New York: Harper & Row, 1965).

28. John Wisdom, *Philosophy and Psychoanalysis* (Oxford: Basil Blackwell, 1964); Anthony Flew, "Psychoanalytic Explanation," in *Philosophy and Analysis*, ed. Margaret Macdonald (Oxford: Basil Blackwell, 1954). See also Sidney Hook, ed., *Psychoanalysis, Scientific Method, and Philosophy* (New York: New York University Press, 1959).

29. Maurice Merleau-Ponty, *The Structure of Behavior*, trans. Alden Fisher (1942; Boston: Beacon Press, 1963), and Paul Ricoeur, *Freedom and Nature: The Voluntary and the Involuntary*, trans. Erazim V. Kohák (1950; Evanston, Ill.: Northwestern University Press, 1966).

30. A good example of this stance toward Freud can be seen in Sartre's change of mind from his first assessment of psychoanalytic insight as merely another instance of "bad faith" (in *Being and Nothingness*) to his more recent and more appreciative recognition of the subtlety and complexity of

Freud's thought. Writing about her own and Sartre's view of psychoanalysis, Simone de Beauvoir recently remarked:

> We looked favorably on the notion that psychoses, neuroses, and their various symptoms had a meaning, and that this meaning must be sought in the patient's childhood. But we stopped short at this point; we rejected psychoanalysis as a tool for exploring a normal human being. We had hardly read any Freud apart from his books *The Interpretation of Dreams* and *The Psychopathology of Everyday Life.* We had absorbed the letter rather than the spirit of these works: we were put off by their dogmatic symbolism and the technique of association which vitiated them for us. Freud's pansexualism struck us as having an element of madness about it, besides offending our puritanical instincts. Above all, the importance it attached to the unconscious and the rigidity of its mechanistic theories meant that Freudianism, as we conceived it, was bound to eradicate human free will. No one showed us how the two might possibly be reconciled, and we were incapable of finding out for ourselves. We remained frozen in our rationalist-voluntarist position: in a clear-minded individual, we thought, freedom would win out over complexes, memories, influences, or any traumatic experience. It was a long time before we realized that our emotional detachment from, and indifference to our respective childhoods was to be explained by what we had experienced as children.

Simone de Beauvoir, *The Prime of Life* (New York: World Publishing Company, 1962). I am indebted to Stuart Charmé of the University of Chicago for pointing out to me this shift in Sartre's thinking.

31. Philip Rieff, *Freud: The Mind of the Moralist* (New York: Viking Press, 1959); Norman O. Brown, *Life Against Death: The Psychoanalytic Meaning of History* (New York: Random House, 1959); Herbert Marcuse, *Eros and Civilization* (Boston: Beacon Press, 1955); and Paul Ricoeur, *Freud and Philosophy*, trans. Denis Savage (1965; New Haven, Conn.: Yale University Press, 1970). For a review of these interpretations of Freud, see Peter Homans, *Theology After Freud: An Interpretive Inquiry* (Indianapolis, Ind.: Bobbs-Merrill, 1970). Like Sartre, Ricoeur has altered his view of Freud radically. In *Freedom and Nature* he viewed Freud as a strict determinist. (He associated the Freudian unconsciousness with "the absolute involuntary.") In *Freud and Philosophy* he argued for a dimension of meaning in Freud, alongside the strand of determinist thinking. Freudianism is seen to have a hermeneutical dimension, as well as being a strict science.

32. Ricoeur is a philosopher with theological commitments, Brown is a classicist turned historian, and Rieff is a sociologist.

33. See Rieff, *Mind of the Moralist,* chap. 10, "The Emergence of Psychological Man."

34. See Ricoeur, *Freud and Philosophy*, esp. the section entitled "Dialectic: Archeology and Teleology," pp. 459–93.

35. See, for example, Sam Keen, *To a Dancing God* (New York: Harper

& Row, 1970), esp. the section entitled "Storytelling and the Discovery of Identity," pp. 70–74.

36. In addition to the epistemological and historical forms of cultural reflection on psychoanalysis, there is a third form, referred to above, that interprets psychoanalysis from the point of view of the sociology of (psychological) knowledge. Since it is only now emerging, and since Erikson's work does not engage it as directly as it does the other two, it is not included here. For examples of such an approach, see Peter Berger, "Toward a Sociological Understanding of Psychoanalysis," *Social Research* 32 (1965): 26–41, and John Murray Cuddihy, *The Ordeal of Civility* (New York: Basic Books, 1974). For a similar sociological interpretation of the psychology of Carl Rogers, see Peter Homans, "Carl Rogers' Psychology and the Theory of Mass Society," in *Innovations in Client-Centered Therapy*, ed. David A. Wexler and Laura North Rice (New York: John Wiley and Sons, 1974), pp. 319–37.

37. See Erikson, *Childhood and Society*, chap 11. In this chapter, entitled "Beyond Anxiety," Erikson discusses the anxieties of contemporary Americans and offers his clinical knowledge as a solution. In doing so, Erikson assumes that a properly reformulated interpretation of psychoanalytic theory can meet the need of a modern world for meaning—a need created by the decline in the power of traditional religion to bind the individual into a meaningful social structure. What modernity lacks is stability, the key to stability is tradition, and the key to tradition is religion.

Childhood and Selfhood

ESSAYS ON
TRADITION, RELIGION, AND MODERNITY
IN THE PSYCHOLOGY OF
ERIK H. ERIKSON

Part I

Erikson's Psychology and Religion

1

Luther and His Father: Observations on Erik H. Erikson's *Young Man Luther: A Study in Psychoanalysis and History*[1]

HEINRICH BORNKAMM

Translated by Christoph Stauder

The conflict between father and son belongs to the painful experiences of mankind. One encounters it not only in the generation problem, as such, but also in the particular encounter between a father and his eminent son, who is unwittingly preparing for his historical role. In retrospect, the father inevitably falls into the weaker position. Therefore, he has a certain right, insofar as the sources permit it, to be treated and examined leniently and with special care, particularly in a case in which the temporary wound not only healed but later even strengthened the mutual bond of love. Certainly it is not always so. But that is how it was with Luther and his father.

A second characteristic must also be considered before one attempts to interpret such a relationship according to psychological analogies, however indispensable they may be.

In contrast to other famous father-son conflicts—such as those between Frederick the Great and his father and between Schleiermacher and his father—the roles of Luther and his father were reversed. In their case it was the father who (*cum grano salis*) had a modern understanding of life, whereas the son, who entered the monastery against his father's wishes, belonged to a world that really was already overcome. Hans Luther was that type of successful modern man for whom the social advancement of his family was of greater account than any religious sacrifice that could be offered to God. Compared to his own father, a farmer in Möhra, he had come a long way. After his early, difficult years as a miner he became co-owner of a copper mine, later even of several of them. In 1491 he became one of the "quadrumvirate," the four representatives of the citizenry who stood alongside the council of Mansfeld. Now the son was supposed to carry things an even greater step forward. For that reason the father had sent him to good schools and then to the university to study law; with Martin's talents, he could hope for a fine career. This was surely compatible with a simple church piety, but it was also the limit of what the father thought should be asked of him, even for the sake of God. The son, on the other hand, wanted to make a step backwards into a monastic life that had long since lost its prestige and was commonly looked down upon. The fact that he fled from the latent secularization that began to permeate the time and took instead a path away from the world, against all common sense and the warnings of his father, was certainly decisive for his future significance.

Upon this path he found his way not only to God but also to himself and, after years of estrangement, back to his father. The psychologist obviously has his share to contribute to an understanding of this event. The historian, who is accustomed to working with the basic sources, will first of all, before he raises questions and objections, want to express gratitude to Erik H. Erikson for the love and knowledge of the person and writings of Luther that he displays in his interpretation. Erikson writes with the awareness that he can contribute something from his background that others have not yet accomplished, as well as with the modest knowledge that his work is only an attempt "to grasp something essential in the reformation which stands at the beginning of our era, something which we have neither completely lived down nor successfully outlived."[2] He adds that "such is the material of psychoanalysis," and thereby characterizes the nature of his work; it is a therapy that seeks to unravel the muddled contents of the soul, to preserve the essential in transmission and to discard the distorted. At this point, however, one must ask whether the means of psychoanalysis are indeed adequate to this task or whether psychoanalysis, when applied as the single key to the problem, must not necessarily come into conflict with history, especially with regard to such a unique and incomparable figure as Luther. Nonetheless, the historian can at first only learn from the abundance of observations and brilliant formulations that are found—along with much that is open to dispute—in Erikson's book. Above all, he can learn from Erikson's sensitivity to the deepest stirrings in Luther's life and to the "utter integrity" with which he reports the stages that characterize the development of his personality as a genuine *homo religiosus*. "I emphasize this . . . because it makes his total experience a historical event far beyond its immediate sectarian significance, namely, a decisive step in human awareness and responsibility. To indicate this step in its psychological coordinates is the burden of this book."[3]

Erikson describes the principal upheaval in the life of the young Luther—his entry into the monastery—with the Freudian concept of *identity crisis*[4]*, the period in which a young person has not yet found his individuality and only painfully becomes himself. The crisis is anticipated by a

---

* Editor's note: Here Bornkamm is mistaken. The concept of *identity crisis* is not, of course, a Freudian concept, but is rather one that belongs to Erikson's conceptual framework.

series of stages (*infancy, early childhood, initiative versus guilt, age of learning*), which Erikson seeks to correlate—not without violence, given the scarcity of the material—with the stages of Luther's early youth. To this he adds still another stage called the *integrity crisis*, "which again leads man to the portals of nothingness." "This integrity crisis, last in the lives of ordinary men, is a life-long and chronic crisis in the *homo religiosus*."[5] Erikson projects these general and timeless categories onto the historical plane of Luther's day, which he refers to as "a period in history when organized religion dominated ideologies."[6] Religion provided him with the support a young person strives for in his state of crisis—namely, a view of the world that offers something new over and beyond the knowledge already acquired. An ideology is "an utopian outlook, a cosmic mood, or a doctrinal logic. . . . What is to be relinquished as 'old' may be the individual's previous life; this usually means the perspectives intrinsic to the life-style of the parents. . . . The 'old' may be part of himself, which must henceforth be subdued by some rigorous self-denial in a private life-style or through membership in a militant or military organization."[7] In the case of Luther all this bears upon the choice of a monastic order.

Ideology is naturally a vague and somewhat suspect term. One should not take exception to it, however, but should accept it in the way Erikson uses it in his fine chapter entitled "The Meaning of 'Meaning It' ": "Meaning it, then is not a matter of creedal protestation; verbal explicitness is not a sign of faith. Meaning it, means to be at one with an ideology in the process of rejuvenation; it implies a successful sublimation of one's libidinal strivings; and it manifests itself in a liberated craftsmanship."[8] Erikson is not referring to the conventional ideology of the Roman Catholic church of the time but, instead, to that of Paul, the early Christians, and Augustine; they alone could provide an answer to what was happening in the depth of Luther's soul. He devotes a lengthy description to these "ideological influences," distinguishing Luther from the

Renaissance and humanism, as well as, with instinctive certainty, from German mysticism.[9] Luther found himself facing a task far greater than that of awakening a mystical mode of experience that might surpass simple gnosis: "The return to a state of symbiosis with the matrix, a state of floating unity fed by a spiritual navel cord. . . . He was intellectually . . . unfit for it."[10] Or, to employ another of Erikson's characterizations, Luther was not fit for mysticism because he, like other intellectual giants, had to do the "dirty work" of his time. Such is not the business of a mystic. Instead, according to Erikson, "Luther accepted for his life work the unconquered frontier of tragic conscience, defined as it was by his personal needs and his superlative gifts. . . . Hans' son was made for a job on this frontier. But he did not create the job; it originated in the hypertrophy of the negative conscience inherent in our whole Judaeo-Christian heritage in which, as Luther put it: 'Christ becomes more formidable a tyrant and a judge than was Moses.' But the negative conscience can become hypertrophied only when man hungers for his identity. We must accept this universal, if weird, frontier of the negative conscience as the circumscribed *locus* of Luther's work."[11]

At this point it also becomes clear why Erikson sets apart his own theory from the psychopathological interpretation of Luther advanced by the Danish doctor Paul J. Reiter.[12] "The psychiatrist" (Erikson assigns role designations to various figures in his work) evaluates a series of conspicuous psychic excitations and character traits as symptoms "of a steady, pitiless, 'endogenous' process which, in Luther's middle forties, was climaxed by a frank psychosis. *Endogenous* really means biological; Reiter feels that Luther's attacks cannot 'with the best of will' be conceived of as links 'in the chain of meaningful psychological development.' "[13] Erikson writes: "I think the psychiatrist misjudges his man when he thinks that endogenous sickness alone could have kept Luther from becoming a well-balanced (*ausgeglichen*) creature when his preaching brought him success. . . . On the frontier of conscience, the dirty work never stops, the lying old words are never done with, and the new purities remain forever dimmed."[14] But even from the standpoint of Luther's mental predispositions, Erikson does not find Reiter's diagnosis convincing. He measures him "with some norm of *Ausgeglichenheit*—an inner balance, a simple enjoyment of life, and an ordinary decency and decided direction of effort such as normal people are said to display. Though the psychiatrist makes repeated allowances for Luther's genius, he nevertheless demands of him a state of inner repose which, as far as I know, men of creative intensity and of an increasing historical commitment cannot be expected to be able to maintain." If such an equilibrium "does exist, I would expect it least of all in such a sensitive, passionate, and ambitious individual as young Luther."[15]

Whereas Luther is not a case for the psychiatrist, according to Erikson, his character and constitution are nevertheless suitable objects for study by the psychoanalyst. Without going so far as to call him sick, he can still refer to him as a "patient" in Kierkegaard's sense of the term: "Luther . . . is a patient of exceeding import for Christendom." By the term *patient* Erikson means "a life style of patienthood as a sense of imposed suffering, of an intense need for cure, and (as Kierkegaard adds) a 'passion for expressing and describing one's suffering.' "[16] In other words, Erikson understands Luther as the character type of a *homo religiosus* by "the inner logic of his way of life, by the logic of his working gifts, and by the logic of his effect on society. To study and formulate this logic seems to me to constitute the task at hand, if one wishes to consider the total existence of a man like Luther."[17]

Constitution and lawfulness, such as they can be observed in young people in accordance with analogous psychoanalytic experiences, are the presuppositions of Erikson's work; the specific task that he sets for himself is an analysis of the origin of the crisis that determined Luther's life. He finds it, in conformity with the teaching of Freud, in Luther's strained relationship with his father and the shadow that this cast over the relationship with his mother. Erikson draws on a considerable number of dark hues belonging to Luther's later memories in order to paint his picture of the relationship of the young Martin to his parents. But he leaves aside many of the lighter colors that could brighten up the picture, painting in, instead, lots of black, which he derives from his knowledge of personal conflict. This, however, considerably oversimplifies the matter. It is far more difficult to sketch a realistic picture of Luther's childhood and youth, one that is faithful to the sources, than it is to draw such a crass one. The historian, grateful as he is for the interpretative aids he has received, will nevertheless not simply capitulate before the clinician's claim to "recognize major trends even where the facts are not available,"[18] least of all when some facts are being overlooked and others added.

There is incontrovertible evidence that Martin's parents reared the boy in a stern manner—indeed too stern for his sensitivity. He never forgot two particularly harsh instances of corporal punishment: once his mother beat him so hard that blood flowed;[19] another time his father struck him so forcefully "that I ran away from him, and he was worried that he might not win me back again."[20] The phrase "he was worried" shows that the father's remorse, too, impressed itself on the boy's memory. Unfortunately Erikson relies upon a poor source in this case; the phrase should read: "I fled and grudged him."[21] That is something quite different.* In reporting the "nut" story Luther himself comes to the conclusion that it was the severe upbringing by his parents that finally led him into the monastery, however well they had meant it. He was extremely timid, he recalls. "They weren't able to keep a right balance between temperament and punishment. One must punish in such a way that the rod is accompanied by the apple. It is a bad thing if children and pupils lose their spirit on account of their parents and teachers."[22] Even if these are not Luther's own

---

* **Editor's note: Bornkamm does not cite Erikson's translation of the disputed phrase, which is to be found in Erikson, *Young Man Luther*, p. 64.**

words but come from what seems to be a faithful account, they nevertheless constitute an important and revealing statement that points not to a simple but rather to a broken and complex connection between Luther and his parents. The parents indeed did not wish to send him to the monastery; he entered against their will. To be sure, their upbringing and religious instruction had fostered in him an acute sense of conscientiousness. But this was now no longer directed at them but, instead, became a response to the higher claim of God, which ultimately abrogated obedience to the parents. In resolving this conflict, Luther was no longer merely the product of misguided parental upbringing but was an independent self who stood squarely on his own individuality with its powerful and extraordinary sensitivity.

Erikson does not entirely ignore this religious core into which Luther's youthful experiences finally consolidated and out of which everything else grew, but he does not take it seriously in its own right. He pictures it as the form in which the conflict with the father, from which such a religious core originated in the first place, accidentally worked itself out. The psychoanalytic interpretation eclipses the more obvious one and deprives it of its significance. Luther himself often enough mentioned his primary motivation for joining the monastery: "I entered the monastery that I might not perish but have eternal life. I wanted to follow my own counsel and help myself by means of the cowl."[23] The stern God and the image of Christ as judge of the world, as frequently depicted on the triumphal arches of the churches, weighed heavily upon his soul. Thus he sought refuge in the security that a life of monastic asceticism seemed to promise. Monasticism itself had impressed him from early childhood on: the inwardness of the *Nullbrüder*;[24] the Brethren of the Common Life, who had been his educators in Magdeburg in 1496–97; the Duke of Anhalt whom he met there roaming the streets in the garb of a Franciscan monk ("without food and sleep, castigated. . . . Whoever looked at him had to smack in reverence and feel ashamed of his worldly condition");[25] and the monks of the Franciscan monastery in Eisenach with whom the pious Schwalbe family, which had taken him into its house, was closely connected. His own, easily stirred heart and the pull of these memories swept him with overwhelming power into the crisis of his youth.[26]

Erikson's almost exclusive preoccupation with Luther's father and with his parental upbringing all too easily leads to a tendency to portray his parents as excessively severe. This is unjust, not only concerning the mother, who is thereby implicated as well, but also with regard to the father. When the son recalls that his parents "sincerely meant well" despite the mistakes they made in his education, he has reason to do so. The sacrifices made by the father to send him to the best schools; the pride with which he followed his progress; the self-evident, unsentimental piety of his parents' home (relatives in Mansfeld report how the father frequently prayed with great fervor at the bedside of his children[27]); his father's inclination to gaiety;[28] his tendency to meditate (as over the imbalance between the grain growing on earth and the number of people);[29] an obvious appreciation for nature, which was transferred to the son—all this accounts for the fact that one finds only statements of love and respect and never a bad word in Luther about the character of his father, the well-meant educational mistakes excluded. The statement that Hans Luther "belonged to the narrow, suspicious, primitive-religious, catastrophe-minded people"[30] goes far beyond what the sources allow one to say. Rather, there were traits of rationality in him: his aversion to monasticism; his concern with the arithmetical problem of the inadequate sheaves of grain; his frank refusal to bequeath something to the church when a clergyman pressed him hard during a severe illness (he had many children, he said, who needed it far more[31]); and his cool rejection of the voice from heaven that his son claimed to have heard in a thunderstorm (it could just as well have been an illusion). What is remarkable is not that he reckoned with some kind of demonic spook—that was a self-evident part of the world-view of his day—but that he was so skeptical about unusual religious experiences of which legends of saints were indeed so full.

It is likewise enormously exaggerated in comparison with Luther's own account, when the father is said to have "expressed some of his native fury . . . in the home itself," or to have beaten "the residue of a stubborn peasant out of his son."[32] In Luther's memories the thrashings were exceptions, even if he added that, for the moment, they could dim a child's consciousness of the kindnesses received from father and mother. His later judgment is more balanced.[33] Erikson is mistaken when he concludes that the notorious alcoholic excesses of the brother of Luther's father, which were known even to the courts, influenced him to "blow off steam" through occasional spanking incidents at home.[34] Similarly, one should no longer pass on the ugly allegation, even if only by repeating it in the narrative, that the father himself committed a murder; there are no reliable grounds for alleging this.[35] Hans Luther enjoyed a secure reputation in his town.

The way in which Erikson pictures Luther's father as a brutal and frightful figure also determines his conception of Luther's relationship to his mother—in two ways. One conception involves the Oedipus complex, "love for the maternal person who awakens [Luther's] senses and sensuality with her ministrations, and deep and angry rivalry with the male possessor of this maternal person"[36]—a rivalry aggravated by "the father's alcoholic, sexual and cruel self-indulgence," which obviously broke "through his moralistic mask."[37] Here, too, Erikson employs violent distortions.[38] Taking Reiter's description of the conditions in the family bedroom, of which nothing is known at all, he constructs a series of pure conjectures concerning what "the boy Martin, already made sleepless by corporal punishment," could have observed of the sexual life of his parents. "Some of the observations made at night may have put the father's moralistic daytime armour into a strange sadistic light."[39]

Luther, who treated sexual matters with great candor, once touched upon this topic in a wholly different sense: one gains the proper appreciation of the natural married life, which so easily lends itself to distorted conceptions, he believed, only when one looks back upon the marriage of one's own parents, who were surely pious people, or upon those of the patriarchs and prophets. In them one sees, he asserted, that marriage is a truly divine estate. The self-evident openness with which he mentions father and mother here puts an end to the idea of cramping and repressive memories.[40]

The reverse side of Erikson's theory about the injured Oedipal love of Luther for his mother is revealed in his question "Didn't the man have a mother?"[41] "Nobody would discuss women and marriage in the way he often did who had not been deeply disappointed by his mother—and had become loath to succumb the way she did to the father, to fate."[42] It would be easy to prove that Luther's image of women and marriage truly brought no discredit to his mother. More important is another of Erikson's inferences—namely, that out of the disappointment in his mother Luther lost access to the Mother of God.[43] The very opposite is true. He frequently mentioned how he fled to Mary in his fear of the angry God and the judging Christ and, "whenever our dear Lady was not enough," to other saints as well.[44] His later opposition was directed not against Mary, whom he still affectionately loved, but, rather, against the Catholic Mariology, which had made the human Lady of the Gospel, herself in need of redemption, into a heavenly fantasy figure.

It is a pity that Erikson has piled up such a heap of exaggerations and groundless speculations before the real figures of Luther's parents. This would not have been necessary at all in order to illustrate the strain that their educational measures did in fact place on his development and on the crisis of his adolescence. No doubt the atmosphere in the home was not infrequently gloomy, and the mother did not have the strength to brighten things up.

Apparently, the workload and the number of her children were too much for her.[45] Her little verse, often quoted by Luther—"For me and you nobody cares. That is our common fault"—clearly bespeaks a life of sadness and resignation, which had its effect on her young son. Luther's predisposition to melancholy seems to have issued from her side, or at least not from his father, who knew how to cope with life.[46] It is understandable that Luther's inner crisis was at once a test of his strength in relation to his father and an identity crisis of his own personality.

The elements, predispositions, and experiences in the soul of the young Luther may have been diverse and manifold, yet, according to Erikson's psychoanalytic interpretation, their relation, which leads to the decisive turning point, is basically a simple one. "Indeed, one may say that by radically transferring the desperation of his filial position into the human condition vis-à-vis God, . . . he forced himself either to find a new avenue toward faith or to fail."[47] But is it so simple to "transfer" and to "force oneself"? The fact that Erikson narrows the problem down to the father and denies the question of God any claim of its own comes strongly into play here. It is by this means that Erikson understands all of the individual experiences that make up the crisis. Especially important for him is the story of an incident that supposedly happened during the choral prayer in the Erfurt monastery. It is said that during the reading of the story of the epileptic child (Mark 9:14–29) Luther broke down, screaming: "Non sum! Non sum!" The question of the historicity of the incident itself is of no significance here.[48] What is important is the way in which Erikson uses this report. He attaches great significance to the fact that *non sum* must mean "I am *not*" (instead of "It is not I"—namely, the possessed one). Grammatically, this is unfounded, but it gives him the opportunity to omit the connection with the biblical text (although, in the context, it is beyond question) and to replace it with what he takes to be Luther's constant problem during his monastic stay: "I am *not* what my father said I was and what my conscience, in bad moments, tends to confirm I am."[49] For Erikson, it is a matter of "the epileptoid paroxysm of ego-loss, the rage of denial of the identity which was to be discarded."[50]

The question of why Erikson keeps bringing in the father forces itself upon the reader again and again. "What he had been unable to say to his father and to his teachers in due time he said . . . , with a vengeance, to the Pope."[51] Luther's notion of the abandonment of Christ and of the passive conforming of the believer to him in the state of judgment is said to belong to a series of "unconscious tricks" with whose help the ego adjusts to the superego under which it suffers. Does Luther really "assume now on a religious level a volitional role towards filial suffering," and is it true that he "makes of his protracted sonhood the victory of his Christlikeness"?[52] Erikson further states: "In view of Luther's relation to his father, it makes sense that his deepest clinical despair emerged when he had become so much of what his father had wanted him to be: influential, economically secure, a kind of superlawyer and the father of a son named Hans."[53] If only it was so easy to explain the somber melancholy under which Luther sometimes suffered! To the reader who is sensitive to the abundance of other features of Luther's memories of his youth, the constant preoccupation with the father seems quite frequently a forcing of the issue.

Erikson's views of Luther's relation to his father leads him to find in it the one and only key to unlock the whole. The fact that Luther failed on his self-chosen way into the cloister—after monastic works, confession, and his experiments with mysticism had not helped—is again interpreted by means of the old scheme: "All of which led to his final totalism, the establishment of God in the role of the dreaded and untrustworthy father. With this the circle closes and the repressed returns in full force; for here God's position corresponds closely to the one occupied by Martin's father at the time when Martin attempted to escape to theology by way of the thunderstorm."[54] Erikson is far from belittling this event; on the contrary, he wants to express, with the aid of psychoanalysis, Luther's most frightful experiences. He understands Luther's statements as a "confession compulsion": "This is . . . an acknowledgment that something had been wrong with that first bolt of lightning [that drove him into the monastery] just as his father had suspected. . . . The praising ended and the blaspheming began. In the face of such contempt and wilful mistrust, God could only appear in horrible and accusatory wrath, with man prostate in His sight."[55] But why should one consider Luther so monomanic as to say that he associated all this only with the father image? Was it not after all, the image of God that looked out upon him from countless biblical texts and from church traditions? This criticism also applies to Luther's exclamation: "Help me, St. Anne . . . I want to become a monk." It did not mean that, as a "motherly mediator," "she might intercede with the father."[56] This and the many other appeals to the saints about which Luther later frequently reminisced represented, rather, a supplication for intercession with the judging God. But St. Anne was also meant to act as a witness to the fact that he vowed to make the greatest expiatory sacrifice a human being can possibly offer. The narrow family framework into which Luther's experience seems regularly compressed hardly does justice to the depth and power of such experiences, although Erikson, too, wants to convey it in these dimensions.

The final word concerning Luther's relationship to his father in the time of crisis comes from the reformer himself. It is found in a detailed letter of 21 November 1521 in which he dedicated the treatise *On Monastic Vows*, written at Wartburg Castle, to his father.[57] At the same time, it is the earliest and most carefully formulated account he gives of the events surrounding his entry into the monastery. The letter therefore serves as an authoritative reference concerning later reminiscences of Luther handed down to us with frequently questionable fidelity in the form of recorded table conversations, sermons, or lectures. The book on vows grew out of a concern that the many monks and nuns who were leaving the monasteries and getting married in the wake of the Reformation were making it too easy for themselves. Some day they might be haunted by pangs of conscience as to whether they had the right to break their vows, which were, after all, made voluntarily. On their behalf—for he himself had, as yet, no intention of breaking his own vows—Luther therefore endeavored to find ways in which they might legitimately stand before God and their own consciences. He supported his conclusions with arguments from God's Word, faith, evangelical freedom, and love and reason, and systematically attacked the grip of monastic vows upon the conscience. The broadly designed, passionate treatise is for him at the same time a settling of accounts with his youth and, from the higher standpoint of freedom, with his father as well, who had once counseled him not to keep the vow that he had made in the fear of death in the thunderstorm.

> I wish you to know that your son has reached the point where he is altogether persuaded that there is nothing holier, nothing more important, nothing more scrupulously to be observed than God's commandment. But there you will say, "Have you been so unfortunate as ever to doubt this, and have you only now learned that this is so?" Most unfortunately indeed I not only doubted it, but I did not at all know that it is so; and if you will permit me, I am ready to show you that this ignorance was common to both of us.
>
> It is now almost sixteen years since I became a monk, taking the vow without your knowledge and against your will. In your paternal love you were fearful about my weakness because I was then a youth, just entering my twenty-second year (that is, to use St. Augustine's words, I was still "clothed in hot youth"), and you had learned from numerous examples that this way of life turned out sadly for many. You were determined, therefore, to tie me down with an honorable and wealthy marriage. This fear of yours, this care, this indignation against me was for a time implacable. [Your] friends tried in vain to

persuade you that if you wished to offer something to God, you ought to give your dearest and your best. The Lord, meanwhile, was dinning in your ears that Psalm verse [Ps. 94:11]: "God knows the thoughts of men, that they are vain"; but you were deaf. At last you desisted and bowed to the will of God, but your fears for me were never laid aside. For I remember very well that after we were reconciled and you were [again] talking to me, I told you that I had been called by terrors from heaven and that I did not become a monk of my own free will and desire, still less to gain any gratification of the flesh, but that I was walled in by the terror and the agony of sudden death and forced of necessity to take the vow. Then you said, "Let us hope that it was not an illusion and a deception." That word penetrated to the depths of my soul and stayed there, as if God had spoken by your lips, though I hardened my heart against you and your word as much as I could. You said something else too. When in filial confidence I upbraided you for your wrath, you suddenly retorted with a reply so fitting and so much to the point that I have hardly ever in all my life heard any man say anything which struck me so forcibly and stayed with me so long. "Have you not also heard," you said, "that parents are to be obeyed?" But I was sure of my own righteousness that in you I heard only a man, and boldly ignored you; though in my heart I could not ignore your word.[58]

That is Luther's famous account of his entry into the monastery. But instead of proceeding to excuse himself in relation to his father, or to prove him right by means of his new insight into the futility of monastic vows, he writes: "See now whether you, too, were not unaware that the commandments of God are to be put before all things." Otherwise the father, by his paternal power, might have taken him completely out of monasticism. Neither one knew that it was the obedience to God's commands that was at stake, for the father worried about the son, whereas the son believed that he had to follow his vow. God alone could help. "Behold how much God (whose mercies are without number and whose wisdom is without end) has made to come out of all these errors and sins! Would you now not rather have lost a hundred sons than not have seen this good?"

And then Luther put himself once more into the original situation that, after all, still existed: "Will you still take me out of the monastery? You are still my father and I am still your son and all the vows are worthless." The father could, to be sure, have demanded that Luther lay aside the monastic gown and enter into marriage. But in the meantime someone else had acted. "But that you would not boast of it, the Lord has anticipated you, and taken me out himself. What difference does it make whether I retain or lay aside the cowl and tonsure? . . . My conscience has been freed, and that is the most complete liberation. Therefore I am still a monk and yet not a monk. I am a new creature, not of the Pope but of Christ." The relationship between Luther and his father was thereby radically changed. "[God], who has taken me out of the monastery, has an authority over me that is greater than yours." If it had been only a matter of the monastic estate, he could no longer have been disobedient without violating his conscience: "So I am now absolutely persuaded." But something else had been added to monasticism: the service in the Word. To him applies the teaching of Jesus that "he who loves father or mother more than me is not worthy of me." In the conflict between the authority of the parents and that of Christ, "Christ's authority must reign alone." "He is himself (as they say) my immediate bishop, abbot, prior, lord, father, and teacher; I know no other. Thus I hope that he has taken from you one son in order that he may begin to help the sons of many others through me. You ought not only to endure this willingly, but you ought to rejoice with exceeding joy—and this I am sure is what you will do." "Farewell in Christ, my dearest father, and greet in Christ my mother, your Margaret, and our whole family."

Luther's letter speaks a language as childlike as it is

sovereign. After carefully reexamining his conscience concerning the fateful problem of his youth, the monastic vows, he rejected for the second time the secret, or perhaps even explicit, wishes of his father. Once he had cleared the way for his fellow monks, he himself was not about to give up the monastic life. The question had become irrelevant for him. While he was aware of his freedom, he nevertheless felt that he should not make visible use of it because he was now called to a higher duty. Forced for the sake of others to publicly deal with the question of vows, to whom should he have presented the reasons for his behavior other than his father, who opposed his conscience at the time? Luther's action is a sign of unblemished filial respect. He admitted to his father that he acted wrongly at the time and that he would not do it again under the same circumstances. Yet at the same time he declared his father guilty, too: neither was aware of God's will in this matter. On the one hand, he put his father in his place, setting him below the law of God and the authority of Christ; on the other hand, he tried to win his father's favor with words of tender love and expressions of grateful recognition of how much his father meant to him and how much to the point he had been in that unforgettable conversation. Finally, he asked his father to open himself to a higher understanding of the meaning of the events that caused them both so much suffering. Was it not, he asked, reason enough for rejoicing and thanksgiving that God has brought about freedom for man despite the cost of erring and suffering?

It is of great consequence for Erikson's analysis of the father–son relationship that he has misunderstood this letter and the revealing paradoxes it contains. "When he had found a new agency to disobey, namely, the Pope, he had to tell his father publicly that he had finally obeyed him; but we cannot overlook the ambivalent wish to be right at all costs, for he adds: 'Would you still want to tear me out [of the monastery]? . . . In order to save you from a sense of vain-glory, God outdistanced you and took me out himself. . . .' Thus Luther stated to all the world (for his works were then best-sellers) not only that his father had opposed the monastic career, but also that the son had belatedly made this opposition his own—to God's glory, not the father's."[59] But Luther was not in the least concerned with obedience to the Pope; he had already freed himself from that several years earlier. Even now he did not obey his father but stayed with his free decision to continue his monastic life. It made really no difference to him whether he was in the right; he confessed to his father that, in human terms, he could not be disobedient to him again. But the God who liberated him from the obligations of his vows had now acquired a claim upon him. God for him was something more than a mere construct for the fulfillment of the ambivalent wish to remain in the right and, at the same time, to justify his father.[60]

In spite of his honest attempts to find information about Luther's crisis in this important document, Erikson is basically not interested in *what* Luther writes, but in *why* he writes. "We can only wonder at the naiveté with which Luther insisted on airing, to the widest possible public, conflicts which seem too ordinary for a man of his stature. Or are they so ordinary? Perhaps only a man of such stature could be sufficiently sensitive to the personal conflicts that contributed to his theological decisions, and would have enough honesty to talk about them. Being a rebellious theologian, not an armchair psychologist, Luther described his conflicts in surprising, sometimes blustering, and often unreliable words. But one cannot help feeling that Luther often publicly confessed just those matters which Freud, more than three hundred years later (enlightenment having reached the psychological point of no return) faced explicitly, and molded into concepts, when, studying his dreams, he challenged and disciplined the neurotic component of his intellectual research."[61] What Luther wrote was anything but naive. At the outset of a treatise that, more than any of his previous writings, dealt with a problem as urgent as monastic vows, both generally and personally, a bit of personal testimony about his own experience was certainly not out of place—quite apart from the fact that in letters of that kind such personal confessions and communications were then very much in style. It proves Luther's great significance, according to Erikson, that his deep sensitivity to the conflicts of his life and the honesty with which he talked about them make him a precursor of Freud. He repeatedly acknowledges this parallel in his book: "Few men before [Freud] gave more genuine expression to those experiences which are on the borderline between the psychological and the theological than Luther, who gleaned from these experiences a religious gain formulated in theological terms."[62] The two would also have agreed on the importance of childhood to one's later development.[63] When used as an interpretative aid, the psychology of personal conflicts, "which played a role in his theological decisions," can indeed be of very significant help. Even less can one object when psychology attempts to "exploit" Luther's theology because it "has striking configurational parallels with inner dynamic shifts like those which clinicians recognize in the recovery of individuals from psychic distress."[64]

The fact that Luther was a psychological genius is beyond question. This would be an important theme and worthy subject matter in its own right, and Erikson has many suggestions to offer regarding the matter. He illustrates the worthiness of the topic for development with reference to some ideas found in Luther's early lectures—ideas that he has studied in great detail: (1) Voice and word are the instruments of faith; the latter arises from hearing, not from seeing.[65] This is an expression of the passivity of faith frequently emphasized by Luther. "The theology as well as the psychology of Luther's passivity is that of man in the *state of prayer*, a state in which he fully means what he can say only to God: *Tibi soli peccavi*, I have sinned, not in relation to any person or institution, but in relation only to God, to *my* God."[66] (2) Christ's life is God's face. "The Passion is all that man can know of God: his conflicts, duly faced, are all that he can know of himself."[67] (3) Luther's frequently misunderstood rejection of "good works" is directed against the obsession of the "negative conscience" with the law, which makes every minute into a "miniature edition of the Last Judgment" and takes refuge in the "little self-deliverances" of virtue. For Luther good works are done for their own sake and out of love, and righteous action is preceded by God's declaring man righteous. These examples serve to illustrate how theological and psychological statements parallel each other.

All understanding ceases, however, when psychology completely takes over and absorbs "theological decisions," a not infrequent occurrence. "[Luther's] theological solution [to the father–son conflict]—spiritual return to the faith which is there before all doubt, combined with a political submission to those who by necessity must wield the sword of secular law—seems to fit perfectly his personal need for compromise."[68] A psychological derivation of Luther's theology explains nothing, especially when it is as banal as this one. Here, indeed, psychoanalysis comes into conflict with history. Erikson agrees with Jacob Burckhardt's statement that Luther "should be taken for what he was."[69] This entails, though, that one should also take Luther's relationship to God for what it meant to him. This is not an unwarranted theological demand. One's own point of view must, of course, retain its freedom; when Erikson expresses his conviction that "it is the smiling face and the guiding voice of infantile parent images which religion projects onto the benevolent sky,"[70] one cannot argue with that. But the historian is still required to grant the ideas of so great a figure their own validity and power, however strange and incomprehensible they may appear to him. Even if he does not understand them, he will always arrive at more fruitful insights by keeping his attention focused on them carefully rather than by thinking that he can explain them in terms of childhood causes. Thus one finds in Erikson's book both elements that unnecessarily oversimplify the subject matter, as well as beautiful observations that manage to convey to the reader the power of Luther's figure.

Whoever attends fully to the power of Luther's feeling, his childhood memories—fragmentary as they are—and his lifelong inner relationship to his parents will understand how much he derived security from them and how much he suffered when he did not find that security at the crucial turning point of his life. It is understandable how a man like Staupitz, about whom Erikson has some excellent things to say,[71] became an especially beloved father figure for him. As sincerely as Luther later praised him for his help, however, he did not owe his deliverance from his monastic ordeal to him. Rather, it came from the depths of an intensely inward personal experience that cannot be explained simply on the basis of his relationship to other people, be they his father or Staupitz. One may describe Luther's deliverance in different ways, but in the final analysis the question of its origin must be kept open. Otherwise, one conceals from oneself the historical Luther. His real crisis, encompassing a range of experiences from passionate desperation to liberating certainty, was a crisis between him and God as he had learned to know him in his youth and in the monastery. The identity crisis that involved his father, which was entwined with his experience of the reality of God, was significant only to the extent that it challenged the power of his decision for God and measured its strength. Had the faith question not been so unconditional, the conflict with the father would never have penetrated beyond the realm of the private.

The story of Luther and his father did not come to an end with the settlement of childhood experiences and the crisis of youth. Little more was said later about this crisis, but the references that do exist are significant since they precede or are referred to in those bits and pieces from Luther's table talk from which the terror-inspiring picture of the father has been somewhat freely constructed. When, after years of hesitation, Luther finally decided to marry in the summer of 1525, it was the wish of the elderly father, whom he had visited in Mansfeld, that gave him the final incentive. In a time when Luther saw the devil raging in the Peasants' War, he no longer counted on a long life and felt that he was close to death. In this condition he decided to lay aside the last vestige of his "former popish life" as well. "And so I married on account of my dear father's wishes."[72]

Five years later Luther's father was himself about to die. Upon hearing of his dangerous illness, Luther wrote him a letter of consolation on 15 February 1530 that ranks, along with the letter of dedication of 1521, among the great letters of sons to their fathers. In it he expressed regret that he could not go and see him, but he sent a nephew to determine if it were possible to have his parents brought to Wittenberg: "It would be a heartfelt joy for me (as would be only right) to be around you in person and to show, with filial faithfulness and service, my gratitude to God and to you." Luther went on in the letter to effectively prepare his father for death. "Herewith I commend you to him who loves you more than you love yourself. He has proved his love by taking your sins upon himself and by paying [for them] with his blood, and he has let you know this through the Gospel, . . . so that you are not permitted to worry about or be concerned for anything except keeping your heart strong and reliant on his Word and faith. For our faith is certain, and we don't doubt that we shall shortly see each other again in the presence of Christ. For the departure from this life is a smaller thing to God than if I moved from you in Mansfeld to here, or if you moved from me in Wittenberg to Mansfeld. This is certainly true; it is only a matter of an hour's sleep, and all will be different."[73] A year later he wrote a similar letter to his dying mother, full of the same filial love and pastoral authority.[74] Luther's expressions of pain at the news of the death of his father exhibit the same tone as these letters. They contain the following sentences important in this context: "Through him God gave me my life and upbringing," and, "The memory of the most loving dealing[s] with him have shaken me in the innermost parts of my being, so that seldom if ever have I despised death as much as I do now. Yet 'the righteous man is taken away from calamity, and he enters into peace'; that is we die many times before we die once and for all."[75] Whoever studies the beginnings of the story of Luther and his father must also keep in mind the direction in which that relationship moved after the letter of 1521. He will then come to see that, as turbulent and as tension-filled as much of that relationship was, hatred ultimately had no place in it.

NOTES

1. Erik H. Erikson, *Young Man Luther: A Study in Psychoanalysis and History* (New York: W. W. Norton & Co., 1958). My essay was originally written for a *Festschrift,* appearing in *Psychologische Beiträge*, on occasion of the seventieth birthday of Gerhard Pfahler. At the request of the editors, however, it is being published separately for reasons of space. The original circle of readers for whom this essay was intended has to some extent determined the character of the investigation. It concentrates entirely on the subject given in the title and focuses on the basic issues rather than on the many minor, and frequently problematic, points and faulty historical data otherwise found in Erikson. But this would indeed seem to be the right path for a fruitful discussion of him. To my knowledge, no such discussion has taken place so far, in spite of the wide recognition that the book has received. Besides several reviews, I know of only three more detailed works: a series of noteworthy critical remarks on individual issues by Roland H. Bainton, "Luther: A Psychiatric Portrait," *Yale Review* 48 (1959): 405–10 (reprinted in *Studies on the Reformation* [Boston, 1963], pp. 86–92), and two essays by H. Faber and W. J. Kooiman, differing in parts, "Een Psychoanalyticus over Luther" I–II, *Nederlands Theologisch Tijdschrift* 20 (1965–66): 17–37, 38–48.

In the wider sense, there have been several attempts at interpreting Luther with the help of the psychoanalytic tools of the time. All biographers of Luther work with certain simple psychological categories (most notably Adolf Hausrath, who uses a rather ill-defined notion of *mental illness* [*Gemütskrankheit*] in *Luthers Leben*, 2 vols. [Berlin, 1904], 1:30–37). A first "psychoanalytic" attempt, if not of full value, according to Erikson, was made by American Luther scholar Preserved Smith in his essay "Luther's Early Development in the Light of Psychoanalysis," *American*

Journal of Psychology 24 (1913): 360–77. In declared contradistinction to the Freudian analysis of the latter, the Danish doctor Paul J. Reiter gives a psychopathological diagnosis in *Martin Luthers Umwelt, Charakter und Psychose,* 2 vols. (Kopenhagen, 1937–41). His specific attack against the psychoanalytic method is found in vol. 2, pp. 75–90. The work met with detailed criticism—not least of all because it revives certain aspects of the older polemic found in Denifle and Grisar—from people like Gerhard Ritter, ed., *Archiv für Reformationsgeschichte* 39 (1942): 177–81; Johannes Bergdolt, *Luthertum* (Leipzig, 1943), pp. 39–61; Josef Lortz, *Die Reformation als religiöses Anliegen heute* (1948), pp. 129–34 (Translated into English as *The Reformation, a Problem for Today* [Westminster, Md.: Newman Press, 1964] pp. 119–25). It was in particular Eberhard Grossmann, though, who showed that Reiter's diagnosis ("manic-depressive psychosis," endogenous cyclophrenia) falls with his own main argument of "Luther's Great Attack of Mental Illness, 1527–28" (vol. 2, pp. 98–112). Despite a nine-month-long series of complaints of Luther stemming from prolonged periods of *Anfechtung* and melancholy, a depressive phase of an organically-grown psychosis, Grossmann believes, is out of the question due to the compensating factor of Luther's busy and active life. We get the same picture, he feels, from Luther's stays at the Wartburg and the Coburg, which Reiter likewise interprets as such phases (Grossmann, "Beitrag zur psychologischen Analyse der Persönlichkeit Dr. Martin Luthers," in *Monatsschrift für Psychiatrie und Neurologie* 132 [1956]: 274–90). Grossmann describes Luther rather according to the constitutional psychology of Ernst Kretschmer, which he applies with certain qualifications. According to this theory, Luther is a pyknic with a cyclothymic character, alternating hyper- and hypothymic stages and a high level of energy not influenced by variations of mood. Kretschmer himself had already read Luther in a similar manner (Kretschmer, *Körperbau und Charakter* [Berlin 1921], 21st–22d ed. [1955], pp. 360, 377 ff, and *Geniale Menschen* [Berlin 1929], pp. 157–60) (Translated into English, respectively, as *Physique and Character* [New York, 1925], pp. 219 ff, and *The Psychology of Men of Genius* [London, 1931], pp. 155–58). There exist but a few fruitful starts to an analysis independent of the standard psychological interpretations: the illuminating essay by Karl Holl, "Luthers Urteile über sich selbst" (1917), in *Gesammelte Aufsätze* 1 (1921): 326–58; fine observations by Ricarda Huch, *Luthers Glaube* (Leipzig, 1916; reprinted ed., 1964); and the profound insights that Nathan Söderbom (*Humor och Melankoli och andra Lutherstudier* [Stockholm, 1919]) has offered into Luther's tension-rich inner life (cf. Peter Katz in *Luther, Mitteilungen der Luthergesellschaft* 5 [1923]: 63–65, and Reiter, *Martin Luthers Umwelt, Charakter und Psychose,* 2: 88, 467–68). Unfortunately, they are little known and have not as yet been carried further. Thus the field is largely dominated by elements borrowed from the formal language of psychology and psychiatry rather than by original interpretations working with the wealth of testimonies of Luther himself. Independent of the psychological theories is the work of

Martin Werner ("Psychologisches zum Klostererlebnis Martin Luthers," *Schweizerische Zeitschrift für Psychologie* 7 [1948]: 1–18, republished in *Glaube und Aberglaube* [Switzerland, 1957], pp. 32–49) who seeks the source of Luther's monastic struggles in a conversation with the adamant father at the occasion of his first Mass in 1507; from which point on he allegedly "projected" this image onto Christ and God. Werner thereby already points in the direction of Erikson, whose psychoanalysis aims indeed at the decisive question of the *entry* into the monastery. Hans Wernle, on the other hand, offers a sort of literary psychology in his perceptive book, *Allegorie und Erlebnis bei Luther* (Switzerland, 1960), which leads, however, to the curious conclusion that an experiential element, stemming from the father, alternates in Luther's life with the motherly penchant for allegory.

[Translator's note: Bornkamm generally quotes the Weimar edition of Luther's works, commonly abbreviated as "WA" for *Weimarer Ausgabe,* "WATR" for the *Tischreden* ("Table Talk"), "WADB" for the *Deutsche Bibel,* and "WAB" for *Briefe* (Luther's letters). This translation refers, wherever applicable, to the American edition of Luther's Works (Philadelphia: Fortress Press), which is abbreviated as "LW."]

2. Erikson, *Young Man Luther*, p. 10.

3. Ibid., p. 39.

4. Ibid., pp. 36, 42–43, 254–60.

5. Ibid., p. 260–63.

6. Ibid., p. 254.

7. Ibid., p. 41.

8. Ibid., p. 210.

9. Ibid., p. 178–95.

10. Ibid., p. 189.

11. Ibid., p. 195. Erikson explains the word *tragic* by the concept of the "negative" conscience (*conscientia cauterisata*), which "burns itself into the soul as a black and hopeless mark." WA 40, no. 1: 562, line 30; according to Otto Scheel, *Dokumente zu Luthers Entwicklung*, 2d ed. (Tübingen, 1929), pp. 70–71, no. 182.

12. Reiter, *Martin Luthers Umwelt, Charakter und Psychose.*

13. Erikson, *Young Man Luther*, p. 27.

14. Ibid., p. 197.

15. Ibid., p. 34.

16. Ibid., p. 13. Kierkegaard, *Efterlade Papirer* 9 (1926), no. 75. Cf. Eduard Geismar, "Wie urteilte Kierkegaard über Luther?", in *Luther-Jahrbuch* 10 (1928): 1-27, and Heinrich Bornkamm, *Luther im Spiegel der deutschen Geistesgeschichte* (Heidelberg, 1955), p. 63. Kierkegaard means something more than Erikson. He thinks that while a patient can describe his suffering and that which is necessary for his relief, he nevertheless lacks the overview of a doctor. Erikson regards Luther as much healthier. To do "dirty work" for one's time is a form of medical work.

17. Erikson, *Young Man Luther*, p. 35.

18. Ibid., p. 50.
19. WATR 3, no. 3566 A (March–May 1537; LW 54: 234–35).
20. WATR 2, no. 1559 (May 1532; LW 54: 157).
21. Since Erikson follows Otto Scheel (*Martin Luther*, 2d ed., 2 vols. [Tübingen, 1917], 1: 11), here he is not to blame. But a small, not unimportant, character trait is thereby lost.
22. WATR 3, no. 3566 A (LW 54: 235).
23. WA 47: 84, lines 18 ff (LW 22: 359). WA 28: 761, lines 17 ff: "I for my part did not run into the monastery because I wanted to serve the devil [Luther is comparing the work ethic with the worship of the golden calf], but in order to gain heaven through my obedience, chastity, and poverty." WA 44: 782, lines 10 ff (LW 8: 276): "Against everyone's will I deserted my parents and relatives and rushed into a monastery, and donned a cowl, because I was persuaded that with that kind of life and those severe hardships I was showing great allegiance to God." WA 49: 713, lines 6 ff: "I became a monk because I wanted to propitiate the strict Judge with my works." WATR 4, no. 4414: 303, lines 15 ff (LW 54: 338) "I took the vow not for the sake of my belly but for the sake of my salvation, and I observed all our statutes very strictly." WA 37: 661, lines 22 ff: "I always thought, when will you finally get pious and do enough that you will obtain a gracious God? By such thoughts was I driven to monkhood." According to Scheel, *Martin Luther*, 1: 313, who cites a transcript (WA 37: 274, lines 14 ff), this frequently quoted passage belongs to the period in the monastery and not the time before. But in terms of its content this passage certainly also indicates why Luther entered the monastery. Further references are found in Scheel, *Dokumente zu Luthers Entwicklung*, and in the index volume WA 58, no. 1.
24. The name has nothing to do with the figure *0* as the symbol of "rock-bottom" (Erikson, *Young Man Luther*, p. 80). It comes either from *noll* ("cowl," "ball"; hence *Kugelherren*) or from *Lollbrüder* (*lullen,* "to sing softly"). As late as in a letter of 31 January 1532 Luther still expressed his high regard for the Brethren of the Common Life.
25. WA 38: 105, lines 8 ff.
26. Speculation concerning the factors that triggered the crisis goes in two directions. The first one has to do with a surprise trip home to see his parents after the start of his law studies. Erikson writes: "Nobody seems to know what happened there. But it stands to reason that Hans demanded an accounting." We know nothing for a fact, though. The reasons one could adduce are pure speculation, including Erikson's own hypothesis that his father's marriage plans for him, which Luther later refers to in the dedication letter to *De Votis Monasticis* of 1521, were occupying his mind (Erikson, *Young Man Luther*, pp. 91, 102). The other conjecture is more helpful. Between his attainment of the master's degree (early February), the start of the lectures he had to give with his degree (23 April), and the beginning of his law studies (20 May) lay a stretch of time in which he was released from his usual academic commitments. "For the first time in

his life Martin had months of time to thoroughly search his mind." (Heinrich Boehmer, *Der junge Luther*, 5th ed. [Gotha, 1962], pp. 37–44. In a table talk of 1537 Luther recalls: "When I was a young master in Erfurt, moving around sorrowfully under the *Anfechtung* of sadness, I immersed myself into studying the Bible." (WATR 3, no. 3593: 439, lines 2 ff; Scheel, no. 366; Luther's other memories of the *tentatio tristitiae* go back to the monastic period). The Japanese Shigeru Taniguchi has aptly spoken of a "psychological protective mechanism," which, in a time of intensive work, held back the inner tensions ("Martin Luthers Eintritt ins Kloster," German in the Yearbook of the Meiji Gakuin University [Tokyo, 1965], pp. 1–26, esp. pp. 14 ff). This protection had now suddenly fallen away, and Luther stood naked before the question of his existence, not only that of his future profession but also his inner existence for which he was seeking direction by reading the Bible. One only needs to add that statements of psychological probability such as these illuminate not *what* would happen but only why it was happening *now*. The rest lies beyond the laws of psychology and belongs to the realm of personal fate.

27. Scheel, *Martin Luther*, 1: 12.

28. See n. 38, below.

29. WA 49: 435, lines 2 ff; WATR 5, no. 5548.

30. Erikson, *Young Man Luther*, p. 77.

31. WA 47: 379, lines 7 ff; 340, line 9.

32. Erikson, *Young Man Luther*, pp. 57, 65, 236.

33. WA 25: 460, lines 10 ff: "My father was angry with me for an hour, but what harm does it do? He after all had ten years of troubles and pains with me."

34. Erikson, *Young Man Luther*, p. 57.

35. Ibid., pp. 57, 66. Here Erikson is evidently following Reiter, *Martin Luthers Umwelt, Charakter und Psychose*, 1: 349. See also Köstlin-Kawerau, *Martin Luther*, 5th ed., 2 vols. (Berlin, 1903), pp. 14–15.

36. Erikson, *Young Man Luther*, p. 73.

37. Ibid., p. 123.

38. The first point is freely invented, and the second is spun out of a charming reminiscence (WATR 4, no. 5050) that his father, when he had drunk a bit too much, "was cheerful and friendly and sang and jested." This stands quite in contrast to the case of a nephew whom Luther reprimanded because drinking made him irascible. "Such people must be on their guard against wine like poison. . . . Cheerful people can safely indulge in wine a little more." (Laeti et suaves, ut pater meus, cantant, iocantur.)

39. Erikson, *Young Man Luther*, p. 63.

40. WATR 2, no. 1659 (LW 54: 161): "When I consider marriage, only the flesh seems to be there. Yet my father must have slept with my mother and made love to her, and they were nevertheless godly people." Likewise no. 1658 and WATR 3, no. 3181.

41. Erikson, *Young Man Luther*, p. 72.

42. Ibid., p. 73.

43. Ibid., p. 123.

44. WA 41: 197, lines 35 ff. This passage, cited by Erikson himself (p. 71), is in no sense meant in mockery but only expresses emphatically what Luther also says in many other places. Cf. Scheel, *Dokumente*, index, pp. 347, 356. In greater detail on that subject also: Hans Düfel, *Luthers Stellung zur Marienverehrung*, vol. 13 of *Kirche und Konfession*, 1968.

45. She once remarked that she would be twice as healthy if she didn't have any children (WADB 4: 29, line 11).

46. The excellent pictures of the parents of Lucas Cranach (1527; found in Hanns Lilje, *Martin Luther, eine Bildmonographie* [Hamburg, 1964], pp. 106–07) reveal something of that which he had from both of them.

47. Erikson, *Young Man Luther*, p. 157.

48. Scheel, *Dokumente*, p. 201, no. 533. The report, passed on by Joh. Cochlaeus (*Commentaria de actis et scriptis Martini Lutheri* [Westphalia, 1549], pp. 1 ff) and taken as a proof of his association with the devil, goes back to Luther's teacher Nathin from Erfurt (Adolf Herte, *Die Lutherkommentare des Joh. Cochläus* [1935], pp. 188 ff). These two embittered enemies of Luther (Nathin since an early personal quarrel in 1514) are not exactly very reliable witnesses, but some such outbreak of his well-known monastic anxieties is indeed not impossible.

49. Erikson, *Young Man Luther*, pp. 23, 38.

50. Ibid., p. 39.

51. Ibid., p. 122.

52. Ibid., p. 212.

53. Ibid., p. 243.

54. Ibid., p. 164.

55. Ibid., pp. 164–5.

56. Ibid. p. 92.

57. WA 8: 573–76 (LW 48: 329–36).

58. Ibid.

59. Erikson, *Young Man Luther*, p. 49.

60. The meaning and the tone of Luther's letter is similarly grossly misunderstood when Erikson hears in it that "God alone could be right; and only Martin could have found this out—by becoming a monk." Ibid., pp. 232–33.

61. Ibid., p. 50.

62. Ibid., p. 256.

63. Ibid., p. 253, in a larger context containing, furthermore, a series of problematical parallels.

64. Ibid., p. 206.

65. *Ex auditu fides, non ex visu.* Lectures on Psalms (1513–15), WA 3: 227, line 28.

66. Erikson, *Young Man Luther*, p. 208.

67. Ibid., p. 213.

68. Ibid., p. 256.

69. Ibid., p. 36. Cf. Bornkamm, *Luther im Spiegel der deutschen Geistes-*

geschichte, p. 191.

70. Erikson, *Young Man Luther*, pp. 265–66.

71. Ibid., pp. 165–69.

72. WAB 3: 531, line 14 (letter to friends in Mansfeld on 15 June 1525).

73. WAB 5: 239 ff (LW 49: 269).

74. WAB 6: 103 ff (20 May 1533).

75. WAB 5 : 349, lines 22 ff; 351, lines 25ff (LW 49: 319). Letters written from the Coburg to Link and Melanchthon on 5 June 1530: "Ex ipso mihi Deus dedit vitam et educationem. . . . Memoria dulcissime conversationis suae viscera mea concussit, ut mortem vix unquam sic contempserim ["despised" as destroyer]. Sed 'ante faciem malorum tollitur iustus, et intrat in requiem' (Isaiah 57:1), toties scilicet morimur, antequam semel moriamur."

2

Erikson, Experimental Psychology, and Luther's Identity

MARK U. EDWARDS, JR.

The historian H. Stuart Hughes has written that both psychoanalytic and historical explanation combine art and science—a combination that distinguishes them from explanation in the physical sciences, on the one hand, and in the literary and visual arts, on the other.[1] Although his argument would not be universally accepted either by historians, psychologists, or philosophers of the two disciplines,[2] his way of thinking seems to suggest a way of assessing Erik Erikson's *Young Man Luther*. As the psychologist Daniel Yankelovich and the philosopher William Barrett remind us in their *Ego and Instinct*, Erikson started his career as an artist, and his psychological work "exhibits the unity of a painting, not that of a formal logical structure."[3] Of course, Erikson claims that his work is also scientific, that he brings to his historical inquiries a theory of psychosocial development based upon experiment and years of clinical experience. He may admit to being a literary artist; he insists that he is a scientist.

It is my conviction, however, that while much of

Erikson's psychohistory is plausible and compelling, the psychological theory he brings to his historical research is not scientific. I shall discuss briefly my reasons for so concluding and go on to argue that there are psychological theories other than Erikson's—theories of cognitive dissonance, person perception, social learning, and roles—that have a better claim to science and can nonetheless assist in historical research. These theories, unlike Erikson's, are not open-ended and all encompassing. Their range is much narrower, and what they offer the historian is accordingly much more limited. This is the price paid for scientific rigor. But within their limits they can aid historical inquiry. To illustrate this last point I shall reexamine the question of Luther's identity, a central issue in *Young Man Luther*, and apply to the problem psychological theories different from those of Erikson.

I

Historians of late have taken to borrowing theories and methods from the social sciences. The purpose of such borrowing seems fairly evident: the historian wishes to bring more rigor to historical explanation. The social sciences, at least in comparison with history, appear more rigorous. In addition, unlike chemistry or physics, which appear still more rigorous, the social sciences, like history, claim man as their subject.

The historian can without embarrassment concede the greater rigor of the social sciences. Both the social scientist and the historian wish to explain human behavior. The social scientist, however, can test his generalizations by controlled observation and repeated experiment, whereas the historian, by the nature of his subject, can rarely do so. But if he borrows a generalization developed and tested by the social scientist, he can hope to add to his historical explanation a precision and force that are otherwise unattainable, for the research of the social scientist provides him with the knowledge of the tested limits of the generalization he is applying, its explanatory power, and the requisite conditions for its proper application.

Even historians much enamored with the social sciences will admit, however, that these sciences have not enabled them to surmount all the challenges of historical explanation. A historian is supposed to explain specific events; he is bound to the individual and to the particular. He may find tested generalizations from the social sciences that can aid him, but he must adjust the generalizations to fit the historical specifics and add the nuance and the qualification that the individual events demand. Often he can find multiple explanations, both complementary and contradictory, for the same events. And, expected to explain a specific event as fully as he can, he will often be forced beyond the tested limits of the generalization that he is employing. At their present level of sophistication, the social sciences cannot provide a complete causal explanation for the events of history. I doubt that they ever can.[4] Common sense, intuition, and a tolerance for ambiguity and pluralism will remain valuable attributes of the historian.

This does not mean that the social sciences bring no added rigor to historical inquiry, for they do. What it does mean is that history remains both art and science and cannot be judged by the same canons of rigor appropriate to the social sciences. History gains by borrowing; it is not transformed.

The historian who turns to the social sciences soon runs against another sobering fact. Social scientists do not agree among themselves. On the contrary, they are split by fundamental disagreements about human behavior and about the proper nature of scientific explanation and verification. The historian who wishes to borrow from the social sciences is forced to choose sides.[5]

Consider psychology. Psychoanalysts, believing that an adult's behavior from situation to situation is largely determined by a stable "core personality" developed for the most part in childhood, try to uncover this core personality hidden beneath the defenses and resistances of the adult.

Many experimental psychologists, on the other hand, believing that an adult's behavior is more properly described as a learned function of the situations that the adult encounters, attempt to determine the particular changes in the adult's environment that account for changes in his behavior. Which approach should the historian choose?

If the historian wishes somehow to choose the more "valid" of the two approaches, he immediately is faced by another difficulty: what are the appropriate criteria for judging validity? Experimental psychologists claim that the validity of a theory must be determined empirically; to that end its terms must be precisely defined, there must be objective referents for at least some of its theoretical constructs, and it must exclude some observable possibilities so that the psychologist has the opportunity to prove it wrong. Psychoanalysts disagree, arguing that such requirements sap theories of their vitality and impose an artificially narrow notion of science on the discipline: training and experience can equip a practitioner with the skills necessary to properly test and use the theory without forcing on it overly precise definitions or lists of objective referents. Which canon does the historian accept, not, of course, for the purpose of applying to his own, different discipline, but for making his choice among competing theories of psychology?

These are some of the problems that historians using psychological theory in historical research should consider. I suspect, however, that few of them have. Within the discipline of psychology, psychoanalytic theory is only one theory among many and has numerous detractors. Yet practically the only psychological theory that one encounters in historical literature is some form of psychoanalysis. It is possible, I suppose, that the arguments and evidence against the validity of psychoanalysis that have convinced so many psychologists have failed to convince the historians who are using it in their work, and that those historians who have been convinced of the invalidity of psychoanalysis have decided that none of what they see as more solidly grounded theories could be of use to them.[6] I prefer to think, however, that historians who are interested in using psychological theory in history have just not examined all the relevant evidence. Or that they have shied away from the implications of these findings in the erroneous belief that to demand that psychological theories used in history be scientifically verified is to expose history to the same demand, one that history cannot fulfill. But history is both art and science, and, while it cannot by the nature of its subject be as rigorous as a social science, it can nonetheless gain in rigor by borrowing from the social sciences and by insisting that the theories that it borrows are as rigorous as possible.

II

The faults that experimental psychologists see in psychoanalytic theory can be briefly summarized.[7] Much of psychoanalytic theory is so open-ended and vague that it excludes no observable possibilities and hence cannot be falsified; that is to say, it gives psychologists little opportunity to test it.[8] In cases where psychoanalytic theory does seem to produce generalizations that can be empirically tested, test results cast considerable doubt on the validity and reliability of the generalizations. Finally, whatever its minimal claims to being scientific, psychoanalytic theory proves less useful in clinical work and research than do other, competing theories of psychology and personality. Rather than elaborating on these criticisms in the abstract, however, I should like now to examine the way in which some of the criticisms bear on Erikson's form of psychoanalysis as revealed in his study of Martin Luther.

Erikson assumes that the foundations of personality are laid in childhood according to a blueprint of psychosocial development. The foundation is built up in stages, each stage being the outcome of a psychosocial crisis. "At a given age, a human being, by dint of his physical, intellectual and emotional growth, becomes ready and eager to face a new life task, that is, a set of choices and tests which are in some traditional way prescribed and prepared for him by his society's structure."[9] His readiness for each task is determined by inner laws analogous to the epigenetic laws of embryonic development.[10] Each life task presents a crisis "whose outcome can be a successful graduation, or alternatively, an impairment of the life cycle which will aggravate future crises."[11] *Basic trust versus mistrust, autonomy versus shame and doubt, initiative versus guilt, industry versus inferiority, identity versus role confusion*—each stage of childhood and adolescent development builds on the outcomes of its predecessors. The edifice of the adult personality conforms to this foundation, revealing the strengths and weaknesses of its underlying base.

It is Erikson's main contention that Luther resolved his identity crisis, the fifth psychosocial crisis, by becoming the spokesman for a new "ideology";[12] that this ideology provided Luther with a spiritual solution to the conflicts arising from the earlier crises of his psychosocial development; and that this ideology found believers among Luther's contemporaries because Luther's domestic problems had parallels in society.[13]

Luther's new ideology reflected his protracted struggle with "the ontogenetically earliest and most basic problems of life":[14] the problems of faith, justice, and conscience.[15] It was also a spiritual solution to the problems arising from Luther's first three psychosocial crises: the nostalgia for his infantile trust in his mother (Margaret Luder);[16] his violent doubts that his father (Hans Luder), with his high temper and wrathful self-righteousness, was, in fact, sincere or just;[17] and his shame over the conflict between his conscience and his inner feelings, caused at least in part by his father's demands on him and by his own wish to please him.[18] By becoming the spokesman for a new ideology, and a compulsive teacher, preacher, and writer, Luther also found a solution to the problems arising from his fourth psychosocial crisis, which had occurred when his natural loquacity in his native German was severely suppressed during his schooling.[19]

Erikson ties Luther's personal problems to the problems of Luther's society:

> The theological problems which he tackled as a young adult of course reflected the peculiarly tenacious problem of the domestic relationship to his own father; but this was true to a large extent because both problems, the domestic and the universal, were part of one ideological crisis: a crisis about the theory and practice, the power and responsibility, of the moral authority invested in fathers: on earth and in heaven; at home, in the market-place, and in politics; in the castles, the capitals, and in Rome.[20]

Luther became a historical figure, a great man, because in solving his own conflicts he also solved a crisis in society over the moral authority of fathers.

Clearly, the psychosocial crises of Luther's childhood play a central role in Erikson's psychoanalytic explanation of the adult Luther's identity crisis and its resolution. True, Erikson appears to have moved away from a mechanistic and deterministic view of psychosexual development that is characteristic of orthodox psychoanalysis. He grants that the explanation of adult behavior is not to be found solely in childhood traumas, and should not be sought there exclusively. And he hedges his statements about the contribution of Luther's infantile development to the adult Luther's problems with qualifications and cautions. Yet when one searches within the narrative, *obiter dicta*, and sage intuitions, for theoretically grounded explanations of the adult Luther's personality and behavior, the only explanations one finds are based on the theory of stages and crises of psychosocial development.

But how does one arrive at the pertinent facts? Erikson himself acknowledges that the evidence for what actually occurred during Luther's first three or four psychosocial crises—the evidence, in fact, for what occurred during the first half of Luther's lifetime—is extremely meager.[21] To reconstruct this lost past, Erikson must frequently rely on his clinical experience and psychoanalytic training to infer from Luther's known behavior and beliefs their probable childhood origins.[22]

Some of these inferences lead to strikingly precise conclusions. Erikson asserts, for instance, that Luther's father possessed a "murderous" temper; that he considered himself the "very conception, the *Inbegriff*, of justice"; that he "had at his disposal the techniques of making others feel morally inferior without being quite able to justify his own moral superiority"; and that he "was possessed by an angry, and often alcoholic, impulsiveness which he loosed against his family (and would dare loose *only* against his family), under the pretense of being a hard taskmaster and righteous judge."[23] On the basis of these assertions, Erikson reaches the following conclusion:

> Here, I think, is the origin of Martin's doubt that the father, when he punishes you, is really guided by love and justice rather than by arbitrariness and malice. This early doubt later was projected on the Father in heaven . . . and it was clear that Martin, searching so desperately for his justification, was also seeking a formula of eternal justice which would justify God as a judge.[24]

This is an interesting conclusion, but one must remember that it is founded on inference. The surviving evidence about Luther's father is too meager to sustain it. And certainly there is no verifiable information about what happened to Luther during his second year of life when, according to Erikson's theory of psychosocial development, his sense of fundamental justice was being shaped.[25]

There is evidence, however, that before his theological breakthrough, Luther conceived of God as an arbitrary wrathful judge who made such impossible demands that Luther doubted his justice and righteousness. It is difficult to escape the conclusion that it is *only* because Erikson's theory predicts that a person's concept of God must reflect his infantile experiences with his parents, and that the development of a sense of fundamental justice derives specifically from experience with the father, that Erikson has inferred that Hans Luder was an arbitrary wrathful father whose behavior belied his pretense of righteousness. This cannot be established historically.[26]

From Luther's concept of God is inferred Luther's early psychosocial crises, which are then used to explain his concept of God. One may feel safe in this circuity only if a person's concept of God always reveals his view of his father as established during the second psychosocial crisis. If this generalization holds in every case, if it expresses a precise deterministic relationship, then we need not fear to rely on it.[27] But if the generalization does not hold in every case, and with the same specificity in every case (if, in other words, it is like other psychological generalizations),[28] then the specificity of Erikson's argument is delusive; the generality no more than plausible, not proved.[29]

If one could solve the problem of evidence, however, and if one knew all about Luther's childhood, one would still have a problem that is fundamental: the generality and even the ambiguity of Erikson's theory. In principle, no scholar should ask another scholar to accept anything that the other scholar with sufficient skill, effort, and good will cannot ascertain for himself. Yet the description Erikson gives of Luther's psychosocial stages, and the terms in which he couches his theory, are often so loose and metaphorical that a historian wishing to use or to test Erikson's argument, or to apply it to other historical figures, is at a loss. There are few if any clear definitions or objective referents for central terms such as *identity*, *identity crisis*, or *ideology*, and such definitions as there are often raise as many questions as they answer.[30]

Erikson and other psychoanalysts will disagree with this criticism on the ground that insistence on objective referents and precise definitions can sap theoretical terms of their vitality. In discussing his term *identity*, Erikson wrote:

> Social scientists . . . sometimes attempt to achieve greater specificity by making such terms as "identity crisis," "self-identity," or "sexual identity" fit whatever more measurable item they are investigating at a given time. For the sake of logical or experimental maneuverability (and in order to keep in good academic company) they try to treat these terms as matters of social roles, personal traits, or conscious self-images, shunning the less manageable and more sinister—which often also means the more vital—implications of the concept.[31]

But a very sound reason for our seeking to have terms precisely defined, and one that Erikson does not mention, is that only then can one investigator understand and replicate the work of another.

A way out of this difficulty of definition, favored by Erikson and other psychoanalysts, is to rely on the experience and training of a clinician to make consistent and reliable inferences from given data, without "lists" of objective referents.[32] But the objection to this handling of the problem is that studies done on groups of experienced clinicians, whose clinical judgments were based on identical data, showed considerable disparity among the inferences drawn.[33] Erikson may know what he means. A reader may feel that he, too, knows intuitively what Erikson means. But how can he know that this meaning, arrived at by intuition, corresponds with Erikson's meaning? If Erikson's theory is so "vital" and protean as to defy clear definition, it can just as easily produce a gross caricature as a subtle portrait, especially in the hands of others less blessed than Erikson with sensitivity, insight, and sound judgment.

In the specific matter of Luther's identity, Erikson centers his attention on the experiences of childhood. While he sees the individual as having a "self-identity" that depends at least in part on self-images and role-images, with respect to Luther his primary interest is in what he calls "ego-identity." This he defines as "the result of the synthesizing function on one of the ego's frontiers, namely, that 'environment' which is social reality as transmitted to the child during successive childhood crises." Erikson devotes his discussion in large part to analyzing the infantile sources, first, of the conflicts Luther experienced during his prolonged identity crisis, and then of the resolution of these conflicts by the formulation of the new "ideology" that supported his identity as God's spokesman to the Germans.

As we have seen, this analysis rests on a number of shaky inferences that in turn are based on a theory lacking clear definition and observable referents. As much as historians might wish to understand Luther's "ego-identity," the meager historical record and the problematic nature of psychoanalytic inference make it unlikely that they will ever be able to agree on its nature. The adult Luther's "self-images" and "role-images" may, however, be more accessible to study. I should now like to suggest how certain theories drawn from experimental psychology can aid the historian in understanding these other facets of Luther's identity.

III

In my research on Luther, the theories drawn from experimental psychology that I have found especially useful as heuristic guides are the theories of cognitive dissonance, person perception, social learning, and roles. These theories have been tested experimentally, their theoretical terms are well defined, and objective referents have been specified and checked for validity and reliability.[35] Within their purview they can offer the historian insights that he might not otherwise have. Moreover, they offer insight into the interaction of the adult with his environment without depending on often questionable reconstructions of childhood experiences, and they help to explain conscious thoughts and intentions without recourse to often problematic inferences about unconscious dynamics. Though less ambitious and wide-ranging in their application than Erikson's theory, they yield an understanding that is far more solidly grounded.

To explain how these theories can help the historian understand some of the adult Luther's "self-images" and "role-images"—that is, Luther's characterizations of himself and the comparisons and contrasts he drew between himself and others—I must first engage in some brief historical narrative.[36] Luther's description of himself developed and changed during his career as a reformer.[37] In 1517, when he attacked indulgences, he was acting as a doctor of the Scriptures with the responsibility for the correction of errors, as a preacher concerned with the spiritual well-being of his Wittenberg congregation, and as an opponent of scholastic theology and the abuses that it supported. He was God's spokesman—Erikson's term—only to the extent that every true teacher and preacher was God's spokesman.

During his seclusion at the Wartburg following his appearance at the Diet of Worms, Luther believed himself to be a teacher and preacher used by the Word to initiate a return to true Christianity, which had been perverted by the papal Antichrist. He believed that God had accomplished a great deal through him (although even more without him), but that he would soon be replaced by Melanchthon, who he felt surpassed him both as theologian and as teacher.

During the 1520s, however, Luther gradually came to believe that he occupied a more significant role in history than he had first realized. An important step in the direction of this new self-perception came with the Wittenberg disturbances caused by Karlstadt and the Zwickau "prophets," who claimed special revelation as authority for their actions. Melanchthon, Amsdorf, and the others in Wittenberg were unable to handle the situation, and they finally begged Luther to return from the Wartburg. Against the express command of his prince to stay in hiding, Luther returned, and in little more than a week had put down the disturbances. His quick success in quieting the storm and gaining control of the reforms was due to a series of powerful sermons. In the initial sermon he reminded his hearers that he had been the first to preach the purified Gospel, an assertion of authority that he was to make with ever more frequency thereafter.

As the years passed, Luther became increasingly preoccupied with answering attacks on his teachings from within the Protestant ranks. And he saw in each successive opponent—first Karlstadt and the Zwickau prophets, then Müntzer and the peasants, finally Zwingli, Oecolampadius, and the other "sacramentarians"[38]—the characteristics of the biblical false prophets and apostles: they were all lying, hypocritical men, minions of Satan who cared more for the flesh and the religious legalism that enslaved men's consciences than for the spirit and God's grace.

As Luther found parallels between his Protestant opponents and the biblical false prophets and apostles, he began also to see similarities between the biblical true prophets and apostles and himself. By the 1530s he was drawing explicit parallels between their experiences and his own, and using these parallels to justify his actions. For example, both Saint Paul and he suffered tremendous doubts and temptations; they both had been forcibly rescued from what they perceived to be a perverted faith; they both had received their authority and message from God, not from men; and they both had their false apostles—their fanatics who attacked their names, attempted to subvert their doctrine, accused them of violating the requirements of Christian charity, and tried to deprive them and their followers of the title of Church. These tribulations, suffered by them both, were the characteristics, the distinguishing marks, the "stigmata" of God's true prophets. And Luther in turn judged, rebuked, and condemned his Protestant opponents as Paul did the false apostles.

In biblical history Luther found additional support for his belief in his special role. There he saw a continual, unchanging struggle between the true and false church, one that had begun with Cain and Abel and that had continued into his own day. God had repeatedly raised up true prophets or apostles to preach the word and protect the church, while the devil countered with false prophets and apostles to subvert the word and attack the church and its ministers. Luther gradually saw himself in a long line of true prophets of God's word.

Luther's fellow Protestants shared in varying degrees this belief in Luther's role. That part of the culture of his day that comprised the Bible, church history, traditions, and popular beliefs, provided the models of true and false prophets and explained their interaction with each other. Luther's contemporaries, therefore, as well as he himself, understood something of what being a true or false prophet entailed. They believed that such men existed, and they thought in terms of God and Satan struggling for the souls of men. Luther's contemporaries wanted a prophet, moreover, and many were willing to accept Luther as the chosen man.

IV

How might a historian explain the timing and nature of these shifts in Luther's characterization of himself? I suggest, by closely examining the context in which the changes occurred and analyzing it with the aid of the theories of cognitive dissonance, person perception, and roles.

Let us begin with the context. In his controversies with Roman Catholics, Luther merely pointed to the different assumptions and authorities on which he and the Catholics based their doctrinal positions. They argued from Scripture and tradition as interpreted by the church and Christ's vicar, while he argued from Scripture as interpreted by the Word acting within the faithful. In these controversies he made no special claims about himself. On the contrary, he tried to separate his name from the beliefs he espoused; he strenuously combated the attempt by Catholic opponents to link the Reformation movement to his name; and he chastised all those who believed something because Luther or anyone else had advocated it. He first began bolstering his theological arguments with special claims about himself when confronted with Protestant opponents. It was in controversies with other Protestants that he used himself as an example of the conduct proper to a minister, and pointed to the fact that he was the first to preach the purified Gospel and that God had accomplished a great deal with him as his instrument. The difference is striking and suggests that there was something about controversies with other Protestants that precipitated the shift in Luther's description of himself.

To explain how cognitive-dissonance theory can help pinpoint this "something," a word must be said about the theory itself. In the most general terms, cognitive-dissonance theory holds that people usually try to maintain at least an apparent consistency, first, among their cognitions (that is, among their ideas, attitudes, beliefs, values, and the like), and second, between these cognitions and the environment. The environment includes the social institutions, the culture, and the other people in the individual's world. When a person perceives an inconsistency among his cognitions, or between his cognitions and his behavior, or between his cognitions and the environment, cognitive-dissonance theory predicts that he will experience "cognitive dissonance" and that he will attempt to reduce this dissonance in a variety of ways: by changing his beliefs, by changing his behavior, by changing his environment, or by changing his perceptions.[39]

Let us now reexamine the context with the aid of cognitive-dissonance theory. When confronted by Catholics, Luther could argue on the basis of the clear and unambiguous differences between the central assumptions and authorities of the two belief systems. The logical reasons for their disagreement were apparent and the significance of the disagreement obvious to both parties. We would expect little cognitive dissonance to be generated.

In controversies with other Protestants the situation was different. The members of the Reformation movement, after all, were generally in agreement on the central principles that differentiated their belief from Catholicism, and most of them accepted the Scripture as the only authority and source of doctrine. They might, as they did at the Colloquy of Marburg in 1529, agree on every article of doctrine but one; yet despite their common use of Scripture as the sole basis for their position, each side was unable to convince the other of its error concerning Christ's presence in the Supper. With the wisdom of hindsight and after years of debate, we can see that profound differences in assumptions underlay the two positions. But in the initial stages of the dispute, these differences were either not clear or seemed insignificant to many. Thus Luther, when confronted by an opponent who shared his basic convictions and recognized the same authorities, found that his followers were distressed, confused, and unable fully to understand or accept the conventional arguments he advanced against the opponent's position. Moreover, since neither Luther nor his Protestant opponents could understand fully why the other was not immediately persuaded by the overwhelming force of his own argument, their frustration was added to the general confusion and distress. According to cognitive-dissonance theory, this is a situation conducive to high dissonance.

The theory suggests a number of ways that this dissonance might be reduced, two of which have bearing on the change in Luther's description of himself. To summarize the situation, Luther and his Protestant opponents disagreed violently, yet to many their assumptions and theological arguments seemed almost identical. How could a confused Protestant judge who was right? And how could the disputants explain the disagreement to themselves? The answer in both cases was to make the two positions clearly distinguishable by manipulating the status of the disputants. One of them claims special authority for himself or attacks the authority of the opponent or both. At this point common sense alone could have told us what happened. Luther was in a better position to claim special authority than were his opponents since he had in fact been the initiator of the Reformation movement. His accomplishments gave him a solid foundation on which to rest his claims, and he advanced them accordingly.

This was one way in which dissonance was reduced. A second way was the converse of the first. The status of the disputants was manipulated not by the self-aggrandizement of one disputant but by his denigration of his opponent. This accounts for Luther's *ad hominem* attacks on his adversaries, but not for the form of these attacks. Here the theory of roles suggests an answer. Luther maligned his opponents—and thus distinguished his position from theirs—by labeling them "false prophets" and by attributing to them the characteristics of "false prophets" as presented in the biblical accounts. Incidentally, this was a most effective indirect attack on his opponents' doctrine and could be readily appreciated and understood by his contemporaries. A false prophet was possessed by the devil, and so his doctrine had to be false, appearances notwithstanding.

In psychological terms, Luther attributed to his opponents the role of "false prophet." Normally, roles are learned by observation. We learn the appropriate and expected behavior of a particular role by watching someone else perform it.[40] We also learn by observation when it is appropriate to assume a given role, and when it is not, and we learn to recognize the behavior, beliefs, dress, and setting appropriate to a given role. Frequently we learn from written sources—codes and even how-to-do-it manuals—and not infrequently we learn roles that are embedded in larger systems. The role of Catholic priest and the practice of *imitatio Christi*, for example, derive vitality and strength from the larger system of which they are a part.

Roles have a cultural, a social, and a psychological dimension. They are cultural in that the characteristics and behavior appropriate to a role are defined by the community. They are social in that they involve interaction with other people. This interaction frequently extends to "complementary" roles, such as those of bishop and priest or of leader and follower. Roles are psychological in that each person fills a role in his own way, bringing to it his own personality, his other roles, and his perceptions.[41]

Luther learned the characteristics of the role of false prophet from Scripture and church history. He attributed this role and its characteristics to his Protestant opponents. He learned the characteristics of the role of true prophet—the role complement to that of false prophet—from the same sources. With time, he appropriated this role to himself. With the aid of the theory of person perception[42] and the already-mentioned theories of cognitive dissonance and roles, the historian can trace through the 1520s how Luther developed his *ad hominem* attacks on his Protestant opponents, how his new role formed in the course of the debate, and how these two processes interacted.[43]

V

I hope that this brief example illustrates some of the virtues, as well as the limitations, of using experimental psychology in historical inquiry. Experimental psychology can assist the historian in explaining causal relations between *known* data, such as the relation between Luther's controversies with other Protestants and his change in self-image. Unlike Erikson's theory, experimental psychology cannot properly—at least at its present level of sophistication[44]—be used to generate new data from known data, to infer, for example, Luther's early relations with his father from his adult views of God. Moreover, by stressing the environmental determinants of behavior and by limiting itself generally to conscious, articulated motivation, experimental psychology undoubtedly slights the contribution of intrapersonal dynamics, and especially of unconscious or unarticulated motives. Of course, the historian usually has more evidence about an individual's environment than about the goings-on in his head and more evidence for his articulated motives than for his unarticulated or unconscious ones, but he cannot honestly maintain that what he cannot document did not exist or was unimportant. He can only claim to be telling part of the story, perhaps at times even the less important part.

Historians may view this limitation to verifiable data as a major drawback. Certainly one of the attractions of Erikson's theory is that it apparently allows the historian to know much more about the past than he can explicitly document. But in light of the unreliability of psychoanalytic inference and the looseness of psychoanalytic theory, the cautious historian may properly question whether the gain is more apparent than real. If other historians using the same evidence can easily reach different, even diametrically opposed,[45] conclusions about the proper psychoanalytic inference, and if each historian is forced to reach his own intuitive understanding of the theory, scholarly debate is liable to dissolve into anarchy with each historian championing his own "facts" and his own "truth." Perhaps I am an old-fashioned historian, but I prefer to remain agnostic about matters I cannot even begin to document. And I think it more useful to concentrate my efforts on better understanding evidence on which I and other historians can agree. Experimental psychology is well suited to assist in this task.

Of course, any form of psychohistory seems a question-able hybrid to some historians. Most practicing historians do, however, make judgments about past human behavior. While they may not use any explicit psychological theory, they work nonetheless with what could be termed *implicit theory*. A theory of this kind consists of a set of generalizations about human behavior that the historian has learned from his culture or developed from his own experience. Explicit theories of psychology have drawbacks and weaknesses, but so, too, do most implicit theories.[46] Underlying both explicit and implicit theories are fundamental orientations that determine where the historian looks for explanations and what he considers significant. In this essay I have discussed two orientations toward psychohistorical explanation. To summarize the major differences, Erikson's orientation is more toward the social environment of the child, and mine is more toward the social environment of the adult. Erikson stresses more intrapersonal dynamics and I stress more interpersonal dynamics. Finally, in considering motivation, Erikson tends to look for causes of which the individual is not conscious—conflicts originating in earlier, unresolved psychosocial crises—and I rely more heavily on the individual's conscious perceptions and intentions.

Neither approach is necessarily wrong. In principle, the two approaches could in fact be complementary, since it is undoubtedly true that behavior and beliefs are affected by childhood experiences[47] and cannot be altogether explained by conscious perceptions and intentions. For the practicing historian, however, Erikson's approach poses some methodological problems. When the historical record is meager, objective referents fuzzy, and clinical judgments inconsistent, the historian is confronted with a formidable question of evidence. Conclusions drawn from inferred childhood experiences, and from inferred unconscious motivation, are to say the least problematical. Moreover, it is very easy, especially with a historical figure like Luther, to lose sight of the context in which he worked and the age in which he lived. By concentrating on childhood experiences and unconscious dynamics, Erikson's approach can easily lead the historian into committing the great-man fallacy. Luther's effect on his culture, society, and contemporaries was profound and lasting. But it is also true that his self-identity changed, and the new belief system developed because of the particular ways in which his culture, society, and contemporaries affected *him*.

NOTES

1. H. Stuart Hughes, *History as Art and as Science* (New York, 1965).
2. For an excellent collection of essays on the issue of history as science,

see Ronald H. Nash, ed., *Ideas of History*, 2 vols. (New York, 1969). Walter Mischel, *Personality and Assessment* (New York, 1968), provides a detailed survey of the psychological research on the validity, reliability, and utility of psychodynamic theory. The classic attack by a philosopher of science on psychoanalytic theory is found in Karl Popper, *The Logic of Scientific Discovery (*first published as *Logik der Forschung* [Vienna, 1935]*)* (New York, 1959). Two recent critiques from different standpoints are Daniel Yankelovich and William Barrett, *Ego and Instinct: The Psychoanalytic View of Human Nature*, rev. ed. (New York, 1971), and the superb review article by Frederick Crews, *"Life History and the Historical Moment* by Erik H. Erikson," *New York Review of Books* 22 (16 October 1975): 9–15.

3. Yankelovich and Barrett, *Ego and Instinct*, p. 120.

4. On this point H. Stuart Hughes and I are in agreement. See his *History as Art and as Science*, esp. chap. 1, and his "The Historian and the Social Scientist," *American Historical Review* 65 (1960): 20–46.

5. Robert F. Berkhofer, Jr., *A Behavioral Approach to Historical Analysis* (New York, 1969), pp. 2–3. Berkhofer argues persuasively for the use of behavioral and cognitive theory in historical research.

6. Such is Hughes's judgment: "Experimental psychology I have found to be the least adaptable to the historian's purposes. Its rigorous criteria of evidence and the narrowly defined level of abstraction on which it operates contrast so sharply with history's loosely metaphorical procedures as to provide almost no points of contact." Hughes, "Historian and Social Scientist," p. 34.

7. For a detailed discussion of the limitations of psychoanalytic theory, as well as some of the other, competing theories of personality, see J. McV. Hunt, "Traditional Personality Theory in Light of Recent Evidence," *American Scientist* 53 (1965): 80–96; Mischel, *Personality and Assessment;* Donald R. Peterson, *The Clinical Study of Social Behavior* (New York, 1968); Philip E. Vernon, *Personality Assessment: A Critical Survey* (London, 1964). For a survey of the field of personality research by a cognitive consistency theorist, see Salvatore R. Maddi, *Personality Theories: A Comparative Analysis*, 2d ed., rev. (Homewood, Ill., 1972).

8. For a discussion of this criterion for an empirical and scientific theory, see Popper, *The Logic of Scientific Discovery.*

9. Erik H. Erikson, *Young Man Luther: A Study in Psychoanalysis and History* (New York, 1958), p. 254.

10. Erik H. Erikson, *Childhood and Society*, 2d ed. (New York, 1963), p. 65.

11. Erikson, *Young Man Luther*, p. 254.

12. To Erikson an *ideology* is apparently both a tendency and the result of this tendency. "In this book, *ideology* will mean an unconscious tendency underlying religious and scientific as well as political thought: the tendency at a given time to make facts amenable to ideas, and ideas to facts, in

order to create a world image convincing enough to support the collective and the individual sense of identity" (ibid., p. 22). "We will call what young people in their teens and early twenties look for in religion and in other dogmatic systems an *ideology.* At the most it is a militant system with uniform members and uniform goals; at the least it is a 'way of life,' or what the Germans call a *Weltanschauung*, a world-view which is consonant with existing theory, available knowledge, and common sense, and yet is significantly more: an utopian outlook, a cosmic mood, or a doctrinal logic, all shared as self-evident beyond any need for demonstration" (ibid., p. 41). As a *tendency, ideology* may be explained by cognitive-dissonance theory (see n. 39 below).

13. Ibid., pp. 15, 77.

14. Ibid., p. 257.

15. These are the contributions to religious beliefs of the first three stages of psychosocial development.

16. See, e.g., Erikson, *Young Man Luther*, p. 255.

17. Ibid., pp. 255–56.

18. Ibid., pp. 123, 257–58.

19. Ibid., pp. 47, 258–59. This also reflects anal expulsive contributions from the second stage (pp. 245–49).

20. Ibid., p. 77.

21. E.g., ibid., pp. 13, 47, 50, 72.

22. E.g., ibid., pp. 65, 72–73, 255, 257.

23. Ibid., pp. 65, 66, 67.

24. Ibid., p. 58.

25. See Lewis W. Spitz, "Psychohistory and History: The Case of Young Man Luther," *Soundings* 52 (1973): 182–209, and Heinrich Bornkamm, "Luther and His Father: Observations on Erik H. Erikson's *Young Man Luther: A Study in Psychoanalysis and History,*" in this volume. In *Young Man Luther* Erikson does present some indirect evidence in support of his inferences: a punishment occurring after the second crisis was resolved (pp. 64–67), rumors about Hans Luder's brother (p. 57), generalizations about probable bourgeois behavior and upbringing (pp. 63, 69–70), and Luther's disagreement with his father about entering the monastery (pp. 95–97, 138–39, 144–46 passim). Aside from errors of fact in these arguments (see the articles just cited), this adduced evidence is insufficient to sustain Erikson's precise conclusions.

26. Furthermore, a historian might justifiably wonder why all this problematic inference is necessary. Luther was raised and trained in a late medieval piety and theology that depicted God as a wrathful judge who demanded as the price of salvation meritorious intentions and deeds beyond the ability of most men. A careful study of this training with greater attention to the specific details of Luther's beliefs and with less reliance on inferred facts can explain Luther's doubts about God's justice. This does not mean that Erikson's inferences are necessarily wrong, merely that they

are both problematic and arguably unnecessary for an understanding of Luther's beliefs. For a sophisticated discussion of the theological school in which Luther was trained, see Heiko Oberman, *The Harvest of Medieval Theology*, rev. ed. (Grand Rapids, Mich., 1967).

27. An interesting question is why the generalization holds before Luther's breakthrough but not afterward. What are the distinguishing factors?

28. See the works cited in n. 7 above.

29. I am unaware of any systematic experimental evidence establishing this link between one's view of God and the outcomes of the first two psychosocial crises. Erikson (*Young Man Luther*, p. 265) cites Freud's *Future of an Illusion*.

30. For an illuminating attempt to pin down Erikson's concept of *identity*, see Yankelovich and Barrett, *Ego and Instinct*, pp. 122–34.

31. Erik H. Erikson, *Identity: Youth and Crisis* (New York, 1968), p. 16.

32. E.g., ibid., pp. 72–73.

33. For a discussion of some of the attempts to establish objective referents for terms in psychoanalytic theory and to test clinical judgments, see the works cited in n. 7 above, esp. Mischel, *Personality and Assessment*, chaps. 3–5.

34. Erikson, *Identity*, pp. 210–11.

35. For guides to the relevant literature, see the works cited in n. 39–42.

36. The material that I shall outline can be found in considerably more detail in Mark U. Edwards, Jr., *Luther and the False Brethren* (Stanford, 1975), where my sources are cited and can be checked by the interested historian.

37. The standard piece on Luther's view of himself is Karl Holl, "Martin Luther on Luther," trans. H. C. Erik Midelfort, in *Interpreters of Luther*, ed. Jaroslav Pelikan (Philadelphia, 1968). See also Hans Freiherr von Campenhausen, "Reformatorisches Selbstbewusstsein und reformatorisches Geschichtsbewusstsein bei Luther, 1517–1522," *Archiv für Reformationsgeschichte* 37 (1940): 128–49; and Hermann Steinlein, *Luthers Doktorat* (Leipzig, 1912). Roland H. Bainton, *Here I Stand* (Nashville, 1950; New York, 1955), is the best biography in English, while Julius Köstlin and Gustav Kawerau, *Martin Luther: Sein Leben und seine Schriften*, 5th ed., rev., 2 vols. (Berlin, 1903), remains the most complete biography of Luther in any language.

38. Generally speaking, the "sacramentarians" were all those who, in Luther's judgment, denied the real presence of Christ's body and blood in the Lord's Supper.

39. Maddi, *Personality Theories*, discusses some of the different cognitive-consistency theories. Used heuristically, cognitive-dissonance theory seems to offer most to the historian. See Elliot Aronson, "The Theory of Cognitive Dissonance: A Current Perspective," in *Advances in Experimental Social Psychology*, ed. Leonard Berkowitz (New York, 1969), 4: 1–34; Jack Williams Brehm and Arthur R. Cohen, *Explorations in Cognitive Dis-*

sonance (New York, 1962); Leon Festinger, *A Theory of Cognitive Dissonance* (Evanston, Ill., 1957); Philip G. Zimbardo, *The Cognitive Control of Motivation* (Glenview, Ill., 1969).

40. For a discussion of observational learning and role modeling, see Albert Bandura, *Psychological Modeling: Conflicting Theories* (Chicago, 1971), esp. the introduction, and idem, *Social Learning Theory* (New York, 1971).

41. For a general introduction to role theory, see Michael Banton, *Roles: An Introduction to the Study of Social Relations* (New York, 1965). I make an eclectic use of the various theories.

42. For an introduction to research in person perception, see Albert H. Hastorf, David J. Schneider, and Judith Polefka, *Person Perception* (Menlo Park, Calif., 1970). See also Fritz Heider, *The Psychology of Interpersonal Relations* (New York, 1958); Harold H. Kelley, "Attribution Theory in Social Psychology," in *Nebraska Symposium on Motivation,* ed. David Levine (Lincoln, Nebr., 1967); Renato Tagiuri and Luigi Petrullo, eds., *Person Perception and Interpersonal Behavior* (Stanford, Calif., 1958).

43. See my dissertation "Luther and the False Brethren" (Stanford University, 1974), where I trace this development using these theories.

44. Present psychological theory accounts for too little of the variance (correlations typically are in the .2 to .5 range) to allow the historian to make such inferences with any real confidence.

45. By invoking the defense mechanism known as *reaction formation,* the analyst may infer that the expression of a particular anxiety-producing impulse is caused by its exact opposite impulse within the unconscious.

46. For a discussion of some aspects of naive psychology and its weaknesses, see Hastorf et al., *Person Perception.* Mischel, *Personality and Assessment,* discusses the weaknesses of various explicit personality theories. See also the works cited in n. 7.

47. For an introduction to the major approaches to child development, see A. L. Baldwin, *Theories of Child Development* (New York, 1968).

3

Understanding Gandhi*

ARJUN APPADURAI

As a scholarly treatise in the social sciences, *Gandhi's Truth*, by Erik H. Erikson, stands in the tradition of works that seek to understand rather than to explain their human and social subjects. Rather than comprising a hypothesis or set of hypotheses, constructed and presented in accordance with the classic scientific criteria of inference, verification, and deduction, it consists of a set of insights provoked by the use of the methodology of psychoanalysis, but ordered so as to produce a compelling personal and humanistic portrait of Gandhi and the political tool of militant nonviolence, called *satyagraha*, that he devised. In this book Erikson continues the enterprise that he began with the publication of *Young Man Luther* (1958), his first systematic attempt to apply the clinical insights of psychoanalysis to historical materials and problems. But *Gandhi's Truth* is far more than an exercise in what is now called the psychohistorical method. It is also Erikson's vehicle and occasion for personal and meta-

* I wish to thank Professor Ronald Inden, Paul Antze, Patricia Pessar, and Franklin Presler, all of the University of Chicago, for suggestions and criticisms made at various stages in the writing of this essay.

scientific reflections of considerable significance. Erikson's psychoanalytic exploration of the roots of *satyagraha* in Gandhi's childhood leads him to make, in the heart of his book, a serious and personal criticism of Gandhi's method. This criticism is made in terms of a juxtaposition of psychoanalysis and *satyagraha* as techniques for the discovery of truth in action, and as a criticism of the latter in terms of the cumulative insights of the former. In turn, this criticism provides the basis for Erikson's reflections on Gandhi as an example of the *homo religiosus*, and on the evolutionary significance of *satyagraha* as a new ritual for redirecting human aggression.

The choice of the Ahmedabad *satyagraha* of 1918 as the pivotal event in Gandhi's career as a leader, seems to me to be, on historical grounds, arbitrary. But a detailed analysis of this event does seem to have been Erikson's personal wedge into Gandhi's life, and, as such, it serves its purpose. In general, Erikson is not concerned as much with the illumination of events in Indian history as he is with the conceptual issues that I have described. I shall therefore deliberately avoid criticizing Erikson from the perspective of the large body of disaggregated, local studies of the Nationalist movement that has been produced by specialists in Indian history and politics in recent years. I shall attempt to address myself to Erikson's argument at a theoretical level, one that strikes me as richer and more in accordance with Erikson's basic strengths and interests than the strictly historiographic problems that the book raises.

Let me briefly state the argument against Erikson's analysis that I shall elucidate in the body of this essay. It is my contention that Erikson is insufficiently sensitive to the cultural presuppositions, generally Judeo-Christian ones, that underlie psychoanalysis as a cognitive instrument and as an epistemological theory. These presuppositions are, in many cases, opposed to or distinct from those cultural meanings, symbols, and assumptions that formed the essentially Hindu cultural universe of Gandhi and his mass constituency. Erikson allows for cultural differences only at the surface level, beneath which he raises no doubt of the universal applicability of psychoanalytic categories. If culture provides the basic units and tools from which men derive the categories of a meaningful universe, then, it seems to me, psychoanalysis is obliged to decode its own cultural underpinnings, as well as those of its subjects, before it can seek to apply its insights cross-culturally. This Erikson fails to do. In what follows I present a detailed examination of Erikson's procedure and supplement my criticism with at least the outlines of a more adequate cross-cultural application of psychoanalysis. Before I discuss the details of Erikson's argument, however, I must provide at least a brief overview of the key terms, concepts, and assumptions of Gandhi's method.[1]

Gandhi defined his central political goal as *swaraj,* a Sanskrit term meaning "one's own rule," which he took over from prior nationalist usage. But in Sanskrit, as in many other Indian languages, it is possible to make a word yield different contextual meanings by manipulating its components. This fact permitted Gandhi also to interpret *swaraj* as meaning "self-rule" or "self-control," in addition to its political meaning of "one's own rule," or "independence." This self-control, in Gandhi's view, was to be attained by curbing such passions as anger, hatred, and selfishness, which held the self in bondage. *Ahimsa*, which means literally "not doing harm to any creature," but which Gandhi endowed with the more general meaning of "nonviolence," became a Gandhian paradigm for self-control. The central Gandhian argument, at once philosophical and tactical, was that the only way to end British rule and to enable Indians to acquire *swaraj* was for them to achieve rule over themselves, self-control. In part, Gandhi was able to make this argument because he saw in British rule a pure case of violence as the basis of the social order, and of the slavery of Indian "selves" to an alien rule.[2]

Thus Gandhi placed self-control, by his own definition and example, at the heart of India's struggle to achieve independence from British rule. He did this by an imaginative synthesis and redefinition of a number of traditional Indian cultural symbols and meanings, and by dedicating himself to their enactment and actualization in twentieth-century politics. His unprecedented success in capturing the imagination of the Indian people was rooted in the absolute credibility and consistency with which he interpreted the twentieth century, and the problem of action within its context, in terms of this traditional cultural system. Though it is beyond the scope of this essay to examine Gandhi's use of this cultural lexicon in great detail, I shall examine some of its basic assumptions regarding truth, action, and self-control.

Gandhi defined *truth* as the prime ontological principle of the universe, and, as such, considered it to be higher than the gods. With this notion of truth, Gandhi intuitively recovered the Vedic concept of *rita*, the divinely ordained course of nature, "which was associated in the minds of the Aryans with truth, honesty, regularity, and carrying out one's resolutions."[3] In this view, truth is the principle that binds men, gods, and the universe together: it was to be sustained by regular invocation, demonstrated in miracles and ordeals, and expressed in action. This existential conception of truth differentiates itself in later Hindu thought into *satya* ("truth"), which indicates the morally proper nature of the world, and *dharma* ("duty, law"), which indicates the natural aspect of moral action in the world. In this view, *is* and *ought,* nature and morality, are two aspects of a single, nondual, universe. *Svadharma* ("one's duty") in this universe is to conduct one's life as a sacrifice to the divinity that is the truth (*sat-brahman*). In the Vedic period, vows (*vrata*) were the surest ways in which to fulfill one's *dharma*, for in acting in accordance with a freely chosen vow, one invoked and actualized divinity, and escaped the bondage of phenomenal, especially sensual, experience. This is why Gandhi held that "God is the essence of the vow." Proper action, in this scheme, binds one to the ultimate truth, while improper action is a capitulation to phenomenal and sensory experience, the essence of falsehood.

How exactly to interpret one's *dharma* and conduct a proper life is the most important question posed and resolved in the *Bhagavad Gita*, a widely known poetic fragment of the great Indian epic known as the *Mahabharata.* The pseudohistorical scenario of the poem involves a failure of nerve on the part of Arjuna, a great warrior, on the eve of an important battle. Krishna, his divine charioteer, enjoins him to perform his warriar's *dharma* and uses the occasion for a philosophical dialogue. The *Gita* poses the problem as follows: if the universe is nondual, if man and Godhead are one, if nature and morality are two aspects of the same thing, what accounts for the manifold appearance of the phenomenal world? The *Gita* maintains that it is *avidya* ("ignorance," "false knowledge") that creates this appearance. In turn, says the *Gita,* it is *karma* ("action") that falsifies the individual consciousness. It does so by obscuring the proper knowledge of the mind—that is, knowledge of the mind's identity with Godhead—with the false products of the senses, especially those that are responsible for such passions as anger, hatred, and desire. But action is held to be the necessary and unavoidable accompaniment of mortal existence, and, furthermore, crucial to the welfare of the universe. So it cannot, and must not, be avoided or renounced. The way out of this vicious circle, and this is the core message of the *Gita*, is to act detachedly, with regard only to one's duty and not with an eye to the fruits or consequences of action. This detached posture, which distinguishes the ideal man (*stitha-prajña*) of the *Gita*, unyokes action from the sensory world, and helps the mind to concentrate on, and ultimately be absorbed in, Godhead. It is this philosophy of a nondualistic universe—a universe in which action must be performed only with regard to one's *dharma* and not for the fruits of action—that underlies Gandhi's deliberate refusal to separate religion and politics, and his consistent wish to enact the truth in politics, rather than in isolation from political life.

Gandhi considered the *Bhagavad Gita* to be the distilled essence of Hinduism, and it was his ethical touchstone throughout his political career. The *Gita,* however, does not provide any consistent or substantive guidelines for the proper conduct of a detached life, although it acknowledges a wide variety of traditional technologies for this purpose. Its main suggestion, which is that one should involve oneself completely in an active life without becoming a slave to the passions and sensory experience, remains a schematic injunction to self-control—an injunction that is difficult to interpret, especially in the light of the *Gita*'s hostility toward traditional forms of asceticism. To fill this hiatus in the *Gita*, Gandhi performed his most brilliant cultural innovation, which was to revive and extend the link of the predominantly Buddhist and Jain concept of *ahimsa* ("nonviolence") to this general Hindu scheme of nonduality, detached action, and self-control.

In the Indian tradition, and especially in Buddhist and Jain praxis, the principle of *ahimsa* had lost some of its connections to the ideals of austerity, asceticism, and self-control, and become a sentimental, though strictly observed, aspect of the life of the Gujarati middle-class into which Gandhi was born. Gandhi extended its minimal interpretation—that is, of doing as little harm as possible to living creatures—in two directions.[4] Firstly, he interpreted it in such a way that it enjoined him positively to "love the enemy," an idea he absorbed from the moral texture of popular Hindu devotionalism, especially in the medieval period. Secondly, he also interpreted it so that it involved positively inviting injury and bearing suffering, in the service of the truth. This latter extension has fewer traditional precedents, but with at least one of them, the Prahlada story, Gandhi had been deeply impressed from his early childhood. In this important and popular story, Prahlada, the young son of the demon Hiranyakasyapu, was so devoted to the Lord Visnu that he invoked his father's jealous wrath. The boy suffered all kinds of torture ordered by his father, and his dedication to Visnu permitted him to endure steel, poison, and flames without complaint, until, eventually, his father was destroyed by Visnu. Erikson notes the influence of this story on Gandhi in the course of his own argument.

It is clear that Gandhi was fully aware of the new centrality that he had given to the concept of *ahimsa* and knew that this was not simply an application of the conventional Hindu understanding. In this respect, the *Bhagavad Gita*, which Gandhi called the "Universal Mother" because of its capacity to nurture his convictions and solve his problems, presented him with a knotty hermeneutical problem. In the poem, as I have previously noted, Lord Krishna presents his philosophical discourse as a rhetorical means of convincing the warrior Arjuna that he must join battle, fulfill the warrior's *dharma*, and, albeit detachedly, perform violent acts. Faced with this blatant contradiction of his own position, Gandhi freely admitted that the *Gita* was written in a time when the contradiction between warfare and *ahimsa* was not understood. He stubbornly insisted, nevertheless, that the lesson of *ahimsa* was not contradicted by the *Gita*. Such a claim, he argued, did not strain the text and, moreover, conformed to a mode of interpretation practiced by the poet of the *Gita* himself. Like many traditional Indian thinkers, the author of the *Gita* extended the meanings of traditional terms and concepts by reinterpreting them in the light of new or different concerns.[5]

However, of the several arguments that Gandhi adduced to support his interpretation, the most powerful and cogent one is not textual but deductive. Gandhi argued that the primary means suggested by the *Gita* for achieving the ideal state of detachment, consisted in a stilling of the passions, especially those of anger, hatred, and desire. It was thus not difficult for Gandhi to yoke this stoical ideal with his own broadened and deepened conception of *ahimsa*, in which eschewing violence is the means of holding on to the Truth, as well as of stoically bearing suffering. Thus, in Gandhi's view, the psychological attributes of the genuine practitioner of *ahimsa* converged with those of the ideal man of the *Gita*. From a slightly different point of view, Gandhi was able to argue that if *ahimsa* is understood as love, especially for one's enemy, then one of its preconditions is selflessness, which he interpreted as yet another convergence with the *Gita*'s ideal of detachment and self-control. Thus, for Gandhi, *ahimsa* became the "soul of Truth," and celibacy (*brahmacharya*), fasting (*upavasa*) and nonpossession (*aparigraha*), among a series of other restraints, became the most important means to its achievement.[6]

Of these various restraints that Gandhi emphasized as being the content of self-control, *brahmacharya*, or celibacy, was the model and mainstay. Gandhi noted that the translation of *brahmacharya* as celibacy was a narrowing of its broader meaning of "the control of the senses" and its still more basic etymological meaning, which is "conduct adapted to the search of Brahma i.e. Truth."[7] It is also important to note that Gandhi connected self-control, *brahmacharya*, and the pursuit of truth, in virtue of a characteristically Indian model of sublimation, which is best described in his own words:[8]

> There must be power in the word of a Satyagraha general—not the power that the possession of limitless arms gives, but the power that purity of life, strict vigilance, and ceaseless application produce. This is impossible without the observance of *Brahmacharya*. It must be as full as it is humanly possible. *Brahmacharya* here does not mean mere physical self-control. It means much more. It means complete control over all the senses. Thus an impure thought is a breach of *Brahmacharya*; so is anger. All power comes from the preservation and sublimation of the vitality that is responsible for the creation of life. If the vitality is husbanded instead of being dissipated, it is transmuted into creative energy of the highest order.[8]

What Gandhi is describing here is *not* a technique for the redemption of the "spiritual" soul from the "carnal" body, as in Western ascetic traditions based on the Judeo-Christian separation of nature and morality, body and soul, into two separate orders. Gandhi's view is rooted in the Hindu view of the universe as a single order, both natural and moral, in which one of the major techniques for the achievement of liberation (*moksa*) is the conservation and transformation of physical (and especially reproductive) substances and powers into others of a different order. This transformation involves the practice of *tapas* ("exercises in austerity") and is calculated to increase both one's control over the powers that govern the universe and one's capacity to concentrate on the ultimate Truth. Indulgence in carnal activity, in this scheme, is not so much sinful as it is wasteful.

It is the preceding body of cultural meanings, as Gandhi interpreted and extended them, that underlies the technique of *satyagraha*, which is the heart of Erikson's concerns. Gandhi coined this term, which has been translated in many ways, but which means literally "holding firmly to the Truth." It came to describe, inclusively, the techniques of passive resistance, conscious and systematic flouting of British law, and the deliberate courting of arrest and imprisonment, in the interest of political resistance. This concept, and the techniques and philosophy that it represented, were part of Gandhi's effort to synthesize and focus the entire set of cultural assumptions that I have described into a powerful political weapon.

In this method, the pivot is *satya* (truth), which retains its Vedic connotation of an immanent ordering principle (*rita*), discovered "experimentally," guided by the individual conscience, and expressed in action. As a method of dealing with one's opponents, *satyagraha* incorporates Gandhi's radicalized interpretation of *ahimsa*, so that loving one's enemy purifies both sides and ensures the discovery of truth in conflict. To act in the proper spirit of *ahimsa*, the practitioner of *satyagraha* cultivates self-control, is always detached in his actions, and, to purify himself, takes such vows as celibacy, fasting, and nonpossession. These vows are not simply the instruments of self-control and detached action, but, as forms of disciplined austerity, (*tapas*), provide the *satyagrahi* with "soul-force," which is really transformed, instinctual power. This transformation invokes divinity, purifies its recipient, and allows him to defeat his physically more powerful opponent by converting him, stubbornly and forcefully, to the truth.

While it is beyond the scope of this discussion to analyze in detail Gandhi's application of this cultural synthesis to the particulars of Nationalist politics in the twentieth century, it must be noted that a large part of Gandhi's energy and imagination was dedicated to the dramatization and dissemination of these beliefs. He was, among other things, a tireless pedagogue and publicist, and all his actions, speeches, and writings were calculated to educate his Indian audiences in his version of their common cultural heritage. Because he described these essential and enduring elements of Hindu culture with enormous simplicity and clarity, and because his own adherence to these models and meanings was tireless and imaginative, Gandhi had direct access to the Indian popular imagination. His audience, on the whole, lived according to these assumptions, albeit unself-consciously, and were likely to know well such texts as the *Bhagavad Gita*, on which Gandhi relied so extensively. It is this shared cultural universe, dramatized and revivified by Gandhi, that must ultimately explain his "charismatic" career. Erikson's own analysis of Gandhi must be evaluated against this cultural background. To do this, however, it is necessary first to understand the contrasting cultural presuppositions that underlie Erikson's own methodology. Since Erikson is a psychoanalyst of the Freudian school, what this amounts to is a consideration of the cultural axioms and meanings that lie behind Freud's work.

On the surface, Freud's thought is in many respects directly hostile to religion, and draws on a number of militantly secular traditions. He shared the Enlightenment temper of criticizing religious faith from an atheistic and rationalist perspective, drew upon the teachings of nineteenth-century biology and physics in his descriptions of psychic mechanisms of stability and change, and stood in the positivist tradition, starting with Comte, that sought to substitute scientific truth for the allegedly depleted claims of Western religion. In these general debts, as well as in a host of particular claims and judgments, Freud sought to distinguish his teachings from those of Western religious theorists and practitioners. Still, despite its claim of having uncovered the universal and ontogenetic truth about human psychic structure and development beneath cultural and historical variation, Freud's psychoanalytic theory bears the unmistakable stamp of Western—specifically Judeo-Christian—cultural symbols and meanings.[9] These meanings severely limit the universal applicability that Freudian theory claims for itself. Let us consider some of the cultural presuppositions that underpin Freudian methodology.

The first of these presuppositions involves a Judeo-Christian model of historical time. In this view, which Philip Rieff has called the "kairotic" view of time,[10] all of history bears the impress of a single crucial moment or event that defines and contains the significance of the rest of time: the birth of Jesus and the creation of Christ's Church would be examples. Specifically, Freud echoed Augustine in locating this pregnant and predetermining moment in the past. The murder of the original patriarchal leader by his primal horde and the Oedipal drama in early childhood are, for Freud, respectively, the phylogenetic and ontogenetic expressions of a key trauma in the human past. All later history is a reenactment of this crucial event, a series of attempts to remember or forget it, expiate it, embroider it, or escape from it. Freud's view of development, both individual and collective, gives a traumatological and clinical cast to this basically Christian model of time.

Freud is even more obviously a child of the Judeo-Christian tradition in his strict conviction of the duality of all human life,[11] of the separation and opposition of mind and flesh, intelligence and instinct, love and death. Although Freud abhorred the religious optimism that proposed deliverance from this duality, he never doubted the validity of dualist descriptions of the human condition. Indeed, a great deal of his own pessimism can be traced to his conviction that this dualism is an irreconcilable aspect of human life, and underlies its misery. This is Freud's most basic debt to Judeo-Christian thought, and to its later (for example, Cartesian) transformations. All Freudian therapy is directed to the management and mature acceptance of this basic and unavoidable feature of human life.

Freud's view of sexuality, furthermore, represents a transformation of demonstrably Judeo-Christian elements. It is true that Freud did a great deal, against the prevailing Victorian puritanism, to expose the nature of sexuality as an aspect of human nature. But there is no doubt that sexuality remained for Freud, as for Christians, an ignoble slavery to nature, an unruly and ineradicable instinctual force that constitutes the essential manifestation of the human problem. Also—and here the Christian derivation is less explicit but more interesting—sexuality was for Freud, inextricably and by its very origins, a problem of authority.[12] The Oedipal drama is essentially a story of the conflict between the child's sexuality and parental domination: the child's wishes are an attempted usurpation of parental power, and human carnality retains the mark of rebellion. Freud also understood the beginnings of human history and religion in parallel terms. The Freudian myth of the primal horde (developed in *Totem and Taboo* [1912]), involves a group of brothers, frustrated by the sexual monopoly of its leader-genitor, who kill him and then consolidate themselves fraternally by the collective guilt of their patricide. This story, with its basic theme of sexual jealousy directed against parental authority, is the strict phylogenetic analogue to the Oedipus conflict in ontogenetic development. Thus, human history and individual biography both begin with a trauma rooted in the conflict of sexuality and authority. This is structurally the same configuration as in Christian thought, wherein sexuality is the Original Sin of the human race, and carnal indulgence is the paradigmatic rebellion against divine and churchly authority. This model of sexuality, in which, qua instinct, it is man's curse and taint, and qua activity, it is his archetypal rebellion against authority, animates Christian and Freudian thought in equal measure.

Freud's treatment of the concept of guilt reveals a great deal about his peculiar relationship to Judeo-Christian thought. Freud sees the human heritage of guilt, paradigmatically for the original father-murder, as ineradicable, and viewed the alleviation of this guilt as being the primary function of religion. Freud, however, reverses the roles that Christianity assigns to morality and nature in its conception of guilt:[13] whereas Christianity roots guilt in man's repression of his "higher," moral being, Freud locates the source of guilt in man's repression of his "lower," instinctual nature. Both theories of guilt, in spite of their diametrically opposed etiologies, see guilt as the essential symptom of man's divided nature. This apparent convergence, however, is only one product of Freud's general theory of the parallelism between the repetitive aspects of religious ritual and the obsessive aspects of neurotic behavior.[14] Here, as in the other parallels he draws, there are crucial distortions of religious behavior: pathological anxiety is seen as identical with the pangs of a cultivated conscience, and the conscious confession of guilt in religious procedure is identical with its unconscious betrayal in the obsessive behavior of neurotics. But Freud's hostility to religious behavior and belief is not the only source for the caricature of religion on which this analogy depends. Freud's misunderstandings are unlikely to have occurred in the absence of another condition: the close connection between several of his basic ideas and the symbols and categories of the Judeo-Christian universe.

This ambiguity in Freud's relation to Judeo-Christian thought comes to a head in his last work, *Moses and Monotheism*, whose argument runs as follows: There were, in fact, two Moseses. The first, an Egyptian, was a zealous follower of the pure monotheism introduced by the Pharaoh Ikhnaton. After the revolution against Ikhnaton's teachings, the first Moses freed the Israelites from Egypt and trained them in the monotheistic teachings of Ikhnaton. The Israelites, subsequently, killed the Egyptian Moses and forsook the new monotheism. Later, they had another leader, whom they also named Moses, who gave them their Yahweh religion. But the monotheism preached by the first Moses remained a powerful force in the racial unconscious of the

Israelites and reappeared hundreds of years later in the monotheism of the prophets. In Freud's opinion, the killing of the first Moses was a reenactment of the murder of the primal father, leaving a powerful residue of guilt in the racial unconscious of the group. The subsequent death of Jesus was an atonement and sacrifice for this primal murder. Christianity acquired, consequently, the character of a religion based on the sacrificing son rather than the authoritarian father. The Holy Communion, thus, was seen as a direct descendant of the primitive totem feast.

Quite apart from its problematic theoretical aspects, such as the notion of the racial unconscious, this entire argument is an extraordinarily biased and cavalier treatment of the views of bilbical scholars and Egyptologists, even of Freud's own time. There is even some indication that Freud was fully aware that he had drawn a picture of early Jewish history that was so arbitrary that it reads like a fantasy. The question then becomes, Why did he fabricate this wholly untenable story? Surely not simply to establish the Egyptian origins of Jewish monotheism. To my understanding, *Moses and Monotheism* was Freud's final attempt to render his own theories about the religious "illusion" consistent with the Judeo-Christian tradition. This attempt, which led to distortions so serious that it virtually renders *Moses and Monotheism* a fairy tale, would not have taken place unless Freud, at the conclusion of his life, sensed his debts to Judeo-Christian thought, and felt obliged to confront it more directly than he ever had in his previous writings. Thus, in one stroke, he managed to give his theory the support of Judeo-Christian history, just as he was able to give the Judeo-Christian tradition, particularly in the matter of monotheism, the legitimation of his own theory.[15] The Judeo-Christian tradition "begat" Freud at the same time that it profoundly alienated him. The ambiguities and distortions in his treatment of religion flow from this tension, and the wildly unscholarly assertions in *Moses and Monotheism* constitute, in Freud's own life, a sure example of the concept of the *return of the repressed.*

These tensions and ambiguities notwithstanding, the two dominant images of the Freudian corpus, the Oedipal trauma and the murder of the primal father, represent a reformulation (however misguided) of all the following latent and powerful Judeo-Christian presuppositions: the dualistic division of all existence into a moral and natural realm; the connection of God and the Father in a monotheistic imagery; the occurrence of a crucial event in the past that predetermines the rest of history; sexuality as the curse of man's lower nature and the sign of his rebellion against parental authority; and guilt as the basic symptom of the human condition. Taken by themselves, any one of these themes has possible counterparts in other cultures. But taken as an interwoven set of meanings and images, they constitute the essence of at least some important aspects of Judeo-Christian culture.

Freud argued that the existence of universal, instinctual configurations, "latent" meanings, and "unconscious" motivations provided the scientific basis for a theory of psychic functioning that transcended cultural and historical particularities. What I have tried to demonstrate is that, in several key respects, this "unconscious" psychic realm represents a transformation of Judeo-Christian cultural elements, and cannot, therefore, be glibly applied to other cultural domains. Freud collapsed two orders of reality. One has to do with the importance of a child's experiments with sexuality and instinct in general, conducted in an environment of interaction with significant others, leading to powerful and paradigmatic "dramas" that influence adult development. This may well constitute the skeleton of what is universally true of Freud's theory of ontogenetic development. But the other order of reality is that constituted by a set of postulates and images derived from the Judeo-Christian lexicon. In collapsing these two sets of propositions into a single theoretical imagery, Freud severely curtailed the applicability of his theory outside of its original cultural domain. Although there have been severe criticisms of Freudian theory from a strictly scientific point of view, in modern

Western contexts its scientific weaknesses are to some extent compensated by the deep cultural chords that it strikes. This cannot be so in other cultural domains.

Erikson, by contrast with Freud, is rarely reductive about religious experience, not often scientific in his clinical work, and is explicitly interested in the convergence of broadly religious values and concerns with his own theoretical elaboration of Freudian theory. Perhaps because of these differences, the Judeo-Christian presuppositions that remain largely tacit in Freud's work, come closer to the surface of Erikson's thought, particularly in his analysis of Gandhi's childhood.

The core of Erikson's strictly psychoanalytic treatment of Gandhi is contained in a section of *Gandhi's Truth* entitled "The Curse," in which Erikson attempts to ground Gandhi's adult emphasis on sexual abstention and nonviolence in his childhood, particularly in his dealings with his father. He does this by concentrating on two incidents in Gandhi's childhood on which Gandhi himself places considerable emphasis in his *Autobiography*.

At the age of fifteen, Gandhi confessed to his ailing father, in a letter, that he had removed a bit of gold from his brother's armlet in order to clear a small debt that the latter had incurred. With considerable trepidation, he handed the slip of paper to his father, in which he confessed to the crime, asked his father not to take the punishment for the theft on himself, and concluded with a pledge never to steal again. Instead of indulging in an outburst of temper against his son, the father read the letter, shed silent tears over it, and then lay it down again. This incident left an indelible impression on Gandhi:

> This was, for me, an object lesson in *Ahimsa*. Then I could read in it nothing more than a father's love, but today I know that it was pure *Ahimsa*. When such *Ahimsa* becomes all-embracing, it transforms everything it touches. There is no limit to its power.
>
> This sort of sublime forgiveness was not natural to my father. I had thought that he would be angry, say hard

things, and strike his forehead. But he was so wonderfully peaceful, and I believe this was due to my clean confession. A clean confession, combined with a promise never to commit the sin again, when offered before one who has the right to receive it, is the purest type of repentance. I know that my confession made my father feel absolutely safe about me, and increased his affection for me beyond measure.[16]

Erikson's analysis of this incident starts with the proper observation that the core of this story is that it is the son who purifies the father. But he follows this insight with an elaboration concerning the lives of many gifted children who early assume responsibility for their parents, and, specifically, feel driven by the sense that "a parent must be redeemed by the superior character of the child."[17] Having introduced, to my mind gratuitously, the theme of the son "redeeming" the father, Erikson naturally goes on to ask, in the same Christian idiom, what "sin" Gandhi felt urged to redeem in his father. Erikson presents the answer to this question as part of his analysis of the second incident in Gandhi's childhood on which he rests his interpretation. Before considering Erikson's analysis of this second incident, however, it must be noted that a more adequate understanding of the first story must start with a more precise reading of Gandhi's recollection of this incident. The connection that Gandhi explicitly makes is between his "clean confession"—that is, his scrupulous adherence to the truth—and his father's apparently uncharacteristic ability to transform anger into forgiveness. What we have here is a dramatic and highly charged incident in a child's life, when two actions converge in a striking causal fashion: the child's determined, though anxious, adherence to the truth, and the father's newly acquired capacity to convert the instinctual energy of anger into the generous sensibility of forgiveness. This incident seems to have been a primordial and, in the child's imagination, magical, foreshadowing of a link that Gandhi later placed at the center of his teaching. This was the link between *satyagraha* ("holding firmly to the truth") and *ahimsa* ("nonviolence"). The notion of Gandhi's "redeeming" his father, in this cultural context, is misleading.

In any case, Erikson goes on to frame the second incident in the context of the "sin" from which Gandhi is alleged to have felt a need to redeem his father. Early in his *Autobiography*, Gandhi suggests that his father "might have been given to carnal pleasures." Erikson construes this to be part of a more general generational dilemma, and infers that this statement contains "the further accusation that the father, by insisting on the son's early marriage, had cursed the son with his own carnal weakness—certainly a powerful argument for the Augustinian stigma of primal sin."[18] Here again, the Judeo-Christian imagery of sexuality and sin is grafted on to Gandhi's thought and we are asked to "recognize in Gandhi's life a son-father and father-son theme of biblical dimensions."[19] This exegesis sets the stage for Erikson's interpretation of the second important event in Gandhi's childhood.

Early in Gandhi's married life, he found himself torn between tending his ailing father and indulging in sexual activity with his young wife. One night, when his father was approaching death, Gandhi left him in an uncle's care and went to his bedroom to join his then-pregnant wife. He was interrupted in his sexual activity by a servant who informed him that his father was in critical condition. Gandhi rushed to the sickroom, only to find that his father had already died, while he himself had been in his wife's arms. This event, which left Gandhi guilty all his life, taught him something fundamental:

> The shame . . . was this shame of my carnal desire even at the critical hour of my father's death, which demanded wakeful service. It is a blot I have never been able to efface or forget, and I have always thought that, although my devotion to my parents knew no bounds and I would have given up anything for it, yet it was weighed and found wanting because my mind was at the same moment in the grip of lust. I have therefore always regarded myself as a lustful, though faithful, husband. It took me

> long to get free from the shackles of lust, and I had to pass through many ordeals before I could overcome it.[20]

Following Kierkegaard, Erikson labels this event a "curse," by which he means an aspect of childhood that comes to represent an existential debt that remains unsettled over the rest of a lifetime. But Gandhi's recollection of this event is also, according to Erikson, a "cover memory"—that is, a condensation and projection of a pervasive childhood conflict onto a single dramatized scene. Erikson suggests that the propensity for such dramatization might well be unavoidable in a species that has an extended period of infantile dependence, is preoccupied with the death of the old, and early acquires the awareness of the succession of generations as well as the sensibility of guilt. This phylogenetic suggestion leads Erikson to the essence of his analysis of Gandhi's early conflicts:

> To better the parent thus means to usurp him; to survive him means to kill him; to usurp his domain means to appropriate the mother, the house, the "throne." If such guilt is, as religions claim, of the very essence of revelation, it is still a fateful fact that mankind's Maker is necessarily first experienced in the infantile image of each man's maker.
>
> This curse, clinical theory would suggest, must be heir to the Oedipus conflict. In Gandhi's case the "feminine" service to his father would have served to deny the boyish wish to replace the (aging) father in the possession of the (young) mother and the youthful intention to outdo him as a leader in later life. Thus the pattern would be set for a style of leadership which can defeat a superior adversary only non-violently and with the express intent of saving him as well as those whom he oppressed.[21]

Here the Judeo-Christian presuppositions that are only tacit in Freud's thought are considerably more obvious: sexuality as the "primal sin" of man's lower nature and the sign of his rebellion against parental authority; the identification of God and father in a distinctly monotheistic imagery; guilt as the characteristic psychoreligious symptom of mankind. In the Hindu cultural universe, by contrast, morality and nature are two aspects of a single order. Sexuality, as I have already argued, is in Hindu culture not so much sinful as it is wasteful. Furthermore, in Hindu thought, the emphasis is generally on an impersonal Godhead, and, at a secondary level of elaboration, on a large pantheon of male and female deities, with no special preference for a male and paternal image of the deity. Finally, the core psychoreligious problem, in the Hindu view, is ignorance, not guilt: most religious ideologies and technologies are directed to the removal of ignorance and not to the expiation of guilt.

To decode Gandhi's development and thought in terms of an essentially Judeo-Christian lexicon is, thus, on prima facie grounds, dubious. As an exercise in cross-cultural translation, it is problematic. As an effort to provide some measure of meaningful, that is, indigenous, understanding, it is plainly misleading. Instead, let us consider this same event with the Hindu cultural cosmos in mind. Here, Gandhi's own conclusions are again extremely astute. The most powerful connection that the circumstances of his father's death seems to have made in Gandhi's mind is between carnal indulgence and failure in duty. The dramatic form in which Gandhi experienced this link is no doubt a unique biographical fact of his own life. But the Hindu view, as I have outlined it earlier in this essay, provides a specific and widely accepted theory of the link between carnal indulgence, construed as a waste of potent bodily substances, and the failure to perform one's duty. It is the cultural context of Gandhi's childhood that transforms this event from a merely mechanical model for later motor behavior to a psychic and moral paradigm and prefiguration of his later convictions. This incident represents, in Gandhi's childhood, a primordial, unique, and traumatic dramatization of a widespread cultural model. It is in this sense that the event is pregnant with Gandhi's future.

Psychoanalysis is unlikely to transcend its cultural limitations unless it cultivates greater self-consciousness and makes a serious attempt to separate its insights about certain psychic processes from the substantive meanings and presuppositions of its own cultural domain. One such insight that we owe to psychoanalysis consists in the observation that certain childhood dramas, usually involving parental figures, are likely to prefigure adult predilections and patterns. The idea of guilt, to take another example, becomes culturally bound if it is used with its full range of Judeo-Christian semantic and symbolic references. If, on the other hand, guilt is viewed simply as an adult sense of imperfection and anxiety, rooted in the psychic outcome of important childhood dramas, then it gains greater universal applicability, especially for such "oversensitive" children as Gandhi. These early dramas represent the products of the child's experiments with his own instincts as they occur in respect to his parents, and within a given cultural and familial context. These events might well be recalled in "cover memories," but it is not adequate to define such memories simply as condensations of pervasive childhood conflicts. They are also hard to imagine without being, in some sense, cultural condensations and projections as well—that is, concentrated displays of powerful cultural models in single, dramatic scenes. It is also important to note that the transition from cultural models to individual biographies is neither abrupt nor unmediated. Folk literature of various sorts provides concrete, simple, and compelling dramatizations of these models. These dramatizations go a long way toward closing the emotional distance between relatively abstract cultural models and the lives of children. The story of Prahlada, which I have already mentioned, is just one example of this sort of socialization into culture, in Gandhi's own childhood.

Thus, it is misleading to interpret these two events in Gandhi's childhood in the way that Erikson does, in terms of the wish to usurp paternal power, the carnal stigma, and so on. Rather, they must be seen as the dramatic foci for two links that Gandhi made in his childhood, probably in a primordial and tacit form: the link between absolute adherence to the truth (which he later described as *Satyagraha*) and nonviolence (*Ahimsa*); and the link between self-control, especially in the sexual sense (*Brahmacharya*), and the performance of duty (*Swadharma*). Out of his early instinctual strivings and these dramatic, later systematic, insights, Gandhi forged a set of cultural meanings that placed self-control at the heart of proper living and that connected faulty self-control with failure in duty and disregard for the truth. If these childhood dramas were of significance for Gandhi's adult life, it is because their original social context and their later deliberate formulation drew mutual sustenance from a common cultural universe. It is his methodological disregard for this universe that constitutes Erikson's single major drawback.

Closely related to Erikson's psychoanalytic presentation of Gandhi's childhood is another strand of *Gandhi's Truth,* which consists of a set of reflections on Gandhi's capacity to capture the imagination and support of the Indian people. These reflections, which together constitute Erikson's psychohistorical analysis of Gandhi as a leader, in fact fall into two types of suggestion, one of which is considerably more satisfactory than the other. The first type of suggestion, which follows directly from Erikson's analysis of Gandhi's childhood, is strictly psychoanalytic. In various parts of the book, Erikson attributes Gandhi's success as a leader to the convergence of his identity crisis with that of his audience, and to the particularly striking way in which he resolved the father-son problem, problems of generativity and guilt, and the conflict between "phallicism and saintliness, and between paternal power and maternal care."[22] Gandhi's success as a leader is thus attributed to his ability to provide a dramatic and public solution to these endemic and universal conflicts. This line of reasoning, I have tried to show, is alien to the Hindu cosmos, and especially inadequate as an explanation of Gandhi's capacity to galvanize the Indian popular imagination. It is considerably more plausible, and less in conflict with the available evidence, to rest such a case on the shared universe of Hindu cultural meanings to which

Gandhi gave such dramatic and convincing shape. This latter type of argument, of which I offered the outlines earlier in this essay, gives sharper analytic value to the oft-quoted observation, which Erikson himself notes, that Gandhi, "when he listened to his inner voice, heard the clamor of the people."[23]

But the second type of suggestion that Erikson makes concerning Gandhi's growth into a leader is considerably richer than the first. It consists of a set of observations on certain behavioral and tactical modes that Gandhi developed as a child and that he apparently succeeded in transferring to considerably larger historical arenas. The general Eriksonian insight that subsumes these particular observations is that the bridge between infantile patterns and adult behavior, especially in creative individuals, is to be found in "playful enactments in childhood."[24] One such pattern that Erikson notices in Gandhi's early childhood is his peculiar tendency to tease people and animals, in a challenging and humorous way, in order to test himself and his early environment. This capacity certainly grew into an adult political tactic, and Erikson is correct in pointing out that it had "matured into a relentless skill in challenging his audience in terms as fearless as they were often mildly humorous."[25] Similarly, Erikson shrewdly notes the connection between Gandhi's early insistence on playing the peacemaker during quarrels between his playmates and his adult insistence on the moral force of his personal mediatorship in a host of political conflicts. These and other observations on the connections between "playful" patterns in Gandhi's childhood and his adult tactical modes, cast genuine light on Gandhi's unique development into a national leader. These suggestions, unfortunately, play a smaller role in Erikson's analysis than his strictly psychoanalytic interpretations of Gandhi's development. They remain, nevertheless, a fruitful subject for further and more detailed investigation.

In the section of *Gandhi's Truth* entitled "A Personal Word" Erikson offers us, in the rhetoric of a letter addressed directly to Gandhi, his central criticism of Gandhi's interpretation of *satyagraha.* This critique is based on a theme that is of primary importance to Erikson—namely, the convergence and complementarity of psychoanalysis and *satyagraha.* The cornerstone of this convergence, as Erikson sees it, is that, whereas *satyagraha,* as a "truth method," confronts the *outer* enemy nonviolently, psychoanalysis works by the nonviolent confrontation of the *inner* enemy. Both methods consider scrupulous adherence to the truth to be axiomatic, and both discover the truth by a risky and experimental process of interaction between practitioner and patient-opponent. Erikson, thus, sees Gandhi and himself as "somehow joined in a universal 'therapeutics,' committed to the Hippocratic principle that one can test the truth (or the healing power inherent in a sick situation) only by action which avoids harm—or better, by action which maximizes mutuality and minimizes the violence caused by unilateral coercion or threat."[26] But the two methods that are juxtaposed in this powerful analogy are not, in Erikson's opinion, exactly mutual and symmetrical with respect to each other. Psychoanalysis, it turns out, has a serious criticism and a lesson to offer to *Satyagraha,* which takes shape as Erikson's fundamental criticism of Gandhi.

As an exponent of the "truth method" of psychoanalysis who is critically confronting the substantive enactment of the "truth method" of *satyagraha* by its founder, Erikson concentrates on two incidents in Gandhi's life. In the first case, Gandhi, as a householder in South Africa, insisted that his wife dispose of the human waste of a Christian Untouchable who was their guest. Kasturba rebelled and Gandhi told her to leave the house. This, and similar incidents, Erikson rightly sees as part of a generally authoritarian and vindictive attitude on Gandhi's part toward his wife and family, whereas Gandhi preferred to see them as examples of "cruel kindness" and "blind love." The other incident, which Erikson analyzes in considerable detail, also took place in South Africa, at Gandhi's communal Tolstoy Farm. In this latter case, Gandhi heard that some of the young boys in the community, during a common bathing hour, indulged in a mild flirtation with a few of the young girls in the community. Gandhi was outraged by this contravention of his already strong views on *Brahmacharya*. He unilaterally decided that the best way to provide a reminder of this breach was to cut off the hair of the offending girls, a punishment he personally undertook. Erikson rightly sees these acts as representative of a vindictive, even sadistic, propensity in Gandhi. But in explaining this propensity, Erikson again falls into a parochial psychoanalytic viewpoint. He sees these incidents as revealing Gandhi's tendency toward blind moralism and his incapacity and refusal to recognize ambivalence in human motivation—that is, that property of the human constitution, explicitly documented and explained by psychoanalysis, that makes actions motivated by one conscious emotion, such as hate, be at the same time, co-determined unconsciously by the opposite emotion, such as love.

But Erikson goes further. Gandhi's refusal to recognize the ambivalence of human motivation is, in Erikson's view, only a general expression of Gandhi's major blindness, which is in the matter of sexuality. This is Erikson's basic quarrel with Gandhi. Erikson can simply neither understand nor accept Gandhi's emphasis on *brahmacharya* as a prerequisite for *satyagraha*. For Erikson, the emphasis on celibacy is ultimately an exotic and atavistic vestige of a repressive moralism that taints the otherwise rich technique of *satyagraha*. Thus, Erikson says to Gandhi, "The important question is whether *satyagraha* will remain irretrievably tied to such ascetic idiosyncrasies as your followers cultivate."[27] In the first part of this essay, I tried to show how such "ascetic idiosyncrasies" as celibacy, fasting, and nonpossession, were, in Gandhi's personal synthesis of the Hindu cultural idiom, absolutely integral elements of a total cultural lexicon, of which *satyagraha* is the political conclusion. It must also be recalled that the model of sublimation behind Gandhi's strictures views the curbing of sexuality not as repressive but as retentive of crucial energies. *Brahmacharya* is not only different from repression, in the

Freudian sense, but is even, from one point of view, directly opposed to it. Where repression connotes an unconscious attempt to stifle the sexual impulse, *brahmacharya* indicates a conscious and deliberate attitude toward sexual energy, in which it is first systematically husbanded and then appropriately transformed.

This misunderstanding flows, in part, from factors that I described in my criticism of Erikson's treatment of Gandhi's childhood. Here, as in that part of Erikson's analysis, the substantive cultural presuppositions of psychoanalysis blind Erikson to the cultural universe that Gandhi inhabited. What constituted an alien and gratuitous superimposition of meanings in the analysis of Gandhi's childhood becomes, in this section, a tendentious criticism of Gandhi's motivation, Erikson's obvious sincerity notwithstanding. But this cultural bias is not the only source of Erikson's misapprehension. The other standpoint from which Erikson finds Gandhi's views on sexuality mistaken consists of an ideological elaboration of his psychoanalytic view of human happiness. The prime components of this ideology are that sexual relations between men and women must be conducted in a spirit of "mutuality" rather than of abnegation. In turn, this "mutuality" must be supported by an understanding of "the Hereness of women as the guardians of an earthly order dedicated to an optimal hospitality toward planned progeny."[28] This is argued to be part of a "better knowledge of the role of sexuality and sensual pleasure in the energy household of men and women."[29] This enlightened attitude toward sexuality, which Erikson suggests as the psychoanalytic corrective to the ascetic excesses of Gandhi's *satyagraha*, is seen as the only way for men to regain their wholeness:

> For men can find what peace there is only in those moments when his sensual, logical and ethical faculties balance each other: this all cultures, at their best, have striven to achieve, and this a world-wide technological culture must help make universal at least as an ideal to be envisaged in a spirit of faith and realism. There is no

doubt, however, that in the world of today a severe disbalance of sensual, logical and ethical experience is upon us.[30]

This recommendation of planned parenthood, sexual mutuality, and universal technology, I submit, is part of Erikson's *ideological* quarrel with Gandhi. However, it supports and is interwoven with his strictly psychoanalytic criticism, and is equally in conflict with Gandhi's explicit ideological preferences on these matters. Taken together, these biases show that Erikson's criticism of Gandhi is not simply a disinterested psychoanalytic corrective to *satyagraha*. Rather, they show the degree to which Erikson's cultural presuppositions, expressed in either clinical or ideological terms, render crucial parts of Gandhi's beliefs and activities, from his point of view, either incomprehensible or unappealing or both.

Erikson is quite right to see certain authoritarian, even sadistic patterns, in Gandhi's behavior, particularly in familial and pseudofamilial contexts. But in explaining these human shortcomings, he casts Gandhi into his own cultural and theoretical molds, so that his own conclusions appear moralistic and exhortative rather than analytic or empathetic. Viewed from the perspective of Gandhi's own beliefs and their indigenous cultural context, these human failures appear as symptoms of Gandhi's difficulties in consistently enacting his own prescriptions. Gandhi's sadism is not so much a matter of his refusal to recognize his own ambivalence about sexuality as it is a response to the tensions of living the life that he chose. As to why his own family and such familylike establishments as the Tolstoy Farm especially sparked these tendencies, Gandhi provides the best clue—one that Erikson notices in another context:

> A reformer cannot afford to have close intimacy with him whom he seeks to reform. True friendship is an identity of souls rarely to be found in this world. Only between like natures can friendship be altogether worthy and enduring. Friends react on one another (affect one an-

> other). Hence in friendship there is very little scope for reform. I am of the opinion that all exclusive intimacies are to be avoided, for man takes in vice far more readily than virtue. And he who would be friends with God must remain alone or make the whole world his friend.[31]

The family, and by implication in the rest of my argument, the pseudofamilial communities that Gandhi organized, is the outstanding example of precisely the sort of "exclusive intimacies" that Gandhi most wished to avoid, but his early marriage was for him a painful fait accompli. The family is the primary social by-product of sexuality, and Gandhi's wife and children were, for him, constant reminders of his adult sexual life before he took the vow of *brahmacharya*. Here Erikson is partly right. But Gandhi's difficulty with the family was not so much a product of his blindness about sexuality as it was the result of a frustrated wish to be unimplicated in sexuality and its social by-products.

But the real problem with the familial model of intimacy was that it confused Gandhi's temperament, as well as his particular reformist tactics. This was so, I suspect, for three reasons. First, the family renders relations of authority ambiguous because of the democratizing tendencies inherent in affection—especially affection rooted in biological or pseudobiological ties. Although Gandhi was quite serious about his egalitarian ideology, as a tactician he thrived on clear-cut and asymmetrical authority relations, which cast him into such unambiguous roles as mentor and rebel. Second, the family blurs conflict, especially of the sort Gandhi used for the conversion of opponents. This is because familial intimacy breeds complexity in the mutual perceptions of its members and renders the motives for many actions ambiguous. This would frustrate the *satyagrahi* in Gandhi, whose notion of conflict rested in part on the clarity, openness, and unambiguity of his own motives, as well as those of his opponents. Last, the familial brand of intimacy is likely to have frustrated love as a political strategy, Gandhi's most distinctive invention. The reason for this is that the family breeds emotional vested interests that complicate love as an emotion and frustrate the uncomplicated, "selfless" love that Gandhi understood to be *ahimsa.*

Thus, the family represented the sort of social arena that Gandhi is likely to have found least tractable to his approach. Unlike larger collectivities, it could not be the ideal audience for Gandhi's reformist techniques. Nor, like his own "self," was it easily open to such technologies as fasting and celibacy, based primarily on the internal exercise of the individual will. Since all action for Gandhi was, from one point of view, political action, the family must have seemed to him a frustrating political arena, since it probably blunted his political weapons and conceivably threatened his thoroughly political identity. It is ultimately this ambiguity in the family, understood as a political arena, that explains Gandhi's sadism in familial and pseudofamilial contexts. Gandhi's family, whether in the form of Kasturba's stubborn insistence on remaining illiterate, his son Harilal's dissolute life, or the juvenile sex-play of his young wards at the Tolstoy Farm, thwarted Gandhi, and his sadism in this context is really an exposure of frustration, an admission of failure. The other side of this problem appears in Gandhi's own attempts to redefine the nature of kinship ("the cow is our mother," "*Gita* my mother") and to provoke such redefinitions in his disciples, one of whom told Erikson that "Gandhi was my mother." Thus these sadistic proclivities represent Gandhi's failure to live up to his own ideals, to his own conception of the universe and right action, not to Erikson's criteria of proper knowledge and the harmonious life.

In a brilliant analogy developed in the concluding portion of *Gandhi's Truth*, Erikson compares *satyagraha*, as a nonviolent political instrument, to the pacific rituals employed by several animal species to handle aggressive instincts in a healthy and minimally harmful fashion. This analogy leads Erikson to recommend *satyagraha* as the political expression of a new evolutionary phase in human development, where men rechannel their aggressive instincts and replace traditional forms of violence by this new "pacification ritual." This evolutionary step, in Erikson's view, would amount to a rediscovery, at a more complex moral level, of what is healthiest in the adaptive arrangements of certain "lower" species. But Erikson's central question is whether, in order to adapt this new ritualization, men are also obliged to accept such practices as *brahmacharya*, which Gandhi saw as inseparable from *satyagraha*. Erikson's implied conclusion is that these "atavisms" are unnecessary and misguided, and that *satyagraha* can, and indeed must, be universally adopted in isolation from them. This recommendation encapsulates Erikson's misunderstanding of Gandhi and his failure to seriously consider the basic methodological questions raised by the cross-cultural application of psychoanalysis. But the fact that Erikson forces one to face this problem and reflect on it is to the genuine credit of *Gandhi's Truth*.

NOTES

1. For my understanding of Gandhi's traditional antecedents, I have relied especially on two sources: Indria Rothermund, *The Philosophy of Restraint: Gandhi's Strategy and Indian Politics* (Bombay: Popular Prakashan, 1963), esp. chaps. 2, 3, and A. L. Basham, "Traditional Influences on the Thought of Mahatma Gandhi," in *Essays on Gandhian Politics: The Rowlatt Satyagraha of 1919*, ed. Ravinder Kumar (Oxford, 1971).
2. Rothermund, *Philosophy of Restraint*, p. 23.
3. Basham, "Thought of Gandhi," p. 26.
4. Ibid., pp 30–32.
5. M. K. Gandhi, *Gita: My Mother*, ed. Anand T. Hingorani (Bombay: Bharatiya Vidya Bhavan, 1965), pp. 50, 54.
6. Ibid., p. 62.
7. M. K. Gandhi, *Non-Violent Resistance (Satyagraha)*, ed. B. Kumarappa (New York: Schocken Books, 1961), p. 45.
8. Ibid., p. 97.
9. My understanding of Freud's cultural roots has been considerably influenced by two works by Philip Rieff: "The Meaning of History and Religion in Freud's Thought," in *Psychoanalysis and History*, ed. Bruce Mazlish

(Englewood Cliffs, N.J.: Prentice-Hall, 1963), pp. 23–44; and *Freud: The Mind of the Moralist* (New York: Viking Press, 1959).

10. Rieff, "Freud's Thought," pp. 26–27.
11. Rieff, *Freud*, p. 344.
12. Ibid., p. 160.
13. Ibid., p. 277.
14. H. L. Philp, *Freud and Religious Belief* (London: Rockliffe, 1956), pp. 21–37 passim.
15. Rieff, *Freud*, p. 201.
16. M. K. Gandhi, *An Autobiography; or, The Story of My Experiments with Truth* (Ahmedabad: Navajivan Trust, 1927), p. 39.
17. Erik H. Erikson, *Gandhi's Truth: On the Origins of Militant Nonviolence* (New York: W. W. Norton & Co., 1969), p. 126.
18. Ibid., pp. 127–28.
19. Ibid., p. 128.
20. M. K. Gandhi, *Autobiography*, pp. 43–44.
21. Erikson, *Gandhi's Truth*, p. 129.
22. Ibid., pp. 401–2.
23. Ibid., p. 397.
24. Ibid., p. 133.
25. Ibid., p. 278.
26. Ibid., p. 247.
27. Ibid., pp. 250–51.
28. Ibid., p. 252.
29. Ibid., p. 251.
30. Ibid., pp. 251–52.
31. M. K. Gandhi, *Autobiography*, p. 14, as quoted in Erikson, *Gandhi's Truth*, p. 139.

Part II

Erikson's Psychology and Methodology

4

A Psychoanalyst in the Field: Erikson's Contributions to Anthropology[1]

WAUD H. KRACKE

Going into a new culture for a long period, one finds oneself alternating between two kinds of experience. At one moment, one feels—after meeting a completely unexpected response in a situation that one thought was familiar—that the people one has come to live among are completely alien, and one despairs of coming to understand them. Yet before long, one may have an experience of meeting of minds, of sympathetic contact, rendering immediate and humanly understandable what had seemed a perplexing way of reacting. One comes to feel that, after all, all human beings share a fundamental ground of experience, and that in the end all people are alike. At successively deeper levels, these alternating experiences are likely to recur throughout one's contact with the culture.

Anthropologists do not often describe such encounters—particularly in their professional writings.[2] Yet this alternation of experiences is perhaps the essence of anthropology. Every science defines certain experiences as "real data" for its schemata and makes its theories about them; for anthropology, such crucial experiences are those of the person immersed in a culture different from his own, struggling to understand it.

Much theoretical controversy in anthropology implicitly boils down to an emphasis on one or the other of the alternating experiences I have just described. Many anthropologists insist that there is a core way of perceiving the world—one that is shared by those who "belong" to any particular culture—so irreducibly different from the way people of another culture perceive the world that empathy across cultural boundaries is at best tenuous, perhaps impossible. Others hold that behind all differences in the way that people express their emotions or suppress them, the feelings and reactions that individuals have in one society are ultimately the same as in any society—ultimately human. As Robert Redfield and Alfonso Villa-Rojas put it in their noted collaborative ethnography of a Mexican village:

> Beneath any culture are the same people one has always known. There are always the shy and the bold, the excitable and the phlegmatic, the intelligent and the stupid, the leaders and the led.[3]

Neither of these positions, of course, is widely held in pure form—at least, not today. Clifford Geertz[4] offers a sophisticated statement that leans toward the position of cultural relativism without espousing it. He argues that culture, in all its variable forms, is an essential part of human nature and that one can never be sure that one can empathize with someone of another culture. Melford Spiro, on the other hand, in a searching and insightful intellectual autobiography,[5] describes how successive fieldwork experiences gradually convinced him that much he had thought culturally relative in human nature was in fact universal.

These issues are of considerable import in Erik Erikson's work. Having undergone repeated sojourns (some by necessity, others of his own volition) for substantial periods in unfamiliar cultures, Erikson can claim considerable experience with the ebb and flow of communicating with someone of another culture. The issues just referred to—the question of how and at what level an individual's experience is shaped or determined by his culture, and the closely related one of the degree of empathic communication possible between people of different cultures—occupy an important place in his writing. My intent here is to appraise his contribution to the discussion of these issues, in the context of current anthropological thinking on them.

As a psychoanalyst, Erikson was at special advantage for approaching these problems. Where personal experiences and communication between individuals are central to the issue, the psychoanalyst's special skill and training in listening to the emotional communications of others, and to his own feelings, give him something special to contribute. Indeed, most of the early anthropologists who interested themselves in such problems—Edward Sapir, Clyde Kluckhohn, and many others—turned particularly to psychoanalytic theory (with varying degrees of understanding) for the tools to glean further insights in this area. Sapir and Kluckhohn did put their knowledge to good use; but theorizing—especially by those not trained in the special kind of attention appropriate to evaluating data in ways relevant to the theory—can go only so far. What is needed are trained psychoanalysts willing to collaborate with anthropologists in gathering data on personalities in other cultures, sharing the experience of coming in contact with an alien culture and the people in it. Sapir closed one of his articles with the plea:

> Perhaps it is not too much to expect that a number of gifted psychiatrists may take up the serious study of exotic and primitive cultures . . . in order to learn to understand more fully than we can out of the resources of our own cultures, the development of ideas and symbols and their relevance for the problem of personality.[6]

Erikson was not the first psychoanalyst to interest himself

in cultural differences; Abram Kardiner[7] was already collaborating with anthropologists in developing his strongly relativistic theory of "basic personality," and Geza Roheim[8] preceded Erikson in exposing himself to field work with primitive cultures. But Erikson undertook the task with a special appreciation for both the theoretical complexity of each discipline and for the subtle differences between their perspectives on man. He exposed himself not only to the cultures that he wrote about, but also to anthropological ideas, through his friendships with the anthropologists who studied those cultures. Perhaps Erikson, himself something of a wanderer in his youth, had some temperamental affinity with anthropologists, who are of necessity mobile. In any case, as much as any analyst who has retained the basic psychoanalytic framework of Freud, he has shown an understanding of anthropologists' ideas, and of some of the uneasiness anthropologists feel, as Sapir put it, about "the particular ways in which psychoanalysts appreciate"[9] anthropologists' data.

Erikson did more than take anthropology seriously; he wove it into the fabric of his thought. Every one of his clinical contributions includes careful consideration of the social context of the case or personal document under discussion; his eye for the mutual relevance of social patterns and individual lives makes each of his case histories a rich social document as well as a clinical one. He is certainly the closest thinker in the field today to Sapir's vision of

> a field of social psychology which is not a whit more social than it is individual and which is, or should be, the mother science from which stem both the abstracted impersonal problems as phrased by the cultural anthropologist and the almost impertinently realistic explorations into behavior which are the province of the psychiatrist.[10]

But while this blend of psychoanalysis with social science offers many insights into the interactions between culture and personality, it also presents a danger: in achieving a blend, one risks losing sight of crucial distinctions between the very different points of view of the two disciplines. Anthropology and psychoanalysis focus on two very different levels of human experience, from totally different perspectives. Their propositions, therefore, apply to quite different kinds of phenomena. Psychoanalysis is directed to the innermost subjective experience of the individual, which in oneself is accessible directly through introspective self-observation, in others less directly through empathic communication.[11] Anthropology, by contrast, formulates the public symbols by means of whose *shared* meanings we communicate with the fellow members of our society, and those shared ideas and orientations that make it possible for us to interact with others in our society in an organized way. While these two aspects of experience are obviously related, the kinds of propositions made from one perspective may be quite meaningless or misleading if they are applied in the domain of the other.

Many psychoanalysts question whether Erikson has not, by focusing his gaze midway between the experiencing individual and his culture, compromised an essential element of the psychoanalytic view—its profound sensitivity to, and sympathy with, the individual's innermost experiences of himself and the world, which may be very much at odds with what his culture defines as "rational" or "correct" or "moral," and which may always retain some patterns and assumptions characteristic of a child's thought. Anthropologists, on the other hand, accuse Erikson of "psychologizing" culture—treating a culture and its institutionalized ways of thinking as if they were the fantasies of an individual.

The difficulty is compounded by the very fluidity of Erikson's style, rich in metaphor and innuendo, which enhances the readability and literary value of his work—making him one of the more readable contributors to current psychoanalytic literature—but not always to the benefit of clarity of communication or precision in his explicit formulations.

Erikson has been keenly aware of these conceptual hazards. He has made a resolute effort to avoid the mistakes of psychoanalysts who preceded him in the endeavor to understand individual psychology in other cultures—Abram Kardiner, Geza Roheim, Theodor Reik,[12] and Freud himself.[13] The extent to which he has managed to avoid the twin dangers of psychologizing culture and of what Dennis Wrong[14] has called "the oversocialized conception of man" is a measure of his contribution to the field.

In this paper, I shall examine the fresh perspectives and experiences that Erikson brings as a psychoanalyst to the questions of cross-cultural communication and understanding, and of the ways in which an individual participates in his culture. I am not concerned here with Erikson's more popularized ideas—the eight stages of life, for example, and the concept of identity—with which other writers have dealt more than adequately. What interests me are his subtler insights into how an individual's unique, subjective experience articulates with the world of beliefs, values, and modes of expression that he shares with other participants in his culture and that forms the ambience of the individual's experience. Many of these insights adumbrate or anticipate ideas now achieving influence in anthropology about the personal use of cultural forms; yet they have been neglected by other writers, and Erikson himself has not developed many of them, at least explicitly, although some of them continue implicitly to guide his thought. In this paper, I shall set Erikson's thought in the context of current anthropological thinking on these problems (with occasional historical excursions into the field of culture and personality for background), showing how Erikson's ideas relate to current trends of thought—how he contributes to such trends, how he has influenced or presaged them, or where he goes against the grain.

Everything that Erikson has written probably bears to a greater or lesser degree on the problem of this paper. From his impressive output, I will limit myself to commenting on those of his writings that deal directly with his experience in cultures quite different from our European-American milieu: his brief but significant contacts with two American Indian cultures, written up in several reports and articles[15] before being encapsulated in *Childhood and Society*;[16] and his visit to India, "in search of Gandhi."[17]

Erikson himself, as I have remarked, has repeatedly undergone the experience of contact with cultures different from his own. Like many European analysts, he suffered politically enforced transplantation from Vienna to the United States in the 1930s. But Erikson went further, and sought out opportunities to expose himself to more radically different cultural contexts, in situations approximating anthropological fieldwork.

To anthropologists today, Erikson's first field experiences seem disappointingly brief—a "part of a summer" with the Sioux, just a few weeks with the Yurok. This brevity must be kept in perspective, however, with the practices of the time: anthropologists may be shocked to learn that Ruth Benedict's and Esther Goldfrank's forceful portraits of Pueblo culture are both based on only a few months of field contact.[18] In each of Erikson's visits, he had the advantage of extensive familiarity with the literature on the particular culture, as well as the company of an anthropologist deeply familiar with the culture.

The visit to the Sioux, in which he came in an official capacity, seems to have gone smoothly. The Yurok, however, presented him with problems of a sort familiar to anthropologists: then at odds with the government over a policy of land ownership, they suspected him of being a government agent, and apparently did not permit him to work in their traditional villages, forcing him to depend almost entirely on interviews with informants for his data on their culture. This had some rather interesting effects, which I will discuss, on his data.

Later in his life, Erikson returned to anthropological interests, and to "fieldwork" of a somewhat different sort, with his visit to India to pursue the life of Gandhi. Now, of course, his focus was not on anthropology as such—that is, it was not on Indian culture, but on one Gujarati—but the work on Gandhi can certainly be seen as the fruit of his lifelong interest in other cultures. A central theme of the book is the relationship of Gandhi the man and the Indian culture in which he was raised, contributing insights that are very much in line with some current thinking in anthropology about the way an individual grows into and uses his culture. Furthermore, one has the impression that Erikson spent considerably more time in India than he did in either American Indian society, and that, while there, he became much more fully absorbed in Indian life and friends.

In his sojourns with the American Indians, brief though they were, Erikson did have an immediate and personal taste of the cultures of which he wrote. At a point of major transition in his life, these experiences certainly had an impact on his intellectual development. Some of the personalities he met among the Sioux, and the situations of culture conflict that he observed there, are vividly described in *Childhood and Society*, while one woman "colleague" whom he met among the Yurok made an impression on him that lasted through his life.

THE SIOUX AND THE YUROK: CHILDHOOD EMOTIONAL PATTERNS AND THE INTEGRATION OF VALUES

When Erikson met Sioux and Yurok—and later Gujarati Indians—he was less impressed with their total difference from people of Euro-American culture than he was with their common humanity. The differences that struck him were in the realm of values, of conceptualization of the world, and of ways in which people of different cultures express themselves—all, to be sure, aspects of personality, but of a somewhat less fundamental nature than the characteristics Abram Kardiner attributed to the Comanche (absence of repressions) or to the Alorese (fragmented ego, no superego). With Roheim, Erikson could see the same conflicts in Sioux and Yurok children that psychoanalysis had discovered in Europeans; through the eyes of his anthropological colleagues, he could also see the importance of the world views and values of the cultures, and how these were adapted to their economy and environment. His observations confirmed Roheim's that "there is a correlation between the habitual infancy situation and . . . the dominant ideas of the group," but he distinguished his position sharply from Roheim's, in not being able to "conceive of the second as being 'derived' from the first, nor of primitive societies as being solutions of specific infantile conflicts."[19] Later, he distinguished his position from Kardiner's as well:

> In describing conceptual and behavioral configurations in the Yurok and in the Sioux world, we have not attempted to establish their respective "basic personality structures." Rather, we have concentrated on the configurations with which these two tribes try to synthesize their concepts and their ideals in a coherent design for living.[20]

A child analyst like Roheim, Erikson was also interested in childhood and in how the child was introduced to his culture. But, with greater respect for the active, self-determination of the individual, and for the economic and historical forces that shape culture, he posed his questions about the process somewhat differently from Roheim and Kardiner. He asked how the culture's values are successively presented to the child, and how a culture permits and encourages certain forms of childhood expression to continue through to adulthood, while discouraging others that are less compatible with its ideal style.

The Sioux: passing on the values. What interested Erikson as a child analyst about the Sioux and later the Yurok was how their "design for living" was itself inculcated into their children, becoming an integral part of each child's personality, but not necessarily molding the child into a "typical Sioux" or a "basic Yurok." Erikson sees the cultural systems of upbringing much more positively than did either Kardiner or Roheim—not as parents unwittingly (and often sadistically) inflicting on their children the same traumata to which they were subjected, but rather as a set of rules that embody a great deal of developmental wisdom. The child-rearing system *builds on* the conflicts and concerns that all children go through, using them as a medium for presenting the culture's values to the child. In a very important passage for understanding his approach, Erikson asserts:

> We are not saying here that their treatment in babyhood *causes* a group of adults to have certain traits—as if you turned a few knobs in your child-training system and you fabricated this or that kind of tribal or national character. In fact, we are not discussing traits in the sense of irreversible aspects of character. We are speaking of goals and values and of the energy put at their disposal by child-training systems.[21]

What a culture "builds into" the personalities of its children are values, attitudes, and cognitive orientations more or less shared by most people in the culture; but these do not constitute all of personality.

This point of view has something in common with Melford Spiro's early "functionalist" formulation,[22] and, insofar as Erikson stresses the importance of economic adaptation as a determinant of world view ("values do not persist unless they work, economically, psychologically, and spiritually"),[23] his formulation is very close to Clyde Kluckhohn's idea that a custom or belief persists only if it is "adaptive for the society and adjustive for the individual,"[24] satisfying individual emotional and physiological needs as it furthers the survival of the society.

Erikson, as a child therapist, is acutely aware of the interplay between a child's needs and capacities at a particular age and the way in which the culture's values are presented to the child at that age. The parents have a timetable for presenting the child with tasks he is ready for, often (in primitive tribes) the more closely geared to the child's *maturational* readiness because they do not insist on measuring a child's performance against his "years." A particular value is presented to the child in a form appropriate to his level of maturation and is presented through the medium of the particular emotional task facing the child at that point, expressed in parental responses appropriate to that task. Thus, the foundation for the later development of generosity, in a society such as the Sioux that stresses this value, is presented first by indulging an infant's needs at the stage when he is learning to cooperate with his mother to fulfill them, which encourages a later conviction that he will be taken care of when in need, so that he can afford to be generous with what he has. A relaxed attitude toward toilet training further encourages a sense of comfort in parting with valuable things, since young children often think of feces as things of great value—babies or parts of their body.

Erikson does not see these "communications" to the child as *causing* him to become generous, but simply as laying the groundwork; the value itself must be presented later in a more explicit form, by example and exhortation to share with his siblings. Ideally, these should be presented at a time when the child is capable of perceiving others as separate people who, like himself, like to have things given to them—and when he is inclined to imitate and identify with adult models.[25]

An important difference between Erikson's formulation and earlier ones is the active role he allows the individual, portraying him as choosing and molding his own destiny rather than simply submitting to his culture's design for it. The child actively integrates into his personality the values presented to him in age-appropriate forms, or if he feels unable to do so, he chooses one of the alternatives that his society offers. The child himself, with his needs and potentialities and capabilities, builds his own particular personality out of the materials that his culture provides.[26]

Childhood emotional expression and its cultural regulation: the illusion of archaism. In his work with the Yurok, Erikson turned to a slightly different aspect of the relationship between personality and culture—the culture's expressive style. He undertook to find in the beliefs, values and conventional behavior patterns of the Yurok an indication of their ideal personality type, or their preferred style of emotional expression—something very close to what Gregory Bateson, in an earlier study of the Iatmul of New Guinea, had termed a people's "ethos."[27]

The task that Erikson chose for his work among the Yurok was subtler than what he was trying to do with the Sioux—and, as we shall see later, more perilous. Instead of merely showing how cultural values are presented to the child, he portrayed the particular kinds of emotional expression permitted by Yurok culture—even prescribed by the culture in certain situations—and the cultural prescriptions for how emotions should be handled. All these he traced back to the culturally shaped situations a Yurok child faces as he grows up; yet he still eschews the notion that culture *molds* the personalities of those who grow up in it, carefully distinguishing his position from Roheim's and Kardiner's. The above quoted disavowal of Kardiner's "basic personality type" is, in fact, taken from Erikson's Yurok discussion in *Childhood and Society*, and his criticism of Roheim's deriving social structure from culturally typical childhood traumata is from an earlier version of the same discussion. He carefully avoids labeling the culture either as consisting of a particular personality type or as producing one. Choosing his words carefully, he speaks of cultures trying "to synthesize their concepts and their ideals in a coherent design for living," and asserts:

> To accomplish this a primitive culture seems to use childhood in a number of ways: it gives specific meanings to early bodily and interpersonal experience in order to create the right combination of organ modes and the proper emphasis on social modalities; it carefully and systematically channelizes throughout the intricate pattern of its daily life the energies thus provoked and deflected; and it gives consistent supernatural meaning to the infantile anxieties which it has exploited by such provocation.[28]

Here again, Erikson stresses the active role of the individual, *using* the modes of emotional expression his culture provides him, and using them for his own ends, rather than being passively "subject" to them (in the involuntary sense that a neurotic may be "subject" to attacks of anxiety). Describing, for example, the "institutionalized helplessness" expected of a Yurok in certain situations, he insists that the ability to dramatize an attitude of helplessness in such situations is not at all the same thing as actual, childish helplessness:

> Such an institutionalized attitude neither spreads beyond its defined area nor makes impossible the development to full potency of its opposite: it is probable that the really successful Yurok was the one who could cry most heartbreakingly or bicker most convincingly in some situations and be full of fortitude in others, that is, the Yurok whose ego was strong enough to *synthesize orality* and "*sense*".[29]

A culture may encourage the expression of a certain childhood attitude and elaborate it into an expected form of behavior; but this kind of dramatization, even though it may involve a kind of intentional "giving way" to the feeling in question—such as our giving way to anger when we are struck with righteous indignation—can be regulated, more or less limited in expression to the appropriate situation. In an effective, mature member of the society, it will be so.

Such culturally patterned differences in the manner of expressing emotions, and of handling and regulating them, may be one of the greatest sources of initial discomfort for someone visiting another culture. A particularly interesting feature of such differences—and one that is rather neatly illustrated in Erikson's description of certain Yurok emotional expressions on particular occasions—is the frequency with which another culture's emotional expressions strike us, strongly, as *childish*—in the very specific sense of reminding us of a child's behavior. Erikson noted that certain instances of institutionalized Yurok behavior—such as the "accepted" manner of claiming recompense in an economic transaction—could so impress even as sophisticated an outside observer as Kroeber, who described the comportment of the Yurok in this transaction in such terms as "whining around," "bickering," and offering "excuses as a child might give." Erikson himself, comparing the Yurok's pleading with the supernatural with their "bickering" transactions with each other, was

> immediately reminded of the way in which a whining child, now so touchingly helpless in the presence of the mother, uses an instant of her absence to turn on his sibling and to protest that this or that object—anything will do—is his.[30]

An earlier generation of psychoanalysts would have seized upon this observation as evidence that, as many of Freud's statements on "primitives" imply,[31] the "primitive mind" is closer to that of the child (or to neurotic ideation) than to the rational thought of our own society. Erikson, however, knowing from personal experience that adults in a primitive society are quite as rational in terms of their world view as we are in ours, is more circumspect: "Such an institutionalized attitude does not interfere with the individual's efficiency in meeting technological demands."[32]

Nor is he satisfied, though, with the simplest explanation that what is different strikes one as childish simply because it is different. The way in which Yurok behavior reminds him and Kroeber of "childish" behavior is far too specific: his practiced eye, as a child analyst, picks up a *real* similarity.[33]

What happens, Erikson suggests, is that a particular culture permits certain ways that children everywhere have of expressing their emotions, and certain universal patterns of childhood thought, to be expressed in specified situations, and even elaborates on them. Such culturally elaborated behavior is "neither a [personality] trait nor a neurotic symptom," but

> a learned and conditioned ability to dramatize an in-

> fantile attitude which the culture chooses to preserve and to put at the disposal of the individual. . . . to be used by him and his fellow men in a limited area of existence.[34]

The reason that these kinds of behavior strike us as "childish," then, is because (since they are not permitted or elaborated in our adult life) we see such behavior only in our children, or in neurotics, "bewildered people who find themselves victims of an overgrown and insatiable potentiality without the corresponding homogeneous cultural reality."[35]

Erikson has a very important point, but where he stops too short, in my opinion, is in limiting it to "primitive" societies. What I think he did not quite fully appreciate, at least at the time that he wrote *Childhood and Society*, is that exactly the same can be said of the way *we* strike people of *other* cultures—including primitive ones. Any ethnographer will tell you that some of our behavior inevitably appears childish to people of the culture he studies. What North Americans regard as being "direct" and "forthright" is often experienced by Brazilians, for example, as childishly and naively blunt, and expressions of anger that we regard as justifiable "righteous indignation" are regarded by Eskimo as embarrassing infantile temper tantrums—as Jean Briggs[36] so beautifully shows in her personal account of fieldwork with the Eskimo. Every society, including our own, dramatizes some emotions and thought patterns that first appear spontaneously in a child's outbursts or fantasies, and suppresses others that are therefore "childish" when seen in adult emotional displays. But since each society chooses different emotions to dramatize, behavior that is acceptable in one society appears childish to people from another.

Claude Lévi-Strauss, in his early opus, *The Elementary Structures of Kinship*, points out an analogous problem—the intercultural distortions of perception by which another culture's thought patterns seem "infantile." He calls this "the illusion of archaism," explaining it as follows: the cognitive "schemata" of adults, he suggests, though varying from culture to culture,

> are all derived from a universal resource which is infinitely more rich than that of a particular culture. Every newborn child provides in its embryonic form the sum total of possibilities, but each culture and period of history will retain and develop only a few of them. . . .
>
> . . . When we compare primitive and child thought, and see so many resemblances between them, we are victims of a subjective illusion, which doubtless recurs whenever adults of one culture compare their children with adults of another culture. . . . The analogies between primitive and child thought are not based on any so-called archaism of primitive thought, but merely on a difference of extension which makes child thought a sort of meeting-place, or point of dispersion, for all possible cultural syntheses.[37]

Erikson similarly sees childhood as a "meeting place" for cross-cultural communication. He sees all human experience as fundamentally similar enough to allow considerable empathy from one culture to another—for someone who is able to relax his defenses, and willing to make the effort. One message of *Childhood and Society* is that since any culture's values are built into the personality through childhood experiences that are in a general way common to all humans, empathy and communication with people of other cultures is possible through childhood. Access to one's childhood experiences, and an acceptance and some understanding of children's ways of thought and expression in one's own culture, may give one an added access to empathy with people in other cultures. At the very least, the experiences and problems of children in growing up are universal, and provide a universally interesting topic of conversation:

> The interesting thing was that all the childhood problems we had begun to take seriously on the basis of pathological developments in our own culture, the Indians talked about spontaneously and most seriously without any prodding. They referred to our stages as the decisive steps in the making of a good Sioux Indian or a good Yurok Indian.[38]

FANNY: DISTINGUISHING THE INDIVIDUAL FROM HER CULTURE

For all these theoretical insights, Erikson's picture of the Yurok in *Childhood and Society* does not come off as well as his study of the Sioux. While his ideas about the Yurok are intriguing, they seem less convincing than his portrayal of Sioux values. His portrait of the "ideal Yurok personality," built up largely of scraps of myths, ritual attitudes, and social institutions described by old informants, along with a rather formal outline of the process of child rearing, seems stereotyped. One has few of those intimate glimpses of individuals, or of apparently trivial but revealing bits of shared behavior, that bring his picture of the Sioux to life.

It is instructive to probe some of the shortcomings of Erikson's treatment of the Yurok, weighing them against the insights I have just discussed; such a balancing reveals some of the dangers inherent in Erikson's otherwise fruitful program of blending an anthropological perspective with a psychoanalytic one.[39]

Erikson was certainly aware of the difference between formally expected behavior and the expressions of personal proclivities in spontaneous acts. In much of his discussion of the Yurok, he carefully draws the distinction. Thus, he comments in the Yurok monograph:

> There is rarely available the material which would indicate whether or not *traditional* traits (such as nostalgia or avarice or retentiveness) are also dominant *personal* traits in typical individuals.[40]

When he compares Yurok "official behavior" with the obsessive or "anal character"[41] described by Freud and Abraham, he goes on to ask himself: "Am I trying to say the Yurok *is* all of this or that he behaves 'as if'?"[42] He answers himself clearly in favor of the latter alternative.

Yet in his actual analysis of the Yurok style, Erikson at points slips into treating the beliefs, institutions, and ethos of Yurok society as if these were personal inclinations or the fantasies of an individual. His thesis that Yurok "retentiveness" is "alimentary" rather than "anal" rests not so much on his observations of personal trends or fantasies of Yurok individuals, or even on observations of Yurok upbringing, as on the myths, rituals, and concepts of the tribe that emphasize bodily fluids, digestive tubes, and the dangers of greediness, and such "oral" attitudes as ritual helplessness before deities. Erikson appears to treat the society as if it were itself a psychological product, derived from a specific infantile conflict—a reduction for which Erikson had earlier taken Roheim to task. Though Erikson takes pains, as I pointed out earlier, to distinguish his position from Kardiner's, it is not easy to see where the analysis itself differs from one Kardiner might have made, or even Roheim. One does not see the nice interplay between the personal and the social that comes across in the Sioux analysis. What led Erikson to court the fallacy of which he was so well aware, characterizing social institutions themselves in terms of ontogenetic development?

One factor, certainly, was the difficulty he encountered in studying the Yurok. As I have mentioned, Erikson was prevented by circumstances from becoming as familiar with the Yurok as with the Sioux. Now, it is a common experience that the less familiar one is with a culture, the more one is apt to personify it—to mistake the culture's style for the spontaneous self-expression of those who adopt the style.[43] At first, all the individuals seem to blend into one another, and one perceives them as all sharing a particular kind of "personality." Gradually, one learns enough of the culture's expressive symbolism to recognize the meanings conveyed by particular acts and gestures, and to distinguish the personal self-expression of individuals from their formalized role behavior. Only then can one detect the individual personalities expressed through their actions.

Accentuating the effect of the brevity of Erikson's contact with the Yurok was the small number of its exemplars to whom he had access. Erikson's psychological study rested on the few representatives of Yurok culture who presented themselves to him as informants. Their individual personalities would undoubtedly tend strongly to color his picture of the Yurok and to magnify his tendency to personify the society.

One informant, in particular—an obviously imposing woman—does stand out as having struck up a warm and communicative relationship with Erikson: the Yurok lady shaman he calls "F." in the original report, "Fanny" in *Childhood and Society*, with whom he reports having such a delightful time comparing professional notes.[44] In Erikson's more comprehensive original report[45] this dramatic and evidently personable old lady is presented in much fuller detail. Her life story and the story of how she became a shaman occupies nearly a fifth of the short monograph.

Fanny made a deep impression on Erikson. In a difficult field situation, she was the one Yurok who opened herself up to him. Other informants seemed to remain opaque to him: "I know little about him," he remarked of the old man who gave him much of his material on myth and the old ways. Fanny presented herself vividly to him and seems to have been an unusual and impressive person. In a paper he wrote fifteen years later on clinical methods,[46] he describes her approach to her patients, and recalls of their conversation: "We felt like colleagues." One senses that meeting with her was of some personal significance to Erikson.

Fanny's story corresponds strikingly to Erikson's portrait of Yurok personality. It is dominated by an alimentary theme: the dream that ushered in her adolescent symptom, which led her to become a shaman, was of eating secretions that dropped from a woman's basket, and the symptom itself was hysterical vomiting—a common enough symptom, Erikson commented, in adolescent girls. The process of her becoming a shaman, again, involved swallowing and vomiting, and prohibitions on eating and drinking, and the profession itself includes sucking out and swallowing the illness. Erikson comments how well her particular choice of profession suits her emotional conflicts, "lifting her oral desires and aversions to a plane of magical usefulness."[47]

Given the situation, it would be highly understandable

that much of what Erikson said about the Yurok might have reflected the one Yurok he knew well and with whom he felt a deep kinship. One may hazard a guess, then, that his sketch of the Yurok may be less a rounded analysis of Yurok culture than it is a kind of psychobiography—or "ethnobiography"—of Fanny.

CULTURE AND INDIVIDUALITY

A culture cannot be portrayed on the basis of a single informant; nor can any single individual be taken as a typical representative of the personality of members of a culture. To do so would be to neglect the widely diverse individualities of the different, actively responding people who make up a society. From birth, different individuals respond quite differently even to very similar situations, increasingly so as they respond to later situations in terms of a past each has carved out for himself by his earlier responses. Even if all family environments in a culture were identical, which is never even approximately the case, people growing up in the same culture would come out different from one another simply because of the active, choosing nature of the human being, each person to some degree molding his own experience. Since parents, siblings, and other significant persons with whom a child interacts in growing up have their own individualities, the scope of variation increases. Some people in a culture, to be sure, may show similar patterns of response on the basis of having experienced in the same way a particular situation typical of their culture early in life; yet others may have experienced even that initial situation quite differently, and gone on to develop quite a different adult personality. Certain situations may call forth identical *outward* responses from all members of the culture, as in following certain customary rules of avoidance; but even in such cases, the feelings and personal ideas associated with the outward behavior may differ considerably from person to person, or people may integrate the pattern quite differently into their lives and overall personalities.[48]

Ethnographers, dealing directly with inidviduals of other cultures, have long been aware of this. Ralph Linton commented more than thirty years ago:

> All anthropologists who have come to know the members of non-European societies intimately are in substantial agreement on certain points. These are: (1) Personality norms differ in different societies. (2) The members of any society will always show considerable individual variation in personality. (3) Much of the same range of variation and much the same personality types are to be found in all societies.[49]

Edward Sapir, the philosopher of early American anthropology, pointed out quite early some of the conceptual dilemmas arising from such variations among individuals in a society. Culture, he points out, consists of beliefs, symbols and their meanings, values, and such, which are shared by a number of individuals. If these "exist" anywhere, they exist only as a part of the experience of the individuals who hold them or believe in them. But if different individuals have quite different experiences, if some are ignorant of the meanings of symbols that are central for the lives of others, or disagree about the meaning or interpretation or implications of a symbol, or about their central values, how can they be said to share the same culture? Quoting a phrase in Dorsey's *Omaha Sociology* that had shocked him as a student—"Two Crows denies this"—Sapir asserted that every informant's opinion, every disagreement with other informants, was as important a cultural datum as the consensus of all the rest.[50]

Kluckhohn almost alone followed his prescription in full in his book on *Navajo Witchcraft*, documenting every disagreement among his informants; but for the most part anthropologists, including those interested in personality, preferred to ignore variation, or sweep it under the rug. Margaret Mead[51] described numerous variations in personality among the Samoan adolescent girls she studied, but dissolved their differences into generalizations in her conclusions. In interpreting Rorschach responses taken by the anthropologist Cora DuBois from her informants on the Pacific island of Alor, Emil Oberholzer observed that "the variability [among] Alorese . . . is considerably larger than [among] Europeans";[52] but his conclusion is dismissed by Kardiner as reflecting accidental variations in childhood conditions, and as being, in any case, minor compared to the differences he postulated between the Alorese and any other culture.

Ruth Benedict, a close friend of Sapir's, was another anthropological theorist who took variation of personalities in a culture more seriously. She proposed a rather interesting relationship between the range of variability of personalities in a culture and the culture's ethos, or most valued personality type. In any society, she suggested, personalities range from those who are temperamentally in perfect accord with the ethos (who become the society's leaders and successful people) to those who are temperamentally incompatible with it (who are the "deviants"), with a range of people in between who are flexible and can be molded to the ethos, or at least persuaded to conform to it.[53] But she does not consider the deviants to have any significant place in the society. In the end, then, her formulation simply becomes one more rationale for ignoring personality differences within a culture.

How societies organize differences. Benedict leaves her "deviant" personalities in limbo. Erikson attributes a little more compassion (or at least flexibility) to the social order —at any rate, to the order of the American Indian societies he visited. Each society, he noted, while encouraging its members to conform to certain values, makes allowances for deviation from them—either through flexibility in their application or through providing alternative roles for those "who feel that they are 'different,' and that the prestige possibilities offered do not answer their personal needs."[54] In discussing Sioux society, for example, he pointed out several alternative roles offered for "those men who do not care to be heroes and those women who do not easily agree to be heroes' mates and helpers"[55]—roles that, though not free from the "ridicule and horror which the vast majority must maintain in order to suppress in themselves what the deviant represents," at least offer some definite status in society for deviant individuals. The culture's central religious rituals, on the other hand, "permit a few exceptional individuals who feel their culture's particular brand of inner damnation especially deeply . . . to dramatize for all to see the fact that there is a salvation."[56] "Each system, in its own way," he states more generally, "tends to make similar people out of all its members, but each in a specific way also permits exemptions and deductions from the demands with which it thus taxes the individuality of the individual ego,"[57] and he concludes with admiration of "the way in which these 'primitive' systems undertook to maintain elastic mastery in a matter where more sophisticated systems often fail."[58]

Erikson was one of the first, then, to take seriously the question now made more explicit by Anthony Wallace:[59] How does a society organize differences within it—the different personalities of the people that make it up, and the variant beliefs that coexist among them? But the framework that Erikson presented in *Childhood and Society* still bowed to the dominant anthropological assumption of the 1950s: that *differences* are equivalent to *deviance.*

Playing with culture. A second way in which Erikson's approach differs from Benedict's and constitutes an important advance lies in his characterization of the type of individual who will become successful in a given culture. Benedict regards culture as fate: the "configuration" of the culture determines which individuals will be successful, in proportion to the closeness of their temperamental predilections with those favored by the culture. Erikson leaves more room for the initiative of the individual, or for the individual's ability to integrate and direct his native propensities with the culture's expressive patterns. In *Childhood and Society* he comments:

> In order to create people who will function effectively as the bulk of the people, as energetic leaders, or as useful

> deviants, even the most "savage" culture must strive for what we vaguely call a "strong ego" in its majority or at least in its dominant minority—i.e. an individual core firm and flexible enough to reconcile the necessary contraditions in any human organization, [and] to integrate individual differences.[60]

This perspective, emphasizing the way an individual member of the society integrates a value into his ego, brings up the possibility that there may be considerable variation among individuals in the way that they integrate a value into their personalities.

From this, it is not a very long step to the idea that people do not simply conform to norms, or hold certain beliefs, but actively manipulate norms and use their beliefs to gain ends—an idea that has been gaining considerable currency in anthropological studies of village politics.[61] As Suzanne and Lloyd Rudolph have put it (in somewhat less Hobbesian language):

> Cultural norms are as much an opportunity as a constraint and "compliance" can take so many forms that the word may lose its meaning in certain contexts. . . .
>
> . . . "Playing" the culture, as a harp with diverse strings, is, we assume, as frequent a relation to culture as being molded and programmed by it; the spectrum from compliance to noncompliance to counter-cultural innovation suggest the myriad possible relations of the individual to the culture.[62]

This perspective is not entirely new. Kroeber, according to Murphy,[63] "liked to annoy his colleagues by saying that people 'played' with the systems," and much of Dorothy Eggan's work[64] expresses this theme. But it is now becoming a focus of anthropological theory, not a provocative comment.

The perspective is developed more fully, as one might expect, in the psychobiographical studies, such as that of Gandhi (to which, in part, the Rudolphs' remarks refer), where the focus is not on how culture deals with differences among individuals, but rather on how individuals use—and change—their own cultural symbols, beliefs, and norms. In discussing Gandhi's life and the lives of those who influenced his personality development, the emphasis is not on how Indian concepts and norms molded Gandhi's personality, and those of his parents, or guided their acts; it is rather on how Gandhi and those around him embodied Indian norms and ideals in their own particular ways, and how they expressed their own personalities through the medium of Indian ideas, Indian norms, and their particular situation in Indian society of that time.

It is not surprising to see the individual's relationship to his culture in such a perspective in a study focusing on the biography of an individual; so it is difficult to say whether this difference in emphasis represents a change in Erikson's view of society, or simply a shift in his focus from the social to the individual level. Nevertheless, this greater emphasis on the individual's actively expressing his individuality by means of cultural forms, which he can manipulate and not simply conform to, corresponds to a new concept of the relationship between cultural concepts and individual thought and action that is gaining some wide currency in anthropology today. Most strikingly formulated by Edmund Leach[65] in his ethnography of highland Burma in which he presents Kachin myth and ritual as a kind of language with which to express personal differences (rather than, as anthropologists have traditionally seen it, as a set of symbols expressing social unity), this point of view has been most explicitly developed, and its philosophical foundations and implications (always wittily) pursued, in a recent book by Robert Murphy, *The Dialectics of Social Life*. In this point of view, the inconsistencies within a cultural system—between thought and act, between social structure and people's concept of it—are all taken as part of the nature of social reality, not to be explained away by a higher unity.

Some comments on identity. The chief concept in which Erikson formulates the active role of the individual in selecting, modifying, and organizing cultural elements as he assimilates them into his personality—and a concept that one cannot avoid in discussing Erikson's work—is *identity*. It is Erikson's best-known concept, and highlights very important issues, but I do not feel that it is one of Erikson's more felicitous additions to the psychosocial vocabulary.

Certainly the concept of identity has focused attention on the key psychosocial problem that I have highlighted: How does the individual initiative that psychoanalysis stresses—the individual's ability to choose between alternatives and put things together for himself, which is both a postulate of psychoanalytic theory and a goal of its therapy[66]—fit with the anthropological tenet that one's minutest perceptions and the course of one's life are manifestations of inescapable cultural orientations? These apparently contradictory orientations, products of the two major discoveries of this century in the study of man, were bound to come into collision—as they did quite promptly, in the controversy between Malinowski and Ernest Jones.[67] The concept of identity is one attempt to bridge these two orientations.

Perhaps the most important contribution of the concept of identity has been to underline an idea that has been around in the background and that may go some way toward providing a way of reconciling the two viewpoints. One does, as W. E. Hocking puts it, "build" a self,[68] though the materials of which one builds it can be only those at hand—the ideas and values of one's culture (in the particular form in which they are presented to one through one's parents),[69] modified by and integrated with one's own particular needs, abilities, and ways of seeing things. As Sapir puts it:

> A personality is carved out by the subtle interaction of those systems of ideas which are characteristic of the culture as a whole, as well as of those systems of ideas which get established for the individual through more special types of participation, with the physical and psychological needs of the individual organism, which cannot take over any of the cultural material that is offered in

> its original form but works it over more or less completely, so that it integrates with those needs.[70]

But, though this idea was around, it did not receive much attention until it received embodiment in a word.

The concept of identity, then, points to a problem area. It is a whole set of questions, not an answer: *How do* people integrate values and shared symbols into their personalities? How differently can two people integrate a particular value? And so on. The problem is that when such questions are embodied in a word—and particularly a catchy one like *identity*—the word very quickly becomes an answer in itself. Intended to raise questions, it is often used, even by Erikson himself, as an explanation: Gandhi stood up to his caste elders, for the "survival" of his identity.[71] Even when it is used to define an area of investigation, a set of questions, *identity* has very wide boundaries: when introduced as an explanatory concept, it leaves at least one reader with more of a sense of blur than of clarification. (Much the same has happened with the word *culture*, as Meyer Fortes has observed.)[72]

Perhaps Erikson intentionally keeps the concept vague, to prevent it from becoming rigidified (as Coles suggests)[73] and to allow himself a certain impressionistic freedom in his style. Others of his images convey a similar sense of things blurring into one another. It is a theme, particularly in *Gandhi*: "It is always difficult to say where, exactly, obsessive symptomatology ends and creative ritualization begins";[74] and a bit earlier in the book he mentions learning

> how difficult it is to differentiate between stubborn and superstitious remnants of an orthodox world image, personal and conscious emphases and omissions, and repressions and denials coming from irrational recesses. The fact is that none of these can be separated, for in any given life they have become intertwined.[75]

Nature knows no boundaries, as the impressionists have taught us, and Erikson, an artist as much as he is a scientist, may wish to point this out as a corrective to our perhaps overly analytic, scientific view of man. But if this is the case—and if this is one reason that he keeps concepts like identity purposefully vague—it only adds a twist of irony to turn and use the very same concept as an analytic and explanatory tool!

Certainly, much of what Erikson discusses under the rubric of identity are fascinating points and humanly moving clinical observations. One cannot but be intrigued, for example by his insights in the discussion of "grandfathers"[76] and recognize in one's own experience the difficulties caused by radical change in the historical situation for an adolescent's identification with his forebears. Yet the concept simply seems to include too much. One fears that Robert Coles is all too correct when he suggests[77] that "identity has to do with everything that Erikson wrote about in *Childhood and Society*"—an awesome range of phenomena!

An additional problem is that the term had a prehistory, or several prehistories. *Identity* had at least one meaning in sociology before Erikson picked it up, and a complex of meanings in psychiatry, and, rather than exclude them from his concept, Erikson seems to have incorporated all of these into it. In social psychology, the term has long referred to those features by which one is identified as a social person—beginning with one's name, address, and social security number, and going on through the cost and style of one's house and the sort of people with whom one associates, and all the other ways by which one is "assigned a specific place in the world."[78] In psychiatry, on the other hand, *identity* has referred (among other things) to that basic sense of being a self—separate from others, the same as one was a moment ago, and in voluntary control over the parts of one's body—whose crucial period of development is in the first year and a half of life, and which an adult can lose, really, only in psychosis or in transient and unusual states of mind.[79] In this sense, it is very close to what is currently much discussed under the term "self-cohesion."[80] Erikson's definitions seem to encompass all of these meanings; and, in addition, he brings in an idea of "group identity," which ranges from a consensus among a number of individuals that they have enough in common to constitute a group, to what Redfield refers to as a culture's "world view."[81] One is still left with the impression expressed by H. C. Rümke[82] after a 1951 conference in which the concept was discussed:

> We all felt that this 'concept of identity' was extremely important, but it was not clear what the exact meaning was, so loaded with significance was the new term.

CONCLUSION

Psychoanalysis is, and must be, the most sedentary of all professions. It requires a constancy of perception of self, other, and reality: skeptical though he must be of his own motivations and of the possibility of distorted perceptions on his own part, the psychoanalyst, ever contending with human emotional upheaval, must at bottom retain a profound conviction of the rightness of his own perceptions of reality and of himself. The greatest challenge he faces every day is to remain open and sensitive to another person through all that person's determined efforts to close off communication, and through onslaughts of vituperative attack. The anthropologist, by contrast, is probably the most mobile of academics. He must steel himself emotionally for long periods of being out of contact with his consociates, often undergoing physical hardship and sometimes danger to his life, but, most difficult, of being deprived of his essential bearings—the coordinates provided by his familiar social and cultural postulates about reality and human relationships. One can see many similarities between the demands of psychoanalysis and of ethnography—similarities that perhaps partly account for the constant intercommunication and sense of mutual relevance that has characterized the parallel developments of the two disciplines.[83]

Both anthropologists and psychoanalysts must ultimately retain their own cultural commitments, their own sense of who they are, through assaults on their identity by intimate association with quite different ways of experiencing the world. Both must at the same time remain open to the other worlds with which they are confronted, maintaining the attitude of "suspension of disbelief," like that more temporarily required (says Coleridge) of the reader of poetry. Yet the essential difference between the demands on the practitioners of the two professions make it difficult indeed to combine them: the one being required to remain constant and emotionally available to a patient torn by his emotions, the other required to adapt himself to very different ways of living and to accept them, at least for the duration of his fieldwork, as the right way to do things.

It takes an unusual person to combine the sedentary occupation of a psychoanalyst with the mobility—one might say wanderlust—necessary for anthropological fieldwork, and to combine the introspective self-awareness and ability to be tuned into others' emotions one needs in psychotherapeutic work, with the social scientist's awareness of social context. Erikson, from his work, seems to combine these qualities well; perhaps the coexistence of such opposites in his character and intellectual framework contributes to his fondness for paradoxical formulations. He is unquestionably an astute and sensitive clinical observer, and at the same time his awareness of the social context makes his case histories most illuminating studies of the social forces impinging on the subjective lives of individuals. To this he adds a literary gift—not an unimportant asset for someone who has chosen to communicate with such a wide audience as has Erikson, particularly in communicating the flavor of a case history to an audience who has had no direct exposure to the clinical situation, and in presenting individuals of other cultures to people with no experience in those cultures.

In dealing with individual life histories, Erikson is on his home ground as a clinician. It is here—from his sketch of "Fanny," the Yurok shaman, to Gandhi's life—that one finds his richest contributions to anthropological thought on how the individual interlocks with his social context. Here, though, more than in the rest of his anthropological work, one must look not primarily for the theoretical formulations that he makes explicit; those on Gandhi are relatively simple and not very different from those in his earlier analyses of great (or infamous) men and their messages. The richest vein of insights in these works lies in his passing comments, or in descriptions that simply bring out (in painterly fashion) particular facets of the interplay between personal emotions and cultural symbols, or psychological themes in social interactions. This kaleidoscopic variety of psychological comments on social process is refreshing, bringing out the various parts that personal psychology can play in the culturally defined social environment—the interplay between the emotional and ideological meanings of symbols,[84] the intricacies of the psychological relationship between a leader and his followers,[85] and many other kinds of relationship between personal emotions and culture.

Some of these strengths also have their dangers, as does the task of relating social with intrapsychic reality. At times, I have suggested, Erikson is guilty of applying psychoanalytic formulations where analysis at the cultural level might be more appropriate, and at other times, as many psychoanalysts accuse, of making the social *context* of an individual's action seem as if it were the *determinant* of his behavior. Such weaknesses, I think, are inherent in the effort to interweave or (as many of Erikson's metaphors suggest) blend psychological and social models into a single "psychosocial" framework (as Sapir advocated). I would prefer, with Caudill,[86] to maintain the complementary separateness of social and psychological perspectives.

Each of Erikson's best-known anthropological works begins with observations on problems of communication engendered by cultural differences, drawn directly from his experiences in that culture. His various accounts of the Sioux[87] begin with accounts of a seminar with both white and Sioux participants, in which Erikson offers observations on the ways in which the two groups' beliefs and values distort their perceptions of one another and block communication. Beginning the book on Gandhi, he shows how such culturally induced distortions of perception impeded communication in his interviews with friends of Gandhi. Their perception of him, he pointed out, was influenced not only by transferences from their childhood, but more immediately by a "transference" to him of attitudes that they had toward individuals in analogous roles in their own culture. In at least one situation—with Ambalal Sarabhai—Erikson was able to see that a certain impediment to their communication arose from their different perception of the situation: "Once fully understood that Ambalal could take our encounter to be only that of two individuals with allegiances to their respective occupational *dharmas*," Erikson says, "things became easier, and he eventually expressed his full confidence in my work."[88]

Erikson certainly seems to feel that, though culturally different modes of expression and ways of thinking may at first hinder communication,[89] once these differences are perceived, empathic communication is possible, and, indeed, enriching. Being able to understand Sioux patterns of emotional expression (better than a cynical teacher who had concluded from their external reserve that Sioux parents did not love their children), Erikson was able to establish enough rapport with a Sioux father to discuss the man's problems in relation to his children—and was able to recognize the "wordy praise" in the man's laconic comment: "I guess you have told me something."[90]

The very differences of another culture can, once one sees the perspective implicit in them, offer personal rewards for such communication. Mary Catherine Bateson, in a beautiful article on her fieldwork in the Philippines, learned that the Philippine way of dealing with mourning can be more satisfying than the personal isolation to which we in our culture subject the mourner.[91] The readiness with which some people can come not only to understand another culture, but also to adapt to its style of expression and to learn to communicate with its members, suggests that—for them at least—there is no insuperable barrier between different cultures' patterns of thinking and feeling. Thus, Napoleon Chagnon, whose descriptions of Yanomamö bring them to life as live and distinct individuals,[92] knew he had been long enough among the Yanomamö when he found himself having all *too* appropriate Yanomamö responses in situations where these responses could have cost him his life.[93]

Chagnon spent an unusually long time, even for an anthropologist, among the people he studied. Yet other anthropologists of equal experience and perceptiveness assert just as firmly that there *is* an unbridgeable difference between, say, a Balinese individual's way of experiencing the world and our own.[94] The testimony of these ethnographers certainly is not to be dismissed.[95]

The issue we are talking about is essentially one of human experience and human communication. The observer is an essential part of the phenomenon itself. It may well be that the reality of intercultural communication and sympathy (in the literal sense of sharing feelings) across cultural boundaries, may differ from one person to another. One person may experience a deep communication with individuals of another culture, where another experiences a subtle barrier; one person may be more keenly aware of the common experiences with members of the other culture, another more attuned to aspects of the experiences of members of the other culture intrinsically alien to his own. Or two individuals may have different degrees of personal affinity for the way members of a particular culture experience the world.

The psychoanalyst is not only a person trained in certain empathic skills; he is also apt, if he is good at his trade, to be a certain kind of person—one who values the timid, tender core of another's experience, and is able to communicate an appreciation for those personal experiences of the other. He may be especially apt, therefore, to elicit some of the more hidden human feelings of an individual—

perhaps more universal ones. These, if they are universal, would not necessarily be those of greatest interest to the anthropologist looking for the experiences his informant has that are distinctive to members of his culture. The anthropologist is more likely to be a tough romantic, willing to undergo hardships to pursue in distant and difficult terrains some personal quest—perhaps, as Susan Sontag[96] said of Lévi-Strauss, pursuing his vision of the ideal society he does not find at home. He is not likely to take kindly to the suggestion that what he has gone so far to uncover is a mere replica of his own society, in which people pursue the same, humdrum human problems.

A point that Erikson might add to this discussion—though it is only to be teased out of his writings, never made explicit—is that the experience, or experiences, we share most initmately as human beings, are those of having been a child. Perhaps the people who can most easily find common emotional ground with someone of a very different culture from their own, are those who have access to the whole range of their own childhood experiences.

NOTES

1. This article was largely written while I was a fellow of the Center for Psychosocial Studies in Chicago, Autumn Quarter, 1973. I am indebted to the Center staff for their help and support, and I would like to express appreciation for the opportunity to exchange ideas with the Center staff and fellows: Robert LeVine, George Pollock, Bernard Weissbourd, John and Virginia Demos, Mark Gehrie, and Marvin Zonis. Conversations with all of these persons contributed considerably to my appreciation and understanding of Erikson's work, and of the issues discussed in this article. I also owe special thanks to my wife, Laura Huyssen Kracke, for her patient editorial work.

2. What I am here formulating is poignantly described by Kenneth Read in *The High Valley* (New York: Scribner's, 1965), esp. pp. 73–87. He describes a moment of communication with a Gahuku (New Guinea) headman, Makis, in which he suddenly understood the man's feelings for his pregnant wife, who was in danger of dying—feelings hitherto masked by

a callous exterior of Gahuku manliness. Another excellent account of such experiences is Laura Bohannon's fictional account of fieldwork with the Tiv, written under the pseudonym of Elenore Smith Bowen, *Return to Laughter* (New York: Harper & Row, 1954). See also Jean Briggs, *Never in Anger* (Cambridge, Mass: Harvard University Press, 1970), pp. 225–310; William Caudill, "Some Problems in Transnational Communication (Japan-United States)," in *Application of Psychiatric Insights to Cross-Cultural Communication,* Symposium no. 7, Group for the Advancement of Psychiatry (1961), pp. 409–21. (See also nn. 91–93 below.)

3. Robert Redfield and Alfonso Villa-Rojas, *Chan Kom: A Maya Village* (1934; reprint ed., Chicago: University of Chicago Press, 1962), p. 212. Redfield was an anthropologist, Villa-Rojas a school teacher of the village.

4. Clifford Geertz, "The Impact of the Concept of Culture on the Concept of Man," in *New Views of the Nature of Man,* ed. J. Platt (Chicago: University of Chicago Press, 1966), pp. 93–118. See also idem, *Person, Time, and Conduct in Bali,* Yale University Southeast Asia Studies Cultural Report Series, no. 14 (New Haven, Conn., 1966). Both are reprinted in idem, *The Interpretation of Cultures* (New York: Basic Books, 1973). For another view with a relativistic emphasis, see Robert Levy, *The Tahitians: Mind and Experience in the Society Islands* (Chicago: University of Chicago Press, 1973). A psychiatrist, Levy stresses that "one must understand something about shared or prevalent psychological qualities before one can study and understand variations," but he acknowledges that his "interest in *Tahitian* qualities [produces] a partial portrait," and that his subjects' "common humanity" is the "first basis of our relationships and of my understanding of them" (p. xxiv).

5. Melford Spiro, "Culture and Human Nature," unpublished paper.

6. Edward Sapir, "Cultural Anthropology and Psychiatry," *Selected Writings of Edward Sapir,* ed. David Mandelbaum (Berkeley: University of California Press, 1949), p. 521.

7. Abram Kardiner, *The Psychological Frontiers of Society* (New York: Columbia University Press, 1963).

8. Geza Roheim, "The Psychoanalysis of Primitive Culture Types," *International Journal of Psychoanalysis* 13 (1932): 1–224; idem, *Children of the Desert,* ed. Warner Muensterberger (New York: Basic Books, 1974).

9. Sapir, "Cultural Anthropology and Psychiatry," p. 514.

10. Ibid., p. 513.

11. Erik H. Erikson, "The Nature of Clinical Evidence," in *Insight and Responsibility* (New York: W. W. Norton & Co., 1964), pp. 47–80. See also Heinz Kohut, "Introspection, Empathy, and Psychoanalysis," *Journal of the American Psychoanalytic Association* (1959): 459–83. For excellent expositions of the psychoanalytic method, see Alexander L. and Juliette George, *Woodrow Wilson and Colonel House* (New York: Dover, 1964), pp. v–xiv, and Robert LeVine, *Culture, Behavior, and Personality,* (Chicago: Aldine, 1973), pp. 182–202.

12. Theodor Reik, *Ritual: Four Psychoanalytic Studies,* trans. Douglas Bryan (New York: Grove Press, 1946).

13. Sigmund Freud, *Totem and Taboo, Standard Edition of the Complete Psychological Works of Sigmund Freud,* ed. James Strachey, vol. 13 (London: Hogarth Press, 1955); idem, "On Narcissism," *Standard Edition,* vol. 14 (London: Hogarth Press, 1957), p. 75. LeVine, *Culture, Behavior, and Personality,* pp. 48-52, 204–5, gives a sound critique of early psychoanalytic writing on primitive cultures.

14. Dennis Wrong, "On the Oversocialized Conception of Man in Modern Sociology," *American Sociological Review* 26 (1961): 183–93.

15. Erik H. Erikson, "Observations on Sioux Education," *Journal of Psychology* 7 (1939): 101–56; idem, "Observations on the Yurok: Childhood and World Image," University of California Publications in American Archeology and Ethnology, Monograph 35 (Berkeley, 1943), pp. 257-301; and idem, "Childhood and Tradition in Two American Indian Tribes," *Psychoanalytic Study of the Child* 1 (1945): 319–50.

16. Erik H. Erikson, *Childhood and Society,* 2d ed. (New York: W. W. Norton & Co., 1964).

17. Erik H. Erikson, "Gandhi's Autobiography: The Leader as a Child," *American Scholar* 35 (1966): 632–46; idem, *Gandhi's Truth: On the Origins of Militant Nonviolence* (New York: W. W. Norton & Co., 1969); and idem, "On the Nature of Psychohistorical Evidence: In Search of Gandhi," in *Life History and the Historical Moment* (New York: W. W. Norton & Co., 1975), reprinted in *Explorations in Psychohistory: The Wellfleet Papers of Erik Erikson, Robert Jay Lifton, and Kenneth Kenniston,* ed. Robert Jay Lifton and Eric Olson (New York: Simon and Schuster, 1974), pp. 42-77. For a thoughtful review of *Gandhi's Truth,* see Clifford Geertz, "Gandhi: Non-Violence as Therapy," *New York Review of Books,* 20 November 1969, pp. 3–4.

18. Ellen Sack, "The Anthropologist as Individual: Ruth Benedict and Esther Goldfrank" (Master's thesis, University of Illinois at Chicago Circle, 1975).

19. Erikson, "Childhood and Tradition," p. 330.

20. Erikson, *Childhood and Society,* p. 185.

21. Ibid., p. 137–38.

22. Melford Spiro, "Social Systems, Personality Theory, and Functional Analysis," in *Studying Personality Cross-Culturally,* ed. Bert Kaplan (New York: Harper & Row, 1961), pp. 93–127.

23. Erikson, *Childhood and Society,* p. 138.

24. Clyde Kluckhohn, *Navaho Witchcraft* (Boston: Beacon Press, 1944). Kluckhohn later abandoned this formulation as *too* functionalist, implying a greater degree of harmony among the parts of a society than is usually the case, and a degree of satisfaction provided by a social system for its members that is rarely observed. Idem, "The Limitations of Adaptation

and Adjustment as Concepts for Understanding Cultural Behavior," in *Culture and Behavior: The Collected Essays of Clyde Kluckhohn,* ed. Richard Kluckhohn (New York: Free Press of Glencoe, 1964), pp. 254–64.

25. Erikson conceded, though he did not stress or take fully into account, that the same custom of child rearing may have different effects on different children, depending on the child, the parent, and the circumstances. This point is discussed later.

26. Meyer Fortes, writing around the same time (1938) about the bringing up of Tallensi children in Africa, put a similar emphasis on the child's native mastery of his culture. "Social and Psychological Aspects of Education in Taleland," reprinted in idem, *Time and Social Structure and Other Essays* (London: Athlone Press, 1970), pp. 201–59.

27. Gregory Bateson, *Naven* (Cambridge: At the University Press, 1936).

28. Erikson, *Childhood and Society,* p. 185.

29. Erikson, "Observations on the Yurok," p. 295, Erikson's italics; repeated with some slight variations in idem, *Childhood and Society,* p. 183.

30. Erikson, "Observations on the Yurok," p. 295; idem, "Childhood and Tradition," p. 340.

31. See, for example, Freud, "On Narcissism," p. 75.

32. Erikson, *Childhood and Society,* p. 183.

33. For those who do not have access to a strikingly different culture to test this kind of observation, ethnographic films—a medium gaining considerable place in anthropology (cf. Paul Hockings, ed., *Principles of Visual Anthropology,* The Hague: Mouton, 1975)—provide an opportunity for vicarious cross-cultural experience in cultures quite different from our own. In *The Feast,* for example, a film by Timothy Ash and Napoleon Chagnon portraying a festive visit by one village of a South American Indian tribe to another, one scene depicts a trading session during the visit, showing one individual almost jumping up and down, complaining in a whiny, sulky voice, "Doesn't anybody see I need a hammock?" and another, "I'm tired of nobody paying any attention to me!" The emotional tone of these outbursts strikes most viewers of our culture as decidedly childish; yet in the society portrayed (Yanomamö), and in that situation, I suspect that the behavior was perfectly appropriate. Close observation suggests that the men were performing for a calculated effect rather than being "carried away" by a childish tantrum. In our society, we do not see such behavior except in a child (or in a very "childish" person), so that, though the man's fellow Yanomamö seemed to regard it as perfectly normal, it strikes us as "childish."

34. Erikson, "Observations on the Yurok," p. 295; idem, *Childhood and Society*, p. 183.

35. Erikson, "Observations on the Yurok," p. 296; idem, *Childhood and Society*, p. 183.

36. Jean Briggs, *Never in Anger.*

37. Claude Lévi-Strauss, *The Elementary Structures of Kinship*, trans. James Bell, John von Sturmer, and Rodney Needham (Boston: Beacon Press, 1969), pp. 93–95.

38. Richard Evans, *Dialogue with Erik Erikson* (New York: E. P. Dutton & Co., 1969), p. 62.

39. Robert LeVine offers a comprehensive discussion of methodological problems in the psychoanalytic understanding of social phenomena in his recent book, *Culture, Behavior, and Personality*. See esp. pp. 203–48 for discussion of problems of field methodology. See also Herbert Phillips, "The Use and Misuse of Psychoanalysis in Anthropology" (paper delivered at the Seventy-third Annual Meeting of the American Anthropological Association, Mexico City, November 22, 1974).

40. Erikson, "Observations on the Yurok," p. 295.

41. Erikson, *Childhood and Society*, p. 178.

42. Ibid., pp. 182–83.

43. Thus an Italian might at first strike an Anglo-Saxon as "expressive," though he may in fact, for all his expansive gestures, be "as reserved as an Englishman." Edward Sapir remarks:

> It is the failure to understand the relativity of gesture and posture, the degree to which these classes of behavior are referable to social patterns while transcending merely individual psychological significances, which makes it so easy for us to find individual indices of personality where it is only the alien culture that speaks.

Sapir, "The Unconscious Patterning of Behavior in Society," *Selected Writings*, p. 557.

44. Erikson, *Childhood and Society*, pp. 171–75.

45. Erikson, "Observations on the Yurok." I was fascinated to discover this original report of Erikson's visit, the impressions of a psychoanalyst soon after his first encounter with the Yurok, which I read for the first time in preparing this article. Erikson's presentation in this report of his cultural analysis of myths, rituals, and cosmological beliefs of the Yurok renders far clearer and more convincing some of the cryptic statements he makes in the much-abbreviated analysis in *Childhood and Society*. The metaphor in which he summarizes the Yurok world view—"peripheral wombs" whence come fish and game, "joined by the human womb" ("Observations on the Yurok," p. 275)—shows an intriguing resemblance to the imagery of the universe that Gerardo Reichel-Dolmatoff worked out with his gifted Desana informant, Antonio Guzmán, in Colombia, South America: *Amazonian Cosmos* (Chicago: University of Chicago Press, 1971).

For all its rough edges (and a few unguarded bows to psychoanalytic mythology, such as the "primal horde" story), it is unfortunate that this fresh document, so much more immediate than Erikson's later, more polished discussions of the Yurok, should have been left lying in the comparative obscurity of the technical monograph series where it first appeared. Of particular value is the vivid and forceful portrait of Fanny.

46. Erikson, "Nature of Clinical Evidence," pp. 47–80. The remarks about Fanny are on p. 55.

47. Erikson, "Observations on the Yurok," p. 266.

48. Herbert Phillips made similar points in his paper, "The Use and Misuse of Psychoanalysis in Anthropology." See also idem, *Thai Peasant Personality* (Berkeley: University of California Press, 1965). An overview of the rising emphasis on diversity of personalities within a culture is to be found in Pertti J. Pelto's review article, "Psychological Anthropology," in *Biennial Review of Anthropology: 1967*, ed. Bernard J. Siegel and Alan R. Beals (Stanford, Calif.: Stanford University Press, 1967), pp. 140–208. For an earlier statement of this point of view, see George Devereux, "Two Types of Modal Personality Models," in *Studying Personailty Cross-Culturally*, pp. 227–42. William Caudill presents a somewhat different perspective on the question of individual variation within a culture in his "Psychiatry and Anthropology: The Individual and His Nexus," in *Cultural Illness and Health*, ed. Laura Nader and Thomas Maretzki (Washington, D.C.: American Anthropological Association, 1973), pp. 67–77.

49. Ralph Linton, *The Cultural Background of Personality* (New York: Appleton-Century Crofts, 1945), pp. 127–28.

50. Sapir, "Why Cultural Anthropology Needs the Psychiatrist," *Selected Writings*, pp. 569–77.

51. Margaret Mead, *Coming of Age in Samoa* (New York: Morrow, 1928).

52. Emil Oberholzer, "Rorschach's Experiment and the Alorese," in Cora DuBois, *The People of Alor* (New York: Harper and Row, 1961), p. 630.

53. Ruth Benedict, *Patterns of Culture* (Boston: Houghton Mifflin, 1934), chap. 8, "The Individual and the Pattern of Culture."

54. Erikson, *Childhood and Society*, p. 150.

55. Ibid.

56. Ibid., p. 149.

57. Ibid., p. 185.

58. Ibid., p. 153.

59. Anthony Wallace, *Culture and Personality* (New York: Random House, 1970).

60. Erikson, *Childhood and Society*, p. 186.

61. See, for example, Victor Turner, *Schism and Continuity in an African Society* (Manchester: Manchester University Press, 1957), and Ralph Nicholas, "Rules, Resources, and Political Activity," in *Local Level Politics*, ed. Marc Swartz (Chicago: Aldine, 1968), pp. 295–321. For a more theoretical elaboration, see Edmund Leach, *Political Systems of Highland Burma* (Boston: Beacon Press, 1964).

62. Suzanne and Lloyd Rudolph, "Comments on 'The Study of Life His-

tory: Gandhi,' by David Mandelbaum," *Current Anthropology* 14 (1973): 201–3.

63. Robert Murphy, *The Dialectics of Social Life* (New York: Basic Books, 1971), p. 158.

64. Dorothy Eggan, "The Significance of Dreams for Anthropological Research," *American Anthropologist* 51 (1949): 177–98, and idem, "The Personal Use of Myth in Dreams," *Journal of American Folklore* 68 (1955): 67–75.

65. Leach, *Political Systems of Highland Burma.*

66. See, for example, Freud's succinct statement of the goals of a psychoanalysis in a highly important footnote to *The Ego and the Id, Standard Edition*, vol. 14 (London: Hogarth, 1957), p. 50.

67. Bronislaw Malinowski, *Sex and Repression in Savage Society* (1927; reprint ed., New York: Meridian, 1959). This work contains both his attack on the psychoanalytic position and his counterattack to Ernest Jones's reply, "Mother Right and the Sexual Ignorance of Savages," *International Journal of Psychoanalysis* 6 (1925): 109–30. The entire controversy is a study in misunderstanding. Malinowski could not understand that psychoanalytic propositions refer to inner subjectivity rather than directly to observable interpersonal behavior as such. As many anthropologists still do, for example, he took "repression" to be synonymous with moral condemnation or prohibition of a behavior—that is, in the interpersonal sense, as in "political repression"—whereas in psychoanalysis it refers to the subjective act of (involuntarily) banishing an idea from one's *own* thoughts. Jones, on the other hand, could not understand that anthropologists objected to attributing the existence of an institution to its presumed psychological defensive function. The gap between the two points of view is scarcely narrowed. Cf. LeVine, *Culture, Behavior, and Personality*, pp. 48–50.

68. William Ernest Hocking, *The Meaning of Immortality in Human Experience* (New York: Harper & Row, 1957), p. 146.

69. Melford Spiro, "Culture and Personality: The Natural History of a False Dichotomy," *Psychiatry* 14 (1951): 19–46.

70. Edward Sapir, "Cultural Anthropology and Psychiatry," pp. 518–19.

71. Erikson, *Gandhi's Truth*, p. 141.

72. Personal communication.

73. Robert Coles, *Erik H. Erikson: The Growth of His Work* (Boston: Little Brown, 1970), pp. 82, 166.

74. Erikson, *Gandhi's Truth*, p. 157.

75. Ibid., p. 76.

76. Erikson, "Ego Development and Historical Change," *Psychoanalytic Study of the Child* 2 (1946): 359–96.

77. Coles, *Erik H. Erikson*, p. 166.

78. Peter L. Berger and Thomas Luckman, *The Social Construction of Reality* (Garden City, N.Y.: Doubleday, 1966), p. 132. In this sense, the concept has been particularly developed by social psychologists of the "social interactionist" orientation.

79. For a review of the meaning of the term in psychiatry and psychoanalysis—including a critique of Erikson's usage—see Edith Jacobson, *The Self and the Object World* (New York: International Universities Press, 1964), chap. 2.

80. Heinz Kohut, *The Analysis of the Self* (New York: International Universities Press, 1971).

81. Robert Redfield, *The Primitive World and Its Transformations,* (Ithaca, N.Y.: Cornell University Press, 1953). Cf. William Caudill, "Anthropology and Psychoanalysis: Some Theoretical Issues," in *Anthropology and Human Behavior*, Anthropological Society of Washington (Washington, D.C., 1962), pp. 177–78.

82. H. M. Rümke, Preface to *The Concept of Identity,* by David de Levita (Paris and The Hague: Mouton, 1965).

83. This can be seen in the number of scholars who combine the two disciplines, as well as in the degree of interest psychoanalysts have shown in anthropology and vice versa. W. H. R. Rivers, one of the pioneers of British anthropology, was a dynamically oriented psychiatrist, and Meyer Fortes was first trained in clinical psychology—to say nothing of the many anthropologists who had psychoanalytic training after becoming anthropologists, including Alfred Kroeber and Weston LaBarre, as well as, more recently, Robert LeVine and Melford Spiro. The Institute for Psychoanalysis in Chicago has been especially active in giving research training to anthropologists and other social scientists, particularly through the efforts and interest of its director, George Pollock.

84. Cf. Victor Turner, *The Forest of Symbols* (Ithaca, N.Y.: Cornell University Press, 1964), esp. chap. 1, "Symbols in Ndembu Ritual"; and Clifford Geertz, "Deep Play: Notes on the Balinese Cockfight," *Daedalus* (Winter 1972): 1038, reprinted in idem, *The Interpretation of Cultures,* for some insightful studies in the interplay between personal emotion and cultural ideology.

85. Cf. Neil Smelser, "Social and Psychological Dimensions of Collective Behavior," in idem, *Essays in Sociological Explanation* (Englewood Cliffs, N.J.: Prentice-Hall, 1968), pp. 92–121; Fritz Redl, "Group Emotions and Leadership," *Psychiatry* 5 (1942): 573–96; and more recently, Heinz Kohut, "Creativeness, Charisma, and Group Psychology," in *Freud: The Fusion of Science and Humanism*, ed. John Gedo and George Pollock (New York: International Universities Press, 1976), pp. 379–425, for other psychoanalytic perspectives on the leader's relationship with his followers.

86. William Caudill, "Anthropology and Psychoanalysis: Some Theoretical Issues," pp. 176–78. See also idem, "The Influence of Social Structure and Culture on Human Behavior in Modern Japan, *Ethos* 1: 343–82.

87. Erikson, "Observations on Sioux Education," "Childhood and Tradition," and *Childhood and Society*, chap. 3.

88. Erikson, *Gandhi's Truth*, p. 76.

89. The observation that cultural differences can magnify problems of communication and empathy is by no means a new one in psychoanalysis.

Commenting on a Russian patient—the now famous Wolf Man—Freud observed that "a national character that was foreign to ours made the task of feeling one's way into his mind a laborious one"—but not an impossible one! "From the History of an Infantile Neurosis," *Standard Edition,* vol. 17 (London: Hogarth Press, 1955), p. 104.

90. Erikson, *Childhood and Society,* pp. 120–24.

91. Mary Catherine Bateson, "Insight in a Bicultural Context," *Philippine Studies* 16 (1968): 605–21, quoted at length in LeVine, *Culture, Behavior, and Personality,* pp. 16–18. "This is a case," Bateson says in a passage not included in LeVine's excerpt, "where a lack of knowledge would clearly have been painful and led to further misunderstanding, whereas, given sufficient insight, I was even grateful that my loss had occurred here, since I found the Filipino tolerance for the rhythms of life deeply healing" (p. 613). "A sense of discomfort" at the response of people of an alien culture, she concludes, "can be transcended . . . by anthropologists or by any layman who is prepared to look critically at his own responses" (pp. 612–13).

92. Napoleon Chagnon, *Yanomamö: The Fierce People* (New York: Holt, Rinehart and Winston, 1968), pp. 14–17, and idem, *Studying the Yanomamö* (New York: Holt, Rinehart and Winston, 1974), pp. 1–45, 162–197.

93. Chagnon, *Studying the Yanomamö,* pp. 194–97.

94. Geertz, "Concept of Culture."

95. One could suppose that different cultures differ in penetrability to members of our culture, but one sometimes finds different individuals making opposite assertions in this regard, even about the same culture.

96. Susan Sontag, "The Anthropologist as Hero," in *Against Interpretation* (New York: Dell, 1966), pp. 69–81.

5

Psychohistory and Historical Genres: The Plight and Promise of Eriksonian Biography

DONALD CAPPS

There is general agreement among psychohistorians that psychohistory came into being in 1958. Psychohistorians with historical training credit William Langer's presidential address to the American Historical Association in December 1957 with giving birth to the psychohistorical movement.[1] Psychohistorians with training in the psychological sciences have been more inclined to give the credit to Erik Erikson, whose *Young Man Luther* appeared in 1958.[2] Regardless of disagreement on this matter of attribution, however, there is no disputing the fact that the birth of psychohistory can be rather precisely dated, a fact that is of no great significance in itself, but that is well worth keeping in mind as one attempts to assess the contribution of psychohistory to date. Psychohistory has been in existence for close to two decades, a period of sufficient duration to warrant a critical assessment of its past accomplishments and future prospects.

The sheer fact that psychohistory has survived this long ought not be taken lightly. More typically, emergent intellectual movements of this type are aborted before they come to birth, while those that see the light of day usually lack the necessary systems of nurturance to enable them to cope with a demanding, if not hostile environment. It is to psychohistory's credit, therefore, that it has survived when various intellectual movements of comparable potential have not, and that there are clear signs of its continued survival into still another decade.

The subsequent growth of psychohistory has also been quite remarkable. Psychohistorical studies have regularly appeared in the *Journal of Interdisciplinary History*, and, more recently, a journal of psychohistory has been launched under the title *History of Childhood Quarterly*. A working group of psychohistorians within the American Historical Association has been in existence since 1971, and this group publishes a newsletter and regularly sponsors sessions on psychohistory at the annual meeting of the association. Also, under the general editorship of Professor Bruce Mazlish, Basic Books has committed itself to the publication of book-length psychohistorical studies.[3] These and various other developments are illustrative of sustained interest in psychohistory among professional historians.

But perhaps more significant than these developments within academic history are evidences of ecumenical spirit between historians and the psychiatric community. Psychoanalytic institutes regularly sponsor seminars on psychohistory attended by analysts and historians. The Center for Psychosocial Research in Chicago brings historians and psychoanalysts together in a variety of creative ways, including workshops, evening seminars and lectures, a fellowship program, and the publication of a professional directory. There is also increased receptivity on the part of psychoanalytic institutes to the inclusion of historians in various training programs, and, most importantly, these arrangements are mutually beneficial. Historians at the Menninger Foundation take courses in psychiatry, but they also contribute their historical expertise in critiquing case-history methods. Such ecumenical efforts as these have involved scores of people in a wide variety of institutional settings.

These developments point to the continuing strength and vitality of the psychohistorical movement. Both formal and informal structures have been established—journals, books, symposia, and reasonably permanent working groups and organizations. Admittedly, many psychohistorians wish that their enterprises were regarded with more respect in the American Historical Association and that they were taken more seriously by influential historians. However, even in this area, such hopes are standard fare for any young intellectual movement, and even these adversities have their value in challenging the membership to greater initiatives and achievements.

The recent publication of Jacques Barzun's *Clio and the Doctors* poses just such a challenge.[4] While a highly critical assessment of psychohistory, this book does not wholly displease psychohistorians. Their reviews of the book reflect a certain satisfaction that the movement has succeeded in its efforts to draw influential historians into debate over the validity of psychohistory. It seems doubtful that Barzun would have given psychohistorians this satisfaction, however, had he not been genuinely concerned that many younger historians would be unable to resist psychohistory's current appeal. As he points out in his preface to the book:

> My chief aim in making a small book out of a statement has been to lay the issues before the younger generation of students now "taking" history. Their tendency, altogether understandable, is to embrace the new. As in the fine arts, the cult of the new in intellectual matters is now the compulsory, the *conventional* thing, and perhaps it needs to be a little blackened by a devil's advocate, for the same reason that in an earlier generation it was intellectual conservatism which needed to be rebuked and reversed.[5]

Taking at face value Barzun's admission that his attack

against psychohistory is in the nature of devil's advocacy, *Clio and the Doctors* is more an invitation to psychohistory to prove its mettle than an attempt to rout it from the field altogether.[6] In consequence, most psychohistorians believe that they have little to fear from *Clio and the Doctors.* Their reactions to the book in formal reviews and informal conversations indicate that they are not overawed either by the strength or tenacity of Barzun's critique. Thus, the overall effect of such criticisms has been to challenge psychohistorians to greater efforts, certainly not to discourage them altogether. It might even be said that Barzun's critique has given psychohistorians a new sense of group solidarity, for whatever their internal differences, they can agree on their opposition to Barzun.

However—here we begin to address the primary issues with which this essay is concerned—even the most eager proponent of psychohistory must acknowledge that Barzun and his fellow critics cannot be dismissed as benighted old fools. For, whether one wants to admit it or not, the foregoing recital of psychohistory's past successes and future challenges is not the whole story. In addition to past successes and future challenges, the movement has some immediate problems of which some—perhaps most psychohistorians—are more than casually aware. Indeed, it is fair to say that the most formidable critics of psychohistory are not those who parry and thrust from without, but those who are raising rather trenchant questions from vantage points within the movement. Some of these critics from within have actually expressed graver doubts about psychohistory than have the external critics, and this for the simple reason that insiders are often prompted to raise more searching questions about an enterprise to which they have committed much of their own intellectual energy. Outside critics have not proceeded much beyond the sort of criticisms that they were voicing nearly two decades ago, while critics within the movement have begun to identify problems of a more fundamental nature.

The discussion that follows is one insider's critical assessment of the fundamental problems now confronting psychohistory. However, for the very reason that outside critics do not go far enough in their critiques, the discussion begins with these critiques. Furthermore, since this is an essay on Erik Erikson's contribution to psychohistory, we begin with historian David Donald's critique of Erikson's psychohistorical work, a critique delivered as a lecture before the American Psychiatric Association in Dallas, Texas, in 1972.[7]

PSYCHOHISTORY AND HISTORICAL GENRES

Professor Donald points out that Erikson's psychohistorical work suffers from its careless handling of historical evidence, from an excessive indulgence in clinical rhetoric, and from interesting but inappropriate autobiographical intrusions into the historical narrative. In this view, Erikson lacks the primary virtues of the professional historian: objectivity and thoroughness in the collection and sifting of data, caution in the use of an explanatory apparatus, and avoidance of self-indulgence in the writing of the narrative itself. These are not unimportant criticisms of psychohistory, and, in my judgment, the psychohistorian is obliged to take them very seriously. Certainly, a comparison of psychohistorical studies published today as opposed to those published ten or fifteen years ago would show that these kinds of criticisms have made their mark. Psychohistorians writing today make concerted efforts to avoid the procedures that Donald severely criticizes.

On the other hand, these are the same kinds of criticisms that greeted the initial publication of *Young Man Luther*[8] and that, incidentally, followed on the heels of the publication of a psychobiography of Abraham Lincoln in 1921.[9] While the fact that they are not novel does not necessarily mean that they are not true or worth repeating, at least some critics within the movement are persuaded that these historiographical issues fail to address the more serious methodological problems of psychohistory. This means, curious as it may seem, that these psychohistorians are not convinced that critics like Donald, Barzun, and others have uncovered the real vulnerabilities of psychohistory. In their judgment, the psychohistorian can considerably blunt the force, if not entirely refute these arguments against psychohistory. At the same time, however, they believe that such counter argumentation is rather pointless because it does little to confront the more fundamental issues that these criticisms in terms of historical evidence, narrative, and explanatory apparatus address, but fail to penetrate.

In my judgment, the way to begin to address these problems is to view psychohistory in terms of *genre considerations*. This is to say that the real issues confronting psychohistory are not empirical but formal. To be sure, criticisms based on these empirical matters of evidence, explanation, and narrative are not irrelevant to the problem of genre, for the persistence of such criticisms prompts the psychohistorian to address the question of genre. He reasons: If conventional history and psychohistory are as irreconcilable as these outside critics say they are, then perhaps we are confronting formal as well as empirical differences in the two. Thus, the introduction of considerations of genre moves the discussion closer to the really vexing problems that now confront psychohistory, especially in its efforts to gain the acceptance of conventional historians.

However, the assertion that psychohistory is a different genre from conventional narrative history does not settle the issue; it merely joins it. The mere pronouncement that psychohistory is not conventional narrative history is not enough. One must proceed beyond this assertion to set forth arguments for the view that psychohistory is not traditional narrative history but a different genre subject to different criteria. In essaying this particular task, we may appropriately begin with the assumption that, if psychohistory does not belong in the genre of conventional narrative history, it nonetheless has strong affinities with other historical genres. The view that psychohistory fits within an existing historical genre other than conventional narrative history has articulate proponents both inside and outside the movement. However, there is no real consensus among these proponents as to which genre this is; the most persuasive cases are being made for the *special study, family history,* and *biography.* Since any attempt to identify psychohistory generically cannot ignore these arguments, I should like to summarize these arguments in each case and assess their relative merits.

Psychohistory as special study. Barzun argues that psychohistory properly belongs to the genre of special studies—that is, studies that are not conventional narrative history but that use historical materials for other purposes, one of which may be that of contributing to a narrative history.[10] Barzun points out that Stanley Elkins's *Slavery: A Problem in American Institutional Life* is not a history of slavery. As its subtitle clearly states, it is a *study* of a problem in American institutional life. On the other hand, it uses historical materials and has proven to be extremely valuable to historians writing historical accounts of slavery. Such special studies often employ theories and methods derived from the social sciences, and, in Barzun's view, there is therefore no reason in principle for excluding psychohistorical studies from this genre of the special study.

The major distinguishing feature of the special study is that it is shaped by *methodological* as opposed to *narrative* concerns. Thus, David Donald's argument that in Erikson's psychohistories the explanatory apparatus is too much in view is supportive, if unintentionally so, of the view that psychohistory belongs to a genre in which methodological concerns have central importance. In this view, a psychohistory may fail as historical narrative but succeed as a special study because methodological issues take precedence over the requirement of a coherent story line. Thus, the suggestion that psychohistory belongs to the genre of special studies has much to recommend it, not least of which is the fact that it renders inappropriate many criticisms of psychohistory dealing with rhetorical and narrative matters.

But what, precisely, is a special study? And what claims

does psychohistory relinquish in accepting assignment to the genre of special studies? As to what the special study is, Barzun points out that "special studies take up questions that are of small scope, or obscure, or moot, or time-consuming, or requiring uncommon knowledge to pursue." Topics addressed under the heading of special studies and particularly related to the psychological sciences might include the cause and circumstances of death in the "Black Hole of Calcutta," the psychological aspects of shipwreck, the French Revolution's concern with public health, or social histories of epidemics. The special study may involve primary research, but it may also be a distillation from well-known sources never before interrogated on the subject in question. Hence, a psychohistorical study informed by a psychological theory may organize known biographical facts in a new way. Or it might take two or more pieces of evidence that earlier biographers considered contradictory and show how this evidence, when combined, identifies a previously overlooked psychological conflict in the biographical subject.[11] In these examples, psychohistory functions like any other special study in taking up questions that require uncommon knowledge (usually a psychological concept or theory) to pursue. But, more important than the employment of uncommon knowledge, as such, is the fact that psychohistory emphasizes methodological rather than narrative concerns. While the biographer offers a narrative account of the life in question, the psychohistorian takes a methodological approach, applying a psychological theory to historical data. This methodological approach is not a substitute for narrative biography, though the biographer may want to take note of the major findings of the study in his narrative account. Thus, a working relationship between the psychohistorian and the historian can be achieved, with the former pursuing special issues relating to the life of his subject and the latter incorporating into his narrative those features of the psychohistorical study that contribute to the story line.

On the other hand, Barzun himself sees little potential in

this working relationship until psychohistorians accept the fact that psychohistory properly belongs to the genre of special studies and, in accepting this limitation, subject psychohistory to the specific criteria of the special study. He identifies four specific criteria that psychohistory as a special study must meet: (1) the special student's canons of evidence must equal the historian's in rigor; (2) the conclusion or diagnosis must be in the common tongue or translatable into it; (3) any comparative treatment of periods, events, or ideas must be warranted by a preponderance of concrete similarities and must not merely play with abstractions or imagery; and (4) any system or method employed in obtaining the results must not be so embedded in them as to compel belief in both or none,—for example, a special study may use Freudian theory if in the study the elements of description and explanation are readily separable.[12]

Barzun is not persuaded that psychohistorical studies have met these criteria particularly well, but in assigning psychohistory to the genre of the special study, he has taken it seriously enough to demand that it meet criteria appropriate to the special study. Furthermore, this assignment of psychohistory to the special study means accepting the fact that psychohistory is a method and that, as such, it requires continual self-criticism along methodological lines. This latter point is especially important because psychohistorians have frequently been criticised for their preoccupation with methodological concerns, especially when their employment of a heavy explanatory apparatus is contrasted with the graceful descriptive narrative of historical biography. Thus, while many historians, Barzun among them, make clear distinction between history and biography, there is no gainsaying the fact that biography is primarily based on the narrative model, while psychohistory, as a special study, is shaped by methodological concerns. This difference is perhaps best evidenced in Barzun's fourth criterion,—the criterion that *description* of events is separable from the *explanatory* apparatus. In conventional biographical narrative, such separation is neither attempted nor considered desirable.

To illustrate the merits of this view of psychohistory as special study, I should like to consider a psychohistorical work that is especially exemplary of the special study—namely, Peter Loewenberg's "Psychohistorical Origins of the Nazi Youth Cohort."[13] While a thoroughgoing discussion of this study would carry us beyond the scope of the present inquiry, it can be noted that Loewenberg's discussion of Nazi youth is shaped by methodological concerns, with particular attention to developing an explanatory apparatus. The central element in this explanatory apparatus is the notion of the *cohort*, a concept developed by sociological demographers from Karl Mannheim's theoretical work on the sociology of generations. The cohort is an

> aggregate of individuals within a population who have shared a significant common experience of a personal or historical event at the same time. . . . Each cohort is itself unique; its members are different from all those who have preceded it and all who will follow because they have experienced certain traumatic episodes in their collective life at a common time and a specific historical moment.[14]

Lowenberg's cohort group is a birth cohort—that is, German children born during World War I.

Using psychoanalytic theories of childhood deprivation, Loewenberg shows how the war had a traumatic effect on this group and set the stage for the emergence of the Nazi youth movement in the thirties. His study is therefore not a narrative history of the politicization of German youth through the National Socialist Party, but is rather the demonstration of the expanatory uses of the cohort concept conjoined with psychoanalytic theory. That his study is not narrative in the conventional sense is especially well illustrated in Loewenberg's adoption of a "retrogressive" method of explication:

> Rather than proceeding with the story of the Nazi youth cohort chronologically and beginning with its origins, this essay will use what Marc Bloch termed the "prudently retrogressive" method of looking at the outcome first, and then tracking down the beginnings or "causes" of the phenomenon. This, of course, corresponds to the clinical method of examining the "presenting complaints" first and then investigating etiology.[15]

However, even more important than this divergence from the traditional narrative structure is the fact that this study gives great prominence to the explanatory apparatus. The concept of the cohort is explained in great detail, as are the various psychoanalytic theories of childhood deprivation that the study employs. Yet, these concepts and theories are clearly differentiated from the historical data itself. The reader has no difficulty in distinguishing the explanatory apparatus from the historical evidence. Thus, the Loewenberg study easily meets this most critical criterion of the special study. Furthermore, its canons of evidence equal the historian's in rigor, the conclusion is quite devoid of psychological jargonese, and the criterion concerning comparative treatment of periods, events, or ideas does not apply. In short, this pseychohistorical study fits well in the genre of the special study and meets its major criteria with no difficulty.[16]

Psychohistory as family history. A second historical genre with which psychohistory appears to have particular affinities is family history. This genre is itself relatively new. As the editors of *The Family in History*, a collection of essays originally published in the *Journal of Interdisciplinary History*, point out:

> In recent years a variety of subjects largely ignored by earlier generations has captured the attention of historians. One of the most fruitful has been the life of ordinary men and women, whose habits and beliefs were virtually unknown until, during the last two decades, scholars brought to light information about social groups who

> previously had been considered too obscure (or unimportant) to merit exploration. Topics as diverse as popular culture, fertility, and disease have attracted notice and have stimulated the development of such pioneering research techniques as historical demography. . . . The history of the family, a relative newcomer even to so young a body of literature, epitomizes the particular qualities of these seemingly mundane subjects. Nowhere can one perceive more clearly that as our knowledge of prosaic, everyday activities increases, we gain a far richer and more thorough understanding of human behavior in bygone ages. An interest that has long been the preserve of genealogists has thus been transformed, in a few short years, into one of the most lively and influential areas in the study of history.[17]

The editors conclude that family history is a "new genre" that requires "different kinds of evidence and different ways of handling sources."

In the past five years the view of psychohistory as a type of family history has witnessed remarkable growth. The two major historical journals committed to the publication of essays in psychohistory, the *Journal of Interdisciplinary History* and the *History of Childhood Quarterly*, have made major commitments to the psychohistorical study of family life.[18] The rationale for this view of psychohistory as belonging within the genre of family history is not difficult to see, nor is psychohistorians' own enthusiasm for this type of history. Bruce Mazlish put it best in his 1970 essay, "What is Psycho-history?" when he acknowledged that Erikson's life histories are characteristically weak in their exploration of collective acts or mass settings. Mazlish proposes addressing this problem by according the family central importance in psychohistory:

> The family, potentially, is where psychological and sociological theories can best intersect. It can serve as a midpoint between life-history and group-history. In doing a life-history, we can analyse relations in an individual family, e.g. Hitler's family. In working towards group

> history, we can analyse "the German family" as an ideal type or model family. Obviously, the individual family, e.g. Hitler's, its typicality and uniqueness, can only be understood in terms of our understanding of the model family, e.g. the German; and vice-versa.[19]

Mazlish suggests that the peculiar contribution of psychohistory to family history is its use of psychoanalytic theories that "call our attention to certain recurrent and universal features of *all* familial situations." He is quick to add, however, that psychohistory balances this attention to universal features of family life with sociological investigations that address the influence of social and economic class on family practices. He concludes: "In the psycho-historic understanding of the family, sociology is as important as psychology."

Easily the most significant work on psychohistory as family history in America today is John Demos's continuing study of Puritan family life. His studies are of particular importance to readers of this essay because he finds special merit in Erik Erikson's developmental theories. Demos is careful to say that his preference for Erikson is simply that, a preference, but he also makes a persuasive case for the value of Erikson's stage theory in exploring conflict behavior among New England Puritans. Specifically, Demos shows how child-rearing patterns among Puritans had the effect of creating severe conflicts of *autonomy versus shame and self-doubt*. The key element in Puritan child-rearing practice is the fact that for a period of perhaps twelve months the infant was treated indulgently and then, in the second year of life, was subjected to weaning, the arrival of a younger sibling and, most important of all, to a radical shift toward a harsh and restrictive style of discipline that had one primary objective—namely, to curb and even break the child's inherent "willfulness" as soon as it first began to appear. Shaming was characteristically employed as a disciplinary method in this regard, and Demos stresses the role of humiliation in Puritan child-rearing procedures, noting that, "in Erikson's terms, the determination to crush the child's will is nothing less than an effort to deprive him of a chance to develop a lasting and confident sense of autonomy."[20]

Demos is aware that the primary value of this analysis of child-rearing practices is its ability to explain otherwise inexplicable behavior and values in the culture at large. The analysis of child-rearing practices as a study in antinomies (a period of warmth and solicitude followed by humiliating disciplinary procedures) would lead us to anticipate that the society at large manifested a similar dynamic conflict. Indeed, the evidence does not disappoint:

> On the one hand, the Puritans placed a tremendous emphasis on the value of harmony, unity, and concord; one could cite as evidence literally countless sermons, essays, official decrees, and pronouncements. At the level of aspirations, nothing was more important for these people. On the other hand, if one examines in detail the actual record of life in these communities—through various court and personal records—one discovers an extraordinary atmosphere of contentiousness and outright conflict. "Harmony" was always the preeminent value; yet, in trying to attain it, the Puritans always disappointed themselves.[21]

In short, the warmth of the earliest stage of life shapes the society's ideal vision of itself. What makes the application of Erikson's theory persuasive, however, is not simply that the social ideal recaptures the earliest stage of life, but that the *autonomy versus shame and self-doubt* conflict is inherent in the forces that frustrate this societal vision. Evidence that Demos marshals in this regard ranges from disputes over property boundaries to Puritan beliefs about God, the effect of this survey of "some of the larger areas of Puritan life" being a strong argument for the ubiquity of the *autonomy versus shame and self-doubt* conflict in New England Puritan society.

On the other hand, the very ubiquity of the conflict raises a methodological issue. Given the very centrality of this conflict in all areas of Puritan life, Demos asks whether we might not be according child-rearing practices too much explanatory weight by suggesting that "what happened during the second year was critical in the development of these people. . . . Are there not other preferable explanations for the same range of phenomena?" One such explanation would focus on the fact that Puritan New England was a preindustrial society and would consider such conflicts as Puritan boundary disputes as relatively natural in an overwhelmingly agricultural society. This sociological explanation is dubious, however, because the empty lands in the New World ought to have lessened any competitive pressures of this type. We are thus obliged to view these disputes as somehow irrational, as having a psychological function, and this leads us back to child-rearing practices. In Puritan child-rearing practice, few restrictions—such as swaddling clothes—were placed on the infant, and it was a common procedure to allow the infant to sleep in its parents' bed. As noted, however, this indulgence, which might be characterized in terms of almost unlimited boundaries, was brought to an abrupt halt in the second year as the child came under severe restriction. Thus, child-rearing practices provide a more plausible explanation for the peculiar nature of Puritan concerns over boundaries than do concepts of social structure. Of course, this is not to say that there is a single linear connection between child-rearing practices and these larger social conflicts. What Demos and those who view psychohistory as family history are saying is that the family is the primary socializing agent in virtually every society, and because it is, family practices frequently hold the explanatory key to larger social conflicts.

This view of the family as the explanatory key to larger social conflicts might appear to be prompted solely by a disinterested concern to set the historical record straight. However, while less overtly expressed in Demos's studies than in the *History of Childhood Quarterly*, especially in its editorial pronouncements, psychohistorians' understanding of the family extends beyond historiographical to moral concerns. This is to say that psychohistory as family history exposes the deleterious family practices of various societies in various historical periods and in so doing reveals how the family as a social organization has frustrated (as well as inspired) the ideals of the larger society. Thus, an implicit, if not explicit, assumption of much psychohistory, including studies that focus on the individual as opposed to the model family, is that the family and the larger social and political institutions often work at cross purposes. The family is essentially that institution that is responsible for introducing an irrational element into otherwise potentially rational societal processes. Thus, fortunate is the society that is governed by individuals capable of leaving aside these family influences in the execution of their public duty. To be sure, there are psychohistorians who do not view the family as the channel through which irrationality is introduced into the body politic. Even these, however, take particular note of the fact that leaders who view their political roles in terms of family relations invariably oversimplify complex political and social processes. Hence, in a review of Erikson's *Ghandhi's Truth*, Clifford Geertz points out that,

> in attempting again and again to re-enact this family drama on the national stage, [Gandhi's] career revealed both the intrinsic power of attraction that a view of politics as a process of inward change possesses—its ability to move men—and its radical inability, having moved them, to deal with the issues—whether workers' wages or the threat of Partition—thereby raised. The contrast which appeared already at Ahmedabad between Gandhi's extraordinary ability to shape the personal lives of those immediately around him and his inability to control the direction of the strike as a collective act grew greater and greater as he extended himself across India and into larger and larger mass settings.[22]

My purpose here is neither to support nor to dispute this critical view of the family as a socializing agent. However, it is important to point to the fact that where psychohistory is viewed as a type of family history, value considerations take on added importance. Put another way, if the psychohistorian is beginning to give appropriate attention to the role of the family as a socializing institution, he is also according family practices much responsibility for the social conflict and frustrated social visions of any given society.[23]

Psychohistory as historical biography. A third view of psychohistory as belonging to a historical genre is the position that psychohistory is a type of historical biography.[24] At first glance, this view is at least as persuasive as the views of psychohistory as special study and family history. Proponents of this view point out that in both historical biography and in psychohistory the "life history" is central. They acknowledge that psychohistory differs from traditional historical biographies in its use of modern dynamic psychologies, especially psychoanalysis, but they point out that the basic intention of psychohistory is the same as that of all biography—that is, to provide an account of the subject's life. Thus, taking this similarity in intent as a given, most critical discussion of psychohistory as biography has focused on the problem of the use and misuse of psychological concepts in biography. Quite unexpectedly, however, these discussions are beginning to have the effect of challenging the assumption that the primary intent of psychohistory as biography is to provide accounts of lives. This challenge in turn raises serious questions as to whether psychohistory can appropriately be viewed as a type of historical biography.

Questions about the use of psychological concepts in biography were not raised with any real seriousness until the publication of Erikson's *Young Man Luther.* Then, however, the questioning began. Some historians rejected the very idea of using psychoanalytic ideas for biographical purposes on the grounds that these concepts were developed for the treatment of living patients, not for exploration of the psyches of dead heroes. In a slightly modified version of this view, church historian Roland Bainton said that Luther's childhood was virtually irrelevant to his adult career, so why subject Luther to psychoanalytic investigation? He points out that he dissents "from so much in the methodology and more particularly the presuppositions of this book . . . for it seems to me that Luther's theological development might have been just the same if he had been left an orphan in infancy."[25] Other historians, however, have considered the judicious use of psychoanalytic concepts in historical biography appropriate, and a few book-length studies of this kind have received high critical marks from the historical community. In most such cases, psychoanalytic ideas have been used to explain behavior that had the seemingly paradoxical effect of frustrating the very objectives to which the subject was ostensibly committed. The study of *Woodrow Wilson and Colonel House*, by Alexander and Juliette George, inspired by the "personality and politics" school of Harold Lasswell and Nathan Leites, is considered by many historians to be an excellent example of this use of psychoanalytic theory. Its explanation for Wilson's failure to gain congressional support for the League of Nations is universally regarded as a considerably more persuasive analysis of Wilson's "need to fail" than is the study by William C. Bullitt.[26]

On the other hand, the view that this type of study is historical biography needs critical appraisal. While it covers Wilson's life from beginning to end, and would therefore seem to qualify as biography in that it provides an account of its subject's life, it is quite different from conventional historical biography in its employment of a very explicit explanatory apparatus. Its primary concern is to account for Wilson's failures, and it invokes a theory of unconscious motivation to explain these failures. This explanatory apparatus controls the narrative. To be sure, any successful biography must employ an explanatory schema of some sort. No biography is purely descriptive, for, if nothing else, the requirement of a coherent narrative structure necessitates an explanatory apparatus that can account for the continuity of the life over time.[27] In conventional narrative biography, however, this apparatus is more implicit than explicit; events are included or excluded not for methodological but for narrative purposes. Not so with the Georges' study of Wilson. In their view, Wilson's whole career was marked by the seemingly inexplicable failures of his most cherished projects. Their concern is to show that this was indeed the case and to explain in psychological terms why Wilson's life manifested this pattern of self-destructive behavior. Biographical facts are introduced solely to advance this basic argument.

This does not mean, of course, that the Georges' study does not deserve the acclaim that it has received. What it does mean is that its biographical thrust as an account of a life is subordinate to its methodological intent—namely, to explain how irrational processes in the personality of the leader may have a decisive effect on the course of human affairs. In this sense, *Woodrow Wilson and Colonel House* comes closer to the special study than to historical biography for, as we have seen, the special study accords methodology precedence over narrative. On the other hand, the Georges' study is deliberately explanatory, and we need to ask, therefore, whether there are not historical biographies that successfully provide a narrative of a life while employing a consistent psychological perspective in accomplishing this task. Put differently, if the studies like the Georges' possess a coherent psychological perspective but achieve this at the expense of a narrative account of the life itself, then we may appropriately ask whether a historical biography can satisfy the narrative requirement of a life history while at the same time employing psychological concepts in such a fundamental way that the narrative reflects a coherent and consistent psychological perspective.

A number of narrative biographies have been acclaimed for their use of psychological concepts, including David Donald's study of Charles Sumner and Lacey Baldwin Smith's biography of Henry VIII.[28] Both studies have been singled out for their judicious but truly insightful use of psychological ideas. Donald's explanation of Sumner's extended absence from Congress and Smith's account of Henry's declining years and the psychological despair pertaining thereto shed new light on known biographical facts. However, it must be acknowledged that these biographies are not informed throughout by a consistent psychological perspective. Rather, psychological concepts are generally introduced when the more conventional "common sense" explanations employed elsewhere in the book fail to account for the more complex psychological features of the life in question. It would seem to me that a consistent psychological perspective, and not simply the ad hoc use of psychological concepts, no matter how astutely employed, is a necessary characteristic of *psychohistorical* biography. While meeting the narrative criteria of historical biography, these studies by Donald and Smith fail to meet the psychohistorical criteria.

On the other hand, there is nothing in principle that says that a historical biography could not be under the control of a consistent psychological point of view. Various biographies of writers and artists—one of the most successful of which is Aileen Ward's study of John Keats's identity crisis in the formation of his poetic vision—are shaped by such a psychological perspective.[29] Is there nothing comparable in *historical* as opposed to literary biography? By way of answer, it might be argued that Fawn Brodie's controversial *Thomas Jefferson: An Intimate History* has a controlling psychological vision.[30] In this case, it would be difficult to sustain the argument that the author employs a single psychological theory or set of theories. But it could be maintained that, in the course of her narrative, she subjects virtually every episode in Jefferson's life to careful psychological scrutiny. The effect of this procedure is a psychological view of Jefferson built in cumulative fashion, an inductive approach that offers psychological insights into the subject's personality, but not so systematically as to interrupt the narrative line.

On the other hand, it must be acknowledged that the biographer's intention here is not to give us a consistent psychological explanation of her subject, but instead to correct earlier biographical views of Jefferson as a disembodied intellect. To Professor Brodie,

> it was the humanity of Jefferson that fired his genius. The humanity was comprised of more than his loves and his hatreds; there was his fear of enslavement clashing with his habits of benevolent despotism, his affection for power tempered by his extraordinary guilt over its abuse, his normal need for sexual fulfillment coupled with his attraction for the forbidden, his hunger for affection and esteem assuaged not only by his multiple friendships and several loves but also by his fanatical obedience to his larger fantasies of what constituted his duty to the state. His passion, guilt, indignation, and despair, even his weakness, were all tempered by his intellect. They also served to mold and direct it.[31]

Professor Brodie is therefore more concerned to establish the fact that Jefferson's emotions influenced his intellectual activities and vice versa than to provide an explanatory apparatus of sufficient power to account for the development of this remarkable personality. The difference here is, of course, a relative one, and no doubt the *emotion versus intellect* motif constitutes an important formulation of Jefferson's psychological conflicts. In my judgment, however, this motif lacks the necessary explanatory power to enable this biography to claim a consistent psychological perspective such that it might be considered a psychohistorical type of historical biography.

What, then, enables any biography to qualify as psychohistorical? If not the occasional use of psychological concepts or even the constant attention to the psychological dimensions of episodes recounted in the narrative, what makes biography psychohistorical in nature? Our discussion of the Georges' study indicates that what is additionally required is a theoretical structure powerful enough to explain the role of psychological conflicts in the formation and development of the subject's life. Erikson emphasizes this explanatory task of psychohistorical biography when he observes that Luther was a young man "beset with a syndrome of conflicts whose outline we have learned to recognize, and whose components to analyze."[32] Thus, the psychohistory of individual lives involves the recognition and analysis of the "syndrome of conflicts" by which these lives are formed and developed. Narrative is subordinate to the formulation of a conceptual apparatus adequate to explain the subject's psychological conflicts.

Significantly, the American biographer Gamaliel Bradford attempted to distinguish biography based on psychological explanation from narrative biography more than a half century ago. He proposed a new form of biography termed *psychography*, which would not provide a narrative account of the life of the subject but would instead attempt to capture the "psychology" of the subject in a relatively succinct thematic statement.[33] In this concern to formulate the life thematically, Bradford not only anticipated the work of Henry Murray with his Thematic Apperception Test,[34] but more to our purposes here, he also anticipated Erikson's use of thematic analysis in his clinical assessment of patients. In his essay on the nature of clinical evidence, Erikson suggests that the therapist is attentive to "recurrent themes" that, as they continually reapper in the course of therapy, begin to form a pattern. The therapist then hazards an interpretation that attempts to integrate these recurrent themes, and Erikson calls this the *unitary thema*. This unitary thema, like Murray's *simple thema*, is brief, conceptual, and usually imageless and undramatic.[35]

On the other hand, while anticipatory of Murray and Erikson, Bradford's psychographies were not informed by dynamic psychology, and his thematic analyses therefore usually failed to capture the conflictful nature of his subject's basic psychology. Thus, while Bradford characterized Abraham Lincoln as a man of profound isolation, today's psychohistorian would undoubtedly focus on "a syndrome of conflict" that might be thematically formulated in terms of *intimacy versus isolation*. Nonetheless, Bradford recognized and exploited the fundamental generic difference between his psychographies and historical biography by contrasting the explanatory thrust of the one with the narrative emphasis of the other.[36]

Where does all this leave the argument that psychohistory is a type of historical biography? Inasmuch as historical biography is essentially narrative biography, it would appear that the argument is not very persuasive. Psychohistorical biography is not primarily narrative; it is not shaped by narrative but rather by explanatory concerns. Therefore, the arguments that psychohistory is a type of special study or family history are more convincing because both of these historical genres are also shaped by methodological rather than narrative concerns.

On the other hand, if we took this conclusion as the final word on the subject of psychohistory as historical genre, a very important issue would be left unexplored. The problem with this neat differentiation of methodology and narrative is that it neglects the fact that narrative is an extremely important element in psychohistorical studies. They may not be primarily narrative, but they are rarely without narrative features, a fact that the view of psychohistory as historical biography encourages us to recognize. When psychohistory is viewed as a special study or family history, its narrative features are systematically overlooked. Barzun's criteria for the special study and Mazlish's description of family history say little if anything about narrative, and in fact Barzun contrasts psychohistory with conventional narrative history. And yet much psychohistorical work, and especially psychohistories of individuals, involve considerable attention to narrative. As we have seen, in psychohistorical biography the problem is to use narrative without allowing it to shape the study. Any informed discussion of psychohistory in terms of genre must therefore give attention to its dual character as method and narrative.

Until very recently, however, most critical discussion of psychohistory has centered on method.[37] As Erikson's essay on the nature of psychohistorical evidence indicates, psychohistory raises all sorts of methodological issues. He says that a compound name like *psychohistory* tends to designate

> an area in which nobody as yet is methodologically quite at home, but which someday will be settled and incorporated without a trace of border disputes and double names. The necessity to delineate it, however, becomes urgent when forward workers rush in with claims which endanger systematic exploration. Thus, today, psychoanalytic theory is sometimes applied to historical events with little clarification of the criteria for such a transfer.[38]

Erikson goes on to observe that, when *Young Man Luther* appeared, "nothing could have better symbolized the methodological embarrassment on the part even of friendly critics than the stereotyped way in which editors . . . captioned the reviews of my book with the phrase 'Luther on the Couch.'" This concern with method that the publication of *Young Man Luther* virtually forced on the psychohistorian is important and necessary, and one doubts that any serious psychohistorian can proceed very far in his work without confronting the problem of method. However, the foregoing discussion of psychohistory as a genre suggests that, even in his methodological reflections, the psychohistorian must sooner or later confront the problem of narrative. Specifically, he must ask whether narrative in psychohistory is different from conventional historical narrative, and, if so, whether this difference is due solely to self-indulgence on the part of the author (as David Donald suggests) or to more fundamental generic expectations.

PSYCHOHISTORICAL BIOGRAPHY AND NARRATIVE

Among leading psychohistorians, Erik Erikson's psychohistorical work has prompted the most discussion of narrative. This is undoubtedly due to the fact that his two major psychohistorical studies are biographical in nature and therefore raise narrative issues that are more easily circumvented by psychohistorians working primarily in the areas of special studies and family history. Furthermore, Erikson's psychohistorical work raises narrative issues that are especially attractive to students of religion because, while the explanatory apparatus of these studies is psychological, the narratives have a peculiarly religious tonality that is not wholly attributable to the fact that his subjects are religious men. It can be argued that this religious tonality is not an incidental feature of Erikson's narratives, but that it is the major factor in setting his narratives apart from those of conventional historical biography.

We can identify two types of discussion of Erikson's narratives that focus on their religious tonality. The first gives attention to the narrative uses of Erikson's psychological concepts, showing how his employment of such concepts in the narrative enables him to capture the religious nuances of his subject's psychological conflicts. This approach views the psychological concepts employed in the narrative as a means of elucidating the religious features of the subject's personal conflicts. The second approach suggests that Erikson's narratives are informed by theological convictions that are not a self-evident aspect of the study's formal explanatory apparatus, but that nonetheless play a significant role in the structuring of the total narrative. This approach is not so much concerned with the role of the narrative in elucidating the religious features of the subject's psychological conflicts as it is with identifying the implicit theological assumptions that underly the total narrative structure. This approach proceeds according to the conviction that psychological explanations of the life in question are invariably rooted in theological understandings, and that this "deeper" theological level is manifest in the narrative itself.

Psychological concepts as narrative motifs. This first approach to psychohistorical narrative has been well formulated by historian Richard Bushman in his discussions of the uses of psychology in the analysis of autobiographical documents. These discussions, one centering on Jonathan Edwards's boyhood essay on insects and the other on Benjamin Franklin's autobiography,[39] do not address Erikson's own psychohistorical writings. But they do focus on the religious tonality of the narrative in question, and they also show how Erikson's concepts may have a narrative function, how their primary function in this regard is the elucidation of the subject's psychological conflicts.

Bushman begins his discussion of the narrative function of Erikson's concepts with the observation that historians have been too inclined to turn to psychology—much as a doctor turns to pathology books—to discover the nature and cause of the subject's symptoms. In so doing, the historian is inevitably disappointed that the kinds of diagnoses that psychology can offer in this regard are usually based on childhood experiences for which there is little distinctive historical evidence. However, Bushman does not counsel despair, for

> while less helpful in offering crisp diagnoses, psychology may be more helpful than expected in discerning a person's—or a group's—characteristic patterns of acting. Sometimes the historian himself notices the pattern before consulting the psychology book, but often he cannot; finding the pattern may be the most difficult part and the place where personality theory can be of greatest aid. Confronting his materials, the historian's task is to create a coherent picture. Psychology sensitizes the researcher to new connections and draws into a pattern data normally regarded as insignificant.[40]

In Bushman's view, biography is especially exemplary of this use of psychology because every biographer looks for patterns that help explain his subject's life:

> Familiarity instills a more or less vague sense of a characteristic style. The problem is to crystallize these

> feelings into clear propositions which illuminate a large number of specific events. Beginning with a single passage or event, a close analysis using personality theory can often pull together scattered impressions.[41]

Bushman suggests that Erikson's life-cycle theory provides unique possibilities for pulling together these scattered impressions. Specifically, a single life-cycle crisis may provide the conceptual basis for relating the whole series of events recounted in the narrative and, in so doing, illuminate the subject's most prominent psychological conflicts. Bushman's discussion of Benjamin Franklin, for example, centers on the conflict encountered in Erikson's first life-cycle stage—namely, the conflict that the infant experiences when he senses that while obtaining nurturance he must curb the impulse to hurt his benefactor:

> Erikson reports that clinical experience shows this situation to be the origin of a dilemma: the yearning to bite conflicts with the yearning for nourishment and for the continuation of blissful well-being. The child must restrain the urge to bite and learn to obtain food without hurting.[42]

The conflict yields a theme or motif—*getting without hurting*—that does an admirable job of pulling together a whole series of events in Franklin's autobiography,—events in which Franklin went to considerable lengths to obtain his objectives without harming other persons in the process. Thus, the theme of *getting without hurting*, a psychological dynamic that might be described in more sociological terms as *enlightened self-interest*, provides the narrative with its overall coherence and illuminates one of the major dimensions of Franklin's psychological conflicts. That this theme also penetrates the moral features of Franklin's psychological conflicts is perhaps best illustrated by two events that appear to contradict the theme of *getting without hurting*. The first event involved his taking advantage of his brother's legal difficulties to gain control of his business.

The second event involved his making sexual advances toward an Englishwoman and being rebuffed. Significantly, these are the only events in Franklin's narrative in which he confesses to "errata" on his part, and both involved Franklin's efforts to "get" at the expense of someone else. Thus, if the theme of *getting without hurting* penetrates Franklin's psychological conflicts, the moral or possibly religious issue that is involved here is the necessity of avoiding harm to others in his desire to secure advantages for himself.

Now, to be sure, Bushman's analysis of Franklin's autobiography is not itself a biography. However, using Erikson's concepts in getting at the thematic unity of Franklin's own narrative, he has shown how Erikson's concepts can have a narrative function, and how this function is the elucidation of the subject's psychological conflicts. Bushman seriously doubts that he would have been able to identify the narrative's thematic structure had he not been fortified with Erikson's life-cycle theory. Thus, from this demonstration based on Franklin's autobiography, it is a relatively small step to Erikson's own use of life-cycle concepts in the narrative structures of *Young Man Luther* and *Gandhi's Truth.* The similarity is not difficult to see, for in *Young Man Luther* the concept of *identity versus identity diffusion* links together a whole series of events in Luther's life, beginning with the "fit in the choir" episode in chapter 2 and concluding with the "tower experience" in chapter 6. In *Gandhi's Truth* the narrative structure is less clearly organized in terms of a series of thematically related events; rather, a major concern of the book is to justify the selection of a single event as the crucial episode in Gandhi's political and spiritual career. This very concern, however, suggests that the narrative of *Gandhi's Truth* is held together by the theme of *intimacy versus isolation.* To Erikson, this theme not only illuminates Gandhi's own psychological conflicts dating at least as far back as his father's death, but also captures the political and even metaphysical dimensions of Gandhi's leadership role. As Erikson explains, in India

> one moves in a space-time so filled with visual and auditory occurrences that it is very difficult to lift an episode out of the flux of events, a fact out of the stream of feelings, a circumscribed relationship out of a fusion of multiple encounters. If, in all this, I should endow one word with a meaning which unites it all, the word is *fusion*. And I am inclined to indulge in the generalization that Indians want to give and to get by fusing—actively and passively. This may come as a shocking observation to those who, on the basis of one-sided reading, emphasize the *isolation* of the Indian individual and a lifelong nostalgia for solitude and meditation. But fusion and isolation are polar themes. . . . There is, no doubt, a deep recurring need to escape the multitude, and there is a remarkable capacity for being alone in the middle of a crowd. I have, in fact, never seen so many individuals in a catatonic-like isolation in the middle of a chattering crowd. But aloneness, too, is often dominated by a deep nostalgia for fusing with another, and this in an exclusive and lasting fashion, be that "Other" a mentor or a god, the Universe—or the innermost Self.[43]

Throughout *Gandhi's Truth*, therefore, the theme of *intimacy versus isolation* underlies Gandhi's own conflicts, it captures his relations with followers, family, and counterplayers; and it even penetrates Erikson's own responses to Gandhi as expressed in his controversial "personal word," which, unless viewed in terms of the intimacy problem, appears to interrupt the narrative flow.

The foregoing illustrations of Erikson's use of his own concepts in the narrative structures of his psychohistorical biographies should suffice to demonstrate that, if his life-cycle theory provides the overall explanatory apparatus for his psychohistories, particular aspects of the theory are employed in the narrative structure. These illustrations also touch on the relationship between this thematic employment of life-cycle concepts and the religious tonality of the narrative. A more precise statement concerning this relationship, however, is contained in Erikson's account in *Gandhi's Truth* of a seminar discussion in which he participated while in India. This discussion focused on attempts to relate the Hindu life stages to Erikson's life-cycle theory. Erikson indicates that he did not resist these correlations, recognizing that his life stages, for all their seemingly scientific aura, harbored a "mythological trend" of their own.[44] Erikson does not claim that his life-cycle schema qualifies as a "religious world-image," but he does acknowledge that it articulates similar religious meanings and shares with these world-images the conviction that "a pragmatic world-view which shuns all concepts of the cycle of generations can cause widespread disorientation."

The conclusion is inescapable: insofar as Erikson's narratives are under the guidance of his life-cycle concepts, the narrative will manifest a mythological tendency. Furthermore, because the life-cycle concepts (qua themes) are especially designed to identify the personal conflicts of the subject, Erikson's narratives will tend to dramatize the mythic features of such conflicts. Hence, in the hands of the conventional historical biographer, Gandhi's first court appearance marks professional failure; to Erikson, the same event recapitulates the inner conflicts of the ancient warrior Arjuna as he awaited the beginning of his battle against fellow kinsmen. Thus, the "deeper" psychological meaning of Gandhi's experience in the court of small claims is that "he would tend to seek out the smallest and most local situations as a great soul's proper battleground."[45]

In noting the "mythological trend" in Erikson's narratives we see how Erikson has self-consciously allowed his narrative to take on a religious tonality consistent with the life experiences and, more specifically, the psychological conflicts of his subject. We conclude from this that his narratives, through their reconstruction of events, serve as the nodal point at which religion and psychology converge. At the same time, however, his acknowledgment of the "mythological trend" in his life-cycle theory prompts us to ask whether Erikson's narratives are structured by something even more fundamental than these series of convergences—through events—of personal conflict and mythological understanding. Are the narratives informed, in addition, by a theological substructure of which Erikson himself may be largely unaware? This brings us to the second approach to Erikson's narratives, and to a suggestive study of *Young Man Luther* by the theologian Roger A. Johnson.[46]

Theological convictions as narrative substructure. In effect, Johnson's study of psychohistory as religious narrative begins with the previously discussed approach to Erikson's narratives. Focusing on Erikson's portrayal of Hans Luther, Johnson concludes that Erikson's one-sided caricature of Hans as an unmitigated villain, while extremely questionable on historical grounds, ought not be dismissed as sheer fabrication, but instead placed in an appropriate mythological context. Viewed mythologically, Erikson's narrative says that Hans must be wholly evil in order that Luther's conflict over obedience might assume the mythic overtones of a cosmic struggle between good and evil. In this view, Hans is the prototype of Satan as he struggles with God for the soul of young Martin. Here, as in the case of young Gandhi in the court of small claims, events that capture Luther's personal conflicts have mythological overtones.

Then, however, Johnson presses the analysis further and, in so doing, raises the theological issues that are at the heart of the second approach to Erikson's narratives. He asks specifically whether Erikson's narrative in *Young Man Luther* is not under the guidance of a theological structure of which Erikson himself is only dimly aware. The narrative structure of *Young Man Luther*, he suggests, has strong affinities to a paradigm borrowed from classical theology: creation, fall, sin, apocalyptic dread, and prophetic deed. This paradigm is a fleshing out of the cosmic struggle of good and evil, but it carries this mythological trend to its natural theological conclusion. In so doing, it makes explicit certain theological understandings that Erikson, in his explanation of the mythological tendencies in his life-cycle concept, leaves implicit. Thus, says Johnson:

> I have chosen this paradigm for heuristic reasons; the narrative form, ethical focus, and dialectical balance of

> classical theology seem ideally suited to make explicit the distinctive thrust of Erikson's vision of human nature. In addition, the utilization of this format also discloses the strong affinity of Erikson with traditional religious narratives. For the theologian, it suggests that Erikson's psychosocial schema may prove so attractive as a dialogical partner precisely because Erikson, covertly if not explicitly, is already operating within a quasi-theological framework.[47]

Johnson goes on to elaborate this theological paradigm in *Young Man Luther* and shows how its culmination in the "prophetic deed" also figures prominently in Erikson's biographical reconstruction of the life of Gandhi. However, we need not engage Johnson's discussion further, for our primary objective has been to identify the theological view of Erikson's psychohistorical narratives and to distinguish it from the "religious" approach discussed above. Nonetheless, well worth pursuing in this regard would be the suggestion that the theological substructure of Erikson's study of Luther may have insinuated itself into the narrative without conscious intention on Erikson's part. In generic terms, this suggestion may point to a very significant difference between the two approaches to Erikson's narratives.

What can we conclude from this discussion of narrative in psychohistorical biography? Basically, it suggests that psychohistory and historical biography are different not only because the one claims an explanatory apparatus while the other does not, but also because their narratives are significantly different as well. Because the psychohistorical study places a great deal of theoretical emphasis on the psychological conflict, considering it the task of the explanatory apparatus to illuminate these conflicts, we should perhaps not be surprised that such conflicts also play a central role in the narrative structure itself. What does give legitimate cause for surprise, however, is the fact that one prominent psychohistorian, in attempting to come to terms with the complexity of such conflicts, has found himself reverting to the religious themes that have been largely eliminated from modern historical biography. Barzun contends that psychohistorical biographies

> do not constitute a new genre. To be sure, the selection of facts and the ideas that bind them in explanatory ways are not of a kind found in every biography. It can even be agreed that the importance given to psychoanalytic considerations in these works, not written for specialists (for whose purposes full case histories would be required), is a pioneering effort that marks an epoch. But the issue does not lie in these undoubted propositions. It lies in the question whether the special attitude or special capacity of a biographer creates a new discipline when he applies them.[48]

In contrast to many psychohistorians who believe that they are on to something genuinely new, I would agree with Barzun that psychohistory does not constitute a new genre. The real question, however, is whether psychohistorical biography as Erikson understands and practices it is representative of an *old* genre that is struggling to be reborn. Do we have in Erikson's psychological biographies the revival of biographical intentions that were laid to rest with the demise of hagiography? And, without presuming to resuscitate a biographical form that religionists and historians both agree had become moribund, might it not be the case that the future of psychohistory depends in part on its accepting responsibility for the revival of some form of religious biography?

In saying this, I do not wish to be understood as making a plea for religious biography for religious reasons, but rather to express as dramatically as possible the need for a cadre of psychohistorians who are prepared to resist psychohistory's current trend toward the uncritical acceptance of the canons of evidence, method, and narrative enjoined by conventional historians. As psychohistory moves into another decade of its existence, one fears that the legacy of Erik Erikson will increasingly become an anomaly alongside the more respectable special studies and family histories.[49] If this should happen, it will be no more unprecedented than psychohistorical biography itself. Historians have viewed biography from time immemorial as a stepchild among historical genres. Nonetheless, it is not unreasonable to hope that the Eriksonian legacy will receive better treatment from a movement that has known adversity and is still young enough to remember.

PSYCHOHISTORY AS INTERDISCIPLINARY

In attempting to identify the major problems that psychohistory currently confronts, we have focused on genre considerations as one very important means of coming to terms with these problems. More specifically, we have recommended that critics and proponents alike give greater attention to the fact that psychohistory articulates a variety of historical genres, each with its own characteristics and criteria. We have only begun the task of sorting out these various historical genres, and yet even these relatively brief discussions of psychohistory as *special study, family history,* and *historical biography* have enabled us to clear up some of the confusion that psychohistory generates among critics and proponents alike as to its claims, limitations, objectives, and so on.

Another whole set of issues that we have not addressed here, but that are crucial to psychohistory's claim to be interdisciplinary, concerns its affinities with *psychological* genres. While psychologists are less inclined than historians to differentiate their projects according to genres, there is simply no question that psychology has its preferred genres as well. Even the empirical study based largely on statistical findings has a generic formula that proceeds through the review of relevant literature, discussion of methodology or procedures, elucidation of results, and implications for further study. Thus, since psychology also has its genres, we might follow the same procedure as in our discussion of psychohistory as historical genre by identifying those psychological genres with which psychohistory has special affinities. Furthermore we might find that certain psychological genres have characteristics and functions within their own discipline that correspond to the characteristics and disciplinary functions of certain historical genres. The *case study* may have affinities with the *special study*, the *lives-in-progress* model (including moral and cognitive as well as emotional development) may correspond to the *family history*, and *personality theory* may have much in common with *historical biography* (including perhaps their anomalous standing within their respective disciplines). These are merely suggestions that would require careful analysis before we could say with any confidence that they have validity and, equally important, explanatory value. Such suggestions, however, underscore our contention that much work remains to be done in clarifying the relationship of psychohistory to the disciplines from which it derives its name. We cannot assume, merely because psychohistory has been in existence for nearly two decades, that all boundary claims are settled and all disclaimers acknowledged.

NOTES

1. William L. Langer, "The Next Assignment," *American Historical Review* 63, no. 2 (January 1958): 283–304. Reprinted in *Psychoanalysis and History*, ed. Bruce Mazlish (Englewood Cliffs, N.J.: Prentice-Hall, 1963), pp. 87–107.

2. Erik H. Erikson, *Young Man Luther: A Study in Psychoanalysis and History* (New York: W. W. Norton & Co., 1958). Kenneth Keniston recognizes the role of William Langer in pointing to the need for psychohistorical inquiry, but attributes the actual development of the field to Erikson's inspiration: "Until the last decade, most psychohistorical inquiries must be judged a failure from both a psychological and a historical point of view; despite the advocacy of distinguished historians like Langer, the union of history and depth psychology languished. In the last decade, inspired largely by the work of Erikson, new and potentially more fruitful kinds of psychohistorical inquiry have opened up." Keniston, "Psychological Development and Historical Change," in *The Family in History: Interdisciplinary Essays*, ed. Theodore K. Rabb and Robert I. Rotberg (New York: Harper & Row, 1971), pp. 141–57.

3. Mazlish's own psychohistory of Richard Nixon inaugurated the series. See Bruce Mazlish, *In Search of Nixon: A Psychohistorical Inquiry* (New York: Basic Books, 1972). A second book in the series is Walter C. Langer, *The Mind of Adolf Hitler* (New York: Basic Books, 1972).

4. Jacques Barzun, *Clio and the Doctors: Psycho-History, Quanto-History and History* (Chicago: University of Chicago Press, 1974).

5. Ibid., p. x.

6. Barzun struck a similar note in his earlier critique of psychohistory, the essay on which *Clio and the Doctors* is based. In this essay he emphasizes the need to confront fundamental questions of historical theory and practice raised by psychohistory, the purpose of such systematic discussion being to provide both "students of history proper and those of the fused or fusing subject matters . . . clearer choices than emerge from the prevailing exhortations." See Jacques Barzun, "History: The Muse and Her Doctors," *American Historical Review* 77, no. 1 (February 1972): 36–64.

7. David Herbert Donald, "Between History and Psychology: Reflections on Psychobiography" (Benjamin Rush Lecture delivered at the American Psychiatric Association meeting in Dallas, 3 May 1972).

8. See, for example, Roland Bainton's review of *Young Man Luther*, "Luther: A Psychiatric Portrait," *Yale Review* 48, no. 3 (March 1959): 405–10. Bainton expanded his critique of *Young Man Luther* more recently with his essay "Psychiatry and History: An Examination of Erikson's *Young Man Luther*," *Religion in Life* 40 (Winter 1971): 450–78.

9. William E. Barton, a noted Lincoln scholar and minister of the First Congregational Church in Oak Park, Illinois, in the 1920s, observed that a psychological biography of Lincoln by L. Pierce Clark employs a "method of study [that] appears to exhibit certain marked defects." The major such defect "is a very meager and incomplete and quite inaccurate gathering of the material for his induction." Barton's comments occur in a letter intended for publication in the *Psychoanalytic Review* in response to Clark's "Unconscious Motivations Underlying the Personalities of Great Statesmen and Their Relation to Epoch-Making Events (I. A Psychologic Study of Abraham Lincoln)," *Psychoanalytic Review* 8, no. 1 (January 1921): 1–21. This correspondence is inserted in Barton's copy of the Clark paper in his private collection, Joseph Regenstein Library, University of Chicago. Clark later published a full-length study of Lincoln in which he accepted Barton's criticisms on one or two matters of evidence. See *Lincoln: A Psychobiography* (New York: Charles Scribner's Sons, 1933).

10. Barzun, *Clio and the Doctors*, pp. 19–22.

11. H. Stuart Hughes discusses examples of this approach in *History as Art and as Science: Twin Vistas on the Past* (New York: Harper Torchbooks, 1964), pp. 52–55. However, a classic study in the literature is the collaborative study by a psychologist and a historian, Frederick Wyatt and William Willcox, "Sir Henry Clinton: A Psychological Exploration in History," *William and Mary Quarterly* 16 (1959): 3–26. Wyatt discusses the methodology employed in this study in his subsequent article, The Recon-

struction of the Individual and of the Collective Past," in *The Study of Lives: Essays on Personality in Honor of Henry A. Murray*, ed. Robert W. White (New York: Atherton Press, 1963), pp. 305–20. Most psychohistorical literature focuses on conflictful behavior, but Arthur Mitzman in *The Iron Cage* stresses the conflict manifest in Max Weber's intellectual system (New York: Alfred A. Knopf, 1970). Lewis S. Feuer has addressed the same issue in his various essays on major philosophers, the most ambitious being his analysis of Immanuel Kant's epistemology in "Lawless Sensations and Categorical Defenses: The Unconscious Sources of Kant's Philosophy," in *Psychoanalysis and Philosophy*, ed. Charles Hanly & Morris Lazerowitz (New York: International Universities Press, 1971) pp. 76–125. For a critique of the latter type of psychohistorical study, see Gerald Izenberg, "Psychohistory and Intellectual History," *History and Theory* 14, no. 2 (1975): 139–55.

12. Barzun, *Clio and the Doctors*, p. 150.

13. Peter Loewenberg, "The Pyschohistorical Origins of the Nazi Youth Cohort," *American Historical Review* 76, no. 5 (December 1971): 1457–1502.

14. Ibid., pp. 1465–66.

15. Ibid., p. 1468.

16. Another psychohistorian who employs the notion of the cohort is Robert J. Lifton in his studies of atomic bomb survivors and, more recently, Vietnam War veterans. See Lifton, *Death in Life: Survivors of Hiroshima* (New York: Random House, 1968), and idem, "American in Vietnam: The Counterfeit Friend," *History and Human Survival* (New York: Vintage Books, 1971), pp. 210–37. See also idem, *Home From the War: Vietnam Veterans, Neither Victims nor Executioners* (New York: Simon and Schuster, 1973).

17. Rabb and Rotberg, eds., *The Family in History*, p. i.

18. The excellent collection of essays published under the title *The Family in History* originally appeared in the *Journal of Interdisciplinary History*. A well-balanced critical assessment of the *History of Childhood Quarterly* by Louis W. Potts appears in *Group for the Use of Psychology in History Newsletter* 3, no. 3 (1974): 12–13.

19. Bruce Mazlish, "What is Psycho-history?" *Transactions of the Royal Historical Society of London*, 5th ser. 21 (1971): 87–88.

20. John Demos, "Developmental Perspectives on the History of Childhood," in *The Family in History*, p. 133. See also Demos's chapter on infancy and childhood in *A Little Commonwealth: Family Life in Plymouth Colony* (London and New York: Oxford University Press, 1970), pp. 131–44.

21. Ibid., p. 134.

22. *New York Review of Books*, 20 November 1969, p. 4.

23. What the psychohistorian has not given much attention to are instances in which family practices have reduced social conflict. I have suggested that a major element in Abraham Lincoln's greatness as a wartime President was his introduction of traditional family values into a political process that had become increasingly responsive to values represented by

emergent business and legal interests. See Donald Capps, "The Myth of Father Abraham: Psychosocial Influences in the Formation of Lincoln Biography," in *Encounter with Erikson*, ed. Donald Capps, Walter H. Capps, and M. Gerald Bradford (Missoula, Mont.: Scholars Press, 1977).

24. An excellent critical review of psychologically informed historical biographies is John Mack's "Psychoanalysis and Historical Biography," *Journal of the American Psychoanalytic Association* 19 (1971): 143–79. Mack reviews the history of psychoanalytic approaches to biography since Freud, discusses a number of "methodological problems," and gives special attention to the shifting emphasis of psychobiography from literary figures and artists to historical and political figures.

25. Bainton, "Luther: A Psychiatric Portrait," p. 410. It may be worth noting that Bainton's position here, while unpopular with psychohistorians, has theoretical support in Gordon W. Allport's discussion of functional autonomy in the religious sentiment. See Allport, *The Individual and His Religion* (New York: Macmillan, 1960), p. 64. The question, of course, is whether this notion is applicable to Luther's theological development.

26. Alexander L. and Juliette George, *Woodrow Wilson and Colonel House* (New York: Dover Books, 1964). Other shorter-length studies of Wilson include William Carleton, "A New Look at Woodrow Wilson," *Virginia Quarterly Review* 38 (1962): 545–66, and Edwin Weinstein, "Woodrow Wilson's Neurological Illness," *Journal of American History* 57 (September 1970): 324–52. See also Sigmund Freud and William C. Bullitt, *Thomas Woodrow Wilson: A Psychological Study* (Boston: Houghton Mifflin, 1967).

27. On this point, see Wilhelm Dilthey, *Pattern and Meaning in History: Thoughts on History and Society*, ed. H. P. Rickman (New York: Harper Torchbooks, 1961), pp. 90–92. See also Erving Goffman's discussion of biography in *Stigma: Notes on the Management of Spoiled Identity* (Englewood Cliffs, N.J.: Prentice-Hall, 1963), pp. 62–66.

28. David Donald, *Charles Sumner and the Coming of the Civil War* (New York: Alfred A. Knopf, 1960). An excellent excerpt of the relevant psychological passages from the biography appears in Robin W. Winks, ed., *The Historian as Detective: Essays on Evidence* (New York: Harper Colophon Books, 1968), pp. 347–68. See also Lacey Baldwin Smith, *Henry VIII: The Mask of Royalty* (Boston: Houghton Mifflin, 1971). Miles F. Shore focuses on the more prominent features of Henry's personal conflicts in middle age in "Henry VIII and the Crisis of Generativity," *Journal of Interdisciplinary History* 2, no. 4 (Spring 1972): 359–90.

29. Aileen Ward, *John Keats: The Making of a Poet* (New York: Viking Press, 1963). A more classically psychoanalytic biography of an artist is Albert J. Lubin, *Stranger on the Earth: A Psychological Biography of Vincent Van Gogh* (New York: Holt, Rinehart and Winston, 1972). An interesting variation on biographies of artists that are under the control of a single psychological viewpoint is William U. Snyder, *Thomas Wolfe: Ulysses and Narcissus* (Athens: Ohio University Press, 1971). Snyder

combines Rogerian and psychoanalytic theories in developing this psychological portrait of Wolfe.

30. Fawn M. Brodie, *Thomas Jefferson: An Intimate History* (New York: Bantam Books, 1974).

31. Ibid., p. 636.

32. Erikson, *Young Man Luther*, p. 15.

33. See esp. Gamaliel Bradford *Biography and the Human Heart* (Boston: Houghton Mifflin, 1932), which contains a complete reference list of Bradford's psychographs.

34. As will become clear later in a discussion of Erikson's use of narrative, one of the more relevant essays by Henry A. Murray is his "The Possible Nature of a 'Mythology' to Come," in *Myth and Mythmaking*, ed. Murray (Boston: Beacon Press, 1960), pp. 300–53. See esp. his discussion of the role of simple and complex thema in the narrative structures of myths, pp. 324–30.

35. Erik H. Erikson, "On the Nature of Clinical Evidence," in *Insight and Responsibility* (New York: W. W. Norton & Co., 1964), pp. 49–80. An earlier discussion by Erikson of the use of themes in the analysis of children's play constructions appears in Henry A. Murray, ed., *Explorations in Personality* (New York: Oxford University Press, 1938), pp. 552–82.

36. Michael Oakeshott makes this distinction between *explanation* and *narrative* from the historian's perspective when he says: "Change in history carries with it its own explanation; the course of events is one so far integrated, so far filled in and complete, that no external cause or reason is looked for or required in order to account for any particular event. The historian, in short, is like the novelist whose characters (for example) are presented in such detail and with such coherence that additional explanation of their actions is superfluous." See Oakeshott, "Historical Continuity and Causal Analysis" in *Philosophical Analysis and History*, ed. William H. Dray (New York: Harper and Row, 1966), pp. 207–8.

37. Essays on psychohistorical method abound. See, for example, two collections of essays, Benjamin Wolman, ed., *The Psychoanalytic Interpretation of History* (New York: Basic Books, 1971), and Robert J. Lifton, ed., *Explorations in Psychohistory* (New York: Simon and Schuster, 1974). Probably the best book-length treatment of the problem of method, however, is Zevedei Barbu's little-known *Problems of Historical Psychology* (New York: Grove Press, 1960).

38. Erik H. Erikson, "On the Nature of Psychohistorical Evidence: In Search of Gandhi," in *Life History and the Historical Moment* (New York: W. W. Norton & Co., 1975), pp. 114–15. Originally published in *Daedalus* 97, no. 3 (Summer 1968): 695–730.

39. Richard L. Bushman, "Jonathan Edwards as Great Man: Identity, Conversion, and Leadership in the Great Awakening," *Soundings* 52, no. 1 (Spring 1969): 15–46. See also idem, "On the Uses of Psychology: Conflict and Conciliation in Benjamin Franklin," *History and Theory* 5, no. 3 (1966): 225–40. Bushman also has an article on Edwards that, while not

directly related to the narrative issue, bears on Demos's analysis of Puritan family life. See idem, "Jonathan Edwards and Puritan Consciousness," *Journal for the Scientific Study of Religion* 5, no. 3 (Fall 1966): 383–96.

40. Bushman, "Benjamin Franklin," p. 227.

41. Ibid., p. 229.

42. Ibid., p. 232.

43. Erik H. Erikson, *Gandhi's Truth: On the Origins of Militant Nonviolence.* (New York: W. W. Norton, 1969), pp. 40–41.

44. Ibid., p. 38.

45. Ibid., p. 161.

46. Roger A. Johnson, "Psychohistory as Religious Narrative: The Demonic Role of Hans Luther in Erikson's Saga of Human Evolution," in *Psychohistory and Religion: The Case of Young Man Luther*, ed. Roger A. Johnson (Philadelphia: Fortress Press, 1977), pp. 127–61.

47. Ibid., pp. 12–13.

48. Barzun, "History: The Muse and Her Doctors," p. 44.

49. William J. Gilmore has recently recommended a rereading of Donald Meyer's appreciative review of *Young Man Luther* (originally published in *History and Theory* 1, no. 3 (1961): 291–97 and reprinted in Mazlish, ed., *Psychoanalysis and History*, pp. 174–80) because it makes "as strong a case for the larger field and merits of psychobiography as has been made." Yet, says Gilmore, "This is an extremely powerful perspective on psychohistory, *and one at unmistakable variance with present trends within methodological literature." Group for the Use of Psychology in History Newsletter* 4, no. 3 (1975): 52. Emphasis added.

Part III

Erikson's Psychology and Modernity

6

The Significance of Erikson's Psychology for Modern Understandings of Religion

PETER HOMANS

INTRODUCTION

One of the paradoxes of the psychoanalytic study of religion lies in the fact that it has combined vigorous interest in the nature of religion with an equally vigorous critical attitude toward it. On the one hand, religion has occupied a position of prominence in psychoanalytic studies of culture or, as they are sometimes referred to, "applications" of psychoanalysis. In fact, of the various cultural phenomena to which this psychology has been applied, religion has received as much or more attention than any other. On the other hand, this psychology has been as critical of religion as it has been persistent in discussing it.

A second paradox characterizes the psychoanalytic study of religion. This vigorous though critical work on the nature of religion has not been combined with approaches to religion in the social sciences generally, particularly those approaches that have examined Western religious traditions, in both past and contemporary forms. While much work has been done in relating psychoanalytic theorizing to the social sciences generally, and while these sciences have made very definite commitments to the study of religion, there has been little integrative effort between psychoanalytic work on religion and social scientific studies of it. A lack of reciprocal discussion between psychoanalytic writers on religion and scholars in religious studies constitutes a third paradox. These two groups of workers have made little effort to utilize the ideas and findings of the other in order to broaden or unify their own paradigms.

The customary way of accounting for this state of affairs consists of offering the now-commonplace observation that writers on religion in the psychoanalytic tradition have not, for the most part, studied religion as a discrete and particular human experience. Psychoanalytic studies of religion have instead dwelt upon broad generalizations about the nature of religion on the whole, and when these studies have taken it upon themselves to examine concrete and particular manifestations of religion, they have done so largely for the purposes of illustrating an already-formed theory. Such a pattern is unlikely to attract either social scientists who study religion or scholars of religion, both of whom actively strive for a far more flexible and reciprocal relation between interpretive frameworks and specific, historical data. But in all fairness to the psychoanalytic approach, it must be noted that nonpsychoanalytic psychologists of religion display the same weakness. Neither sociologists of religion nor theologians and philosophers of religion have been attracted, for example, to the psychological writings of either James, Allport, or Maslow.

The purpose of this paper is to explore two of these paradoxes—the persistence of psychoanalytic interest in religion despite a wholly critical tone and the lack of interchange between psychoanalytic psychology and religious studies despite a common subject matter—through the writings of one of the most articulate and innovative of contemporary psychoanalytic writers, Erik Erikson. Erikson's work is deeply indebted to classic, psychoanalytic theory; when he recurs to authority in psychological matters, it is always first of all to the Freudian legacy. On the other hand, his work does not simply repeat the psychoanalytic approach to religion, but instead represents a considerable departure from it. Like the classic writers, he too has chosen religion as one of the most suitable objects for the "application" of psychoanalysis. However, unlike his forebears, Erikson has studied specific religious phenomena—such as Luther's writings and their commentaries, and the religious and political circumstances surrounding Gandhi's life work—in considerable detail. But surely the most noticeable feature of Erikson's psychological writings on religion is the positive valuation he accords to it and, in particular, to Protestantism. It is this aspect of his thought that constitutes the particular focus of this paper—namely, how does Erikson transform Freudianism, which is so critical of religion, into a more complex and more generous estimate of it?

This question can be explored only if careful attention is first given to Erikson's psychological theory of religion, and that in turn requires some examination of his psychology. Like others in the psychoanalytic tradition, Erikson makes reference to religion only in the process of pursuing a different end, that of sketching in the various structures and details of the human life cycle. Therefore, clarification of his views on religion requires clarification of his psychology. And since his psychological work represents at every point both a debt to Freud and a transformation of that indebtedness, the relation of his work to Freud's must also be clarified.

All psychologies of religion tend to assess the nature and value of religion in the light of their particular psychological assumptions. Differences in the way that two psychologists interpret religion depend upon the nature of their respective psychologies. For example, James and Freud disagree not only on the meaning of religion but also as to what constitutes the nature of psychology itself. James thought of the unconscious—he called it the "transmarginal"—in a positive way, whereas for Freud the emergence of unconscious material had a negative connotation. Although both associated religion with the unconscious, James accordingly assigned to religion a positive value, and Freud took the negative viewpoint. Erikson's interpretation of religion differs from Freud's because his assumptions about "what is psychological" differ from Freud's. Therefore we need to show Erikson's relation to the psychoanalytic tradition not only in terms of his interpretation of religion but in terms of his psychology as well.

Once Erikson's debt to—and transformation of—Freud's psychology has been clarified, his theory of religion can be stated. This is essential for any interpretive assessment of his positive estimate of Protestantism. I will first discuss religion in relation to the epigenetic principle, giving special attention to the tasks of trust, identity, and integrity. To these I will add two other ways in which Erikson understands religion: religion as "religious actuality"—that is, as a principle uniting psychological reality and historical actuality—and religion as "nostalgia." While both receive only brief treatment by Erikson, the weight of his work as a whole insists that they are significant modes of thought for understanding religion.

With Erikson's psychology and his psychological theory of religion in mind, I will then proceed to the complex question of his positive estimate of religion, despite his debt to the Freudian tradition. This difficult question can be best explored by analyzing the relation of his work to various ways of speaking about religion in contemporary thought. I will first argue that religious studies define religion in three ways: (1) as transcendence (a theological orientation); (2) as order (a sociological orientation); and (3) as spontaneity (a psychological orientation). Each of these discussions is, for the most part, in conflict with the others, creating a kind of pluralism at the level of religious thought.

Second, after identifying the orientations that make up this pluralism, I will show how Erikson's thought on religion is not simply psychological, but, rather, contains aspects of all three orientations. On the grounds of this articulation, I will point out how his psychology incorporates some of the assumptions of the theological definition of religion, thereby making possible a positive interpretation of Protestantism. Finally, I will point out that much of Erikson's appeal to students of religion and to many other readers lies in his capacity to speak of religion in all three ways—ways that are otherwise separated by contemporary thinkers on religion. Then I will conclude by pointing out that, despite innovations in the classic, psychoanalytic view of religion, Erikson also repeats its central shortcoming—the wholly unclarified assumption that religion is a projection of a developmental infrastructure. In this complex web of likeness and difference, which embraces both Freud and current religious thought, lies the essence and significance not only of Erikson's psychological theory of religion, but of his entire psychological system as well.

ERIKSON AND FREUD ON PSYCHOLOGY AND RELIGION

Since a close relation exists between a psychologist's views on psychology and the subsequent stance he takes toward religion, and since Erikson is more indebted to Freud than to any other source, I begin by noting the more important ways in which his psychology differs from Freud's. This is a complex topic that has received considerable attention on the part of psychologists. A brief summary of likenesses and differences is both possible and necessary.

The theory of development is the most important point or issue for comparison between Freud and Erikson, and the most important developmental concept is Erikson's epigenetic principle.[1] Through it he transforms Freud's theory. The term *transformation* suggests that Erikson's thought bears a double relation to Freud's: on the one hand, it is a genuine departure from Freud; on the other hand, it retains a fundamental indebtedness and likeness to

Freud. The epigenetic principle holds that psychological functioning unfolds according to a biologically grounded master plan that is both evolutionary and social in character. Erikson extends and deepens Freud's theory of psychosexual development and relates it to more temporally remote structures, by means of his own psychosocial orientation.

Erikson has extended Freud's psychosexual view of development by specifying a much wider range of social experiences that nevertheless continues to be understood on an evolutionary basis. Freud restricted development entirely to sexual factors in childhood, as these culminated in the Oedipal conflict of the male child during the ages of three to five. Freud understood all subsequent growth in terms of the basic structures laid down during the Oedipal period.[2] Erikson, however, believes that growth extends well beyond the formation of the superego, to include experiences that, while evolutionary both in their basis and in their unfolding, are also highly social. In effect he expands the Oedipal phase to include the more advanced stages of industry, identity, intimacy, generativity, and integrity. Identity occupies for him the position that the Oedipal conflict held for Freud: it is prefigured in the earlier phases but is also the basis of all those following it. It is the fulcrum of the developmental process.

Erikson also deepens Freud's conception of phases by means of his own theory of *developmental task*. Each Freudian phase is largely negative in character—it consists solely of a point of possible fixation of libidinal development. Erikson's understanding of stages differs considerably from this. Each stage possesses a positive value, along with its potential for negative consequences. For example, the first stage is not simply the occasion of oral fixation; it is also a time of both trust and mistrust. But Erikson has done more than simply giving a positive valence to each stage. He has "moralized" and "existentialized" Freud's stages. Each stage possesses a decisional character in addition to its biological and evolutionary significance. For this reason it embodies the character of choice and, by implication, of increased consciousness.

In addition to extending Freud's theory into the realm of

sociality and maturity, and deepening it by adding a moral decisional dimension to it, Erikson has sought to relate the life cycle to temporally more remote historical institutions and traditions. In this he has broadened the social in the direction of the historical, while at the same time fusing it even more closely with bodily modes of expression. In the early stages of life these historical factors are mediated through figures close to the developing person, such as parents and teachers. In this Erikson agrees with Freud, who subsumed the problem of history under the notion of the cultural superego, and in doing so made the family the formative institution of history.[3] But as development extends into a wider range of social relations, historical factors themselves become developmentally significant. Therefore, not only the individual, but also the family, takes much of its later structure from historical institutions such as political and religious groups.

These transformations of Freud's theory of development make it possible to understand Erikson's disagreements with Freud regarding the psychological nature of religion. And because there is a definite relation between the substance of a psychologist's psychology and his understanding of religion, it should also be possible to sense, even at this point in the discussion, some of the major emphases that characterize Erikson's thought on religion. Thus, the departures from Freud's psychology become clues by which Erikson's understanding of religion can be anticipated.

All psychoanalytic theory seeks to discern the child within the adult, and therefore the concept of developmental stages is a central interpretive category. When religion is the object of psychoanalytic scrutiny, the view of development shapes the view of religion, and the basic questions become, What significance is attached to lower and higher stages? and How is religion related to these stages? Freud and Erikson have very different answers to these questions. But a psychological understanding of religion has two facets, beyond the way in which development is understood. First there is the psychologist's view of religion's view of itself—that is, his view of the phenomenon of religion, what it is in itself, quite apart from an interpretation of it. And second, there is his psychological interpretation of religion, which presupposes a particular understanding of the first issue—the nature of the phenomenon called religion.

Freud's views on religion are deceptive, for in one sense they are quite simple, while in another sense they are amazingly complex. Freud thought of religion as a series of beliefs or affirmations about the nature of the real world that were based on clerical authority and not upon reason, as a set of ethical precepts grounded in this (irrational) worldview, and as a series of consolations designed to relieve individuals of the unhappiness that life brings. Religion to Freud was, in effect, an amalgam of doctrine, praxis, and consolation.[4]

Freud also spoke interpretively of religion in a number of different ways—as obsession,[5] as nostalgia for the father,[6] as illusion,[7] and as return of the repressed.[8] And he also spoke of religion in terms of different developmental phases—the oceanic feeling of very early life[9] and the later Oedipal wish for the father.[10] However, despite this apparent variety of references, the cumulative weight of Freud's thought clearly insists that religion was to be understood as an elaboration, on both the cultural and individual level, of the Oedipal stage. Dogma, praxis, and consolation all provide man with a substitute for his wish for a protective, cosmic father, modelled after his biological father. Beneath this wish lies the fundamental psychological dynamic of religion: guilt incurred by the Oedipal wish to murder the father, which creates the subsequent wish for protection and consolation. Freud's many references to religion all devolve back upon the Oedipal conflict, and religion must be seen as an attempt to resolve that conflict. Men are religious insofar as their development remains fixed at this particular stage.

Since Erikson has extended the psychosexual view of development to include later, socially determined phases, and since each task includes an aspect of positively valued choice, both his view of religion's view of itself and his interpretation of that religion differ accordingly from Freud. Erikson associates religion with several stages of development, not simply with one stage. Thus religion is linked with the first stage of life, the stage of trust; with the middle phase of life, that of identity formation; and with the final stage, the stage of integrity. These stages shape Erikson's view of religion's view of itself. In the first case, religion takes the form of faith; in the second it is a belief system; and in the third case it is the reverse of the first, a sense of self-transcendence that results in "being trustworthy."[11] Religion as a belief system resembles Freud's view of religion as belief and praxis, and religion as faith to some extent resembles Freud's view of religion as consolation.

But these similarities cannot be carried very far, for they are contradicted by Erikson's positive valuing of the earlier forms of the developmental process and, as a consequence of this, by his more generous interpretive estimate of religion. Because Freud's stages of psychosexual development were always understood as points of fixation, they always retained their negative moral character, and because he associated religion with these earlier stages, Freud always interpreted religion as a developmental fixation. Erikson, in contrast to Freud, endows even the earliest stages of life with positive, decisional characteristics, and, as a result, arrives at a psychologically positive estimate of religion. Faith, belief, and self-transcendence—the three manifestations of religion —are interpreted in terms of the developmental tasks of trust, ideology, and integrity, and all three are said to support the psychological function of identity formation.

Two important qualifications must be added to these observations. First, Erikson's understanding of the Oedipal basis of religion is complex. For the most part he considers this phase, as did Freud, as contributing negatively to religion. When the Oedipal stage is determinative in religious ideation, it creates harshness, cruelty, and a precocious conscience. At this point Erikson sets forth a psychopathology of religion similar to Freud's.[12] But his overall estimate of religion is mitigated by the positive value that he places upon identity formation—that phase in which the superego is transcended and in which the morality of religion can yield to virtue.[13] Second, Erikson's positive evaluation of religion must not be construed as a psychological defense of religion, as some students of religion, eager to legitimate their own field of study by way of psychological science, might think. For Erikson, is quite clear that religion is not an indispensable ingredient of psychological growth. While he definitely states that religion can serve a positive, psychological function, he is equally clear in asserting that other institutions can perform this function just as well.[14]

Erikson's psychology of religion differs from Freud's in still another important way. Does religion engage purely personal and psychological processes, or is it to be understood as a historical and institutional process, related to, but also separate from, the purely inner life of the individual? Freud's position on this issue is complex, and the extent to which his psychology of the unconscious was also a genuine social psychology has been subjected to extensive debate.[15] It is a well-known fact that Freud considered the family to be the basic human institution. His psychology is in this sense a "family psychology." The individual is understood entirely in terms of his family interactions, and the wider ranges of social and institutional life are substitutive elaborations of family dynamics. Hence, Freud's analyses of culture, tradition, civilization, and religion were all modeled upon his analysis of the family.

It can be argued with considerable success that because Freud's psychology is so oriented to the family, it presents an extremely subtle and intimate weaving together of person and society, and, further, that much of the power of his work lies in its delineation of this interaction. Society is "in" the individual from the very earliest moments of life. The ubiquitous presence of the superego, so knowledgeable about the ego's wishes, and so ready to criticize and limit it at so many points, testifies to this. In another sense, however, Freud's views are strangely ahistorical. He grudgingly concedes to history only the minimal amount of autonomy. His thought is lacking in sociological categories and, as he himself insisted, social psychology is only an extension of individual psychology.[16] For this reason religion could have little to do with historical institutions, separate from the mind of the individual.

While Erikson attempts to retain Freud's subtlety about the presence of familial sociality in individual life, he also builds this view into his own, wider concerns. Freud's emphasis upon the interplay between person and social order, cast at the level of Oedipal conflict, is retained by Erikson, although reformulated and embellished at the level of identity and ideology. Thus, institutions are independent of personal life, but at the same time they exercise perceivable effects upon the psychology of mental life. Ideology is to identity what the cultural superego was to the ego in Freud. And since religion takes the form of ideology, it is unmistakably historical.

ERIKSON'S UNDERSTANDING OF RELIGION

Erikson has not written a systematic statement of his psychological theory of religion. Instead, the theory emerges from psychohistorical observations on religious figures and from comments tangential to these observations. This is true even in the case of *Young Man Luther*, which is subtitled *A Study in Psychoanalysis and History*, but which nonetheless contains a great deal of psychological commentary on religion. This commentary is, however, both here and in other works, sufficiently sustained to make possible the construction of a coherent theory or understanding of religion.

Erikson makes three different types of reference to religion—that is, his many observations and comments fall into three different groupings. The most important of these is the epigenetic type of reference, already touched on above: religion is defined in terms of its effects upon the growth process. A second reference, one less frequently made and far more difficult to comprehend, but one that is easily as important as the first, is to "religious actuality." Religion is associated with the achievement by individuals of historical actuality, which Erikson sets at the opposite pole from psychological reality. A third reference, also infrequently made but also quite easy to grasp, describes religion as a form of nostalgia.

Of the three types of reference, the epigenetic definition of religion receives the most attention in Erikson's thought, and within this developmental framework religion is spoken of most of all in terms of the first stage of life, as trust, hope, and faith. Religion is experienced with great intensity during the earliest phase of growth, and it is mediated by the infant's mother in a form that enables him to adopt an attitude of trust in life.[17] Religion in this case is not of necessity regressive in a negative sense. It is, rather, a means of reaffirming, from time to time, resources derived from the earliest phase of life.

The second epigenetic reference to religion is made in the context of ideology and the associated developmental task of identity formation. At this point religion appears in a very different form and serves a very different function, although it is, finally, an elaboration of the first allusion. Religion as ideology refers, not to a global affective state, but to a system of discrete ideas about the nature and meaning of the contemporary world—ideas that serve to relate the individual in a positive way to the historical order, to the social and political institutions of history. Ideology is the institutional support for the formation of identity. In *Young Man Luther* Erikson gives special attention to the relation between the two:

> This being a historical book . . . religion will occupy our attention primarily as a source of ideologies for those who seek identities. . . .
>
> . . . In this book *ideology* will mean an unconscious tendency underlying religious and scientific as well as political thought: the tendency at a given time to make facts amenable to ideas, and ideas to facts, in order to create a world image convincing enough to support the collective and individual sense of identity. Far from being arbitrary or consciously manageable (although it is as exploitable as all of man's unconscious strivings), the total perspective created by ideological simplification reveals its strength by the dominance it exerts on the seeming logic of historical events, and by its influence on the identity formation of individuals (and thus on their "ego-strength"). In this sense this is a book on identity and ideology.[18]

Because of its rational and conceptual character, ideology is quite different from the predominantly emotional experience of trust. But the former is finally a continuation of the latter. Ideology provides a system of "good reasons" why the world should be invested with a positive attitude of trust rather than with suspicion and alienation. Thus it is simply the conceptual dimension of basic trust; or, to reverse the relation, basic trust is the affective dimension of ideology. Trust and ideology are the psychological infrastructures of faith and doctrine, respectively.

The epigenetic basis of religion is surprisingly symmetrical. Religion appears at the beginning of life, again midway through life, and at the last stage of life as well, where it appears in relation to the task of integrity. In this instance it provides the context for an experience of self-transcendence. Religion discloses to the finite ego-identity the existence of an ultimate reality that derives from beyond finite, conscious experience. The religious support for integrity engages a realm of knowledge and experience that lies beyond the immediacies of either primitive trust or more discerning ideology. Religion is a form of transcendence that is "existential" rather than social. "In the long run," Erikson says, "the 'I' transcends its over-defined ego." Remarking on the limits of Freud's view that the God-image really reflects an infantile image of the father, Erikson asserts that

> a community of I's may well be able to believe in a common fund of grace only to the extent that all acknowledge a super-I. This is a problem of such magnitude that mere intellectual denial hardly touches it.[19]

Belief in the existence of a "super-I" is surely a matter very different from both trust and ideology. Yet just as ideology was an elaboration of trust, this "existential" dimension is successor to both. For through the affirmation of a "super-I"—a commitment that requires both affective and cognitive assets—the individual becomes "trustworthy." That is to say, he becomes deserving of the trust of the young. And with this act the individual life cycle not only completes itself but also articulates the cycle of generations, completing it as well.

The life cycle is made up at every point of a double movement: there is a thrust outward into society and history, and then a movement backward—into selfhood, singularity, and separateness. The two movements achieve a special kind of balance in the stage of identity formation, and religion supports the life cycle, not only at this crucial stage or turning point, but also at the points that precede it and succeed it. But this epigenetic reference to religion, if left to itself, renders all understanding of the life process excessively abstract. Erikson has accordingly adopted an alternate way of describing the relation between the ego and history, especially at the stage of identity formation, which brings to the discussion a more subjective and experiential tone. He distinguishes between "psychological reality" and "historical actuality," and then concludes that there is something religious about historical actuality. Religious actuality thus constitutes his second major reference to religion.[20]

Psychological reality refers to an orientation of the mind that under any given set of circumstances searches for causes and effects. It is synonymous with Freud's conception of the reality principle and of reality testing, and with Heinz Hartmann's redefinition of the former as the capacity to take into account the real features of an object or a situation.[21] It is the instrumental attitude adopted by the ego in order to cope with the "here and now" of the everyday world. *Psychological reality* refers to what common sense has come to call "adjusting to reality." As such, it is the therapeutic goal and epistemological basis of classic psychoanalysis.

Erikson finds this view of reality narrow, constraining, and inaccurate, for it cannot account for the process of mutual activation whereby one person evokes in another—through intuition and active participation—that combination of autonomy and self-recognition that is the mark of a genuine sense of identity. Mutual activation is as much "a fact" as psychological reality, but it is also a process dependent upon a sense of self that is in turn rooted in the historical cycle of generations. Therefore Erikson juxtaposes to psychological reality the notion of historical actuality: to be real is also to be actual. Reality denotes perception based upon the discernment of causes; actuality connotes "the world verified in immediate immersion and interaction." Erikson summarizes this difficult but crucially important concept as follows:

> *Reality*, then . . . is the world of phenomenal experience, perceived with a minimum of distortion and with a maximum of customary validation agreed upon in a given state of technology and culture; while *actuality* is the world of participation, shared with other participants. . . .
> . . . *Mutual activation* is the crux of the matter; for human ego strength, while employing all means of testing reality, depends . . . upon a network of mutual influences within which the person actuates others even as he is actuated. . . . This is *ego actuality*.[22]

The distinction between psychological reality and historical actuality is neither merely a psychological distinction, nor is it restricted to the sphere of ethics alone; actuality is also a religious phenomenon. In *Gandhi's Truth*[23] Erikson describes Gandhi as a "religious actualist," and this discussion makes clear the bond that exists in Erikson's mind between religion and actuality. In suggesting that Gandhi was a religious actualist Erikson remarks that, in his "clinical ruminations," he had found it necessary to "split what we mean by 'real' into that which can be known because it is demonstrably correct (factual reality) and that which feels effectively true in action (actuality)." Gandhi, he continues, "absorbed from Indian culture a conception of truth (*sat*) which he attempted to make actual in all compartments of human life." In other words, Gandhi's religion provided him with the knowledge and ability to produce the "mutual maximization of a greater and higher unity among men," such that "each must begin to become actual by combining what is given in his individual development and in his historical time." This capacity to communicate a "sense of the actual" inevitably leads the creative individual into the role of religious innovation, because "his very passion and power will make him want to make actual for others what actualizes him. This means to create or recreate institutions."

Erikson does not address his psychological questions to the essential core of religious tradition, but instead reflects upon the psychological effects of religion. These reflections lead him to the conclusion that religion creates actuality, so described, or rather that religion produces actuality in the face of a situation that would otherwise be comprised entirely of "mere reality." Just as, in the case of Luther, Erikson sought the psychological infrastructure of identity and ideology beneath Luther's personal faith and his doctrine of justification by faith, so here Erikson seeks and finds actuality beneath the religious leadership and innovation of Gandhi.

It should be clear from this linkage between religion and actuality that the latter includes elements of trust, ideology, and transcendence, that it, in effect, welds these together. And it should be equally clear that actualism is inseparable from the formation, maintenance, and continuation of institutions. Here is further evidence of the centrality of institutions in Erikson's view of life and religion. Actualism, as the essence of human interaction, cannot take place outside of an institutional process, for it constitutes the need for institutions, just as institutions make it possible. The point raises once again the question of the necessity of religion for psychosocial health (actuality). Erikson is clearly ambiguous on this issue. On the one hand, he is taken by the power of religious images (such as those provided by the Hindu life cycle) to construct actuality: "We deny the remnants of old-world images at our own risk. . . . They are not less powerful for being denied."[24] Yet at the same time he insists that, while religions have in the past been the most reliable sources of trust, ideology, and integrity, the modern person may well choose a different mode of access to these processes, so necessary for effective and relatively stressfree living.

The epigenetic principle and the distinction between reality and actuality provide the major references for Erikson's psychological interpretation of religion. However, there is a third approach to religion that, although extremely important, lucid, and informative, is often overlooked because it is so infrequently mentioned. This is the "definition" of religion as nostalgia, a hearkening back, on the part of the individual, to the earliest, most powerful, and impressive experiences in the life cycle. In speaking of religion in this way Erikson once again demonstrates his unique relation to Freud, in which he affirms Freud's assertions, while at the same time giving these affirmations an entirely unique cast. For the process of hearkening back is clearly found in Freud,[25] and the objects for which the individual yearns are clearly infantile; yet, in Erikson's hands, nostalgia is transformed into both a positive and uniquely human activity. In the conclusion to his study of Luther, Erikson reflects upon the nature of religion:

> One may say that man, when looking through a glass darkly, finds himself in an inner cosmos in which the outlines of three objects awaken dim nostalgias. One of these is the simple and fervent wish for a . . . sense of unity with a maternal matrix . . . it is symbolized by the affirmative face of charity . . . reassuring the faithful of the unconditional acceptance. . . .
>
> . . . In the center of the second nostalgia is the paternal voice of guiding conscience, which puts an end to the simple paradise of childhood and provides a sanction for energetic action. . . .
>
> . . . Finally, the glass shows the pure self itself, the unborn core of creation. . . . This pure self is . . . not dependent on providers, and not dependent on guides to reason and reality.[26]

These three "images" Erikson calls "the main religious objects." While this reference to religion may seem different from the other two, it is in fact quite consistent with them. The maternal matrix is the source of trust; the paternal voice is the source of ruling ideas and ideology; and the pure self is the seat of self-transcendence through which the person "comes to himself," free from bondage to both maternal and paternal figures. And actuality, it would seem, is a mode of relation to self and others in which one has creatively integrated, at the level of history, the presence of providers and guides.

ERIKSON'S PSYCHOLOGY AND CONTEMPORARY THEORIES OF RELIGION

Erikson's psychology stands on its own merits as a creative reinterpretation of Freud and of the psychoanalytic theory of religion. Still, much is lost if it is considered in isolation from other systematic attempts to define the nature of religion in contemporary life. On the one hand, Erikson's thought has much in common with current efforts to interpret the nature of religion, and, on the other hand, his psychology offers considerable clarification to the current scene in religious thought. Contemporary theories of religion are in conflict with one another, and there is little interplay or communication between representatives of these theories. Furthermore, situating Erikson's theory of religion in relation to contemporary thought will not only clarify to a considerable extent the several paradoxes, mentioned at the beginning of this essay, that have beset the psychoanalytic study of religion, but will also shed light upon his positive estimate of Protestantism.

Erikson's psychology is above all else a theory of modernity—that is, a theory of how the modern person can live in the modern world. It is therefore best to discuss his thought in relation to those theories of religion that take as their central task the relation of religion to the modern world. While this means the elimination of many historical works on religion, it nevertheless includes much of contemporary religious thought, for modernity—or contemporaneity or secularity—comprises the single great preoccupation of religious scholars.

While schemas or frameworks tend to be oversimplifications, nevertheless they can also help to bring some order and systematization to the flux of religious scholarship. It it possible to break down contemporary theories of religion into three groups, both in terms of their distinctive conceptual style, as well as in terms of the dimensions of religion that they seek to illumine and clarify. In the first group belong theological-philosophical studies that focus upon the ontological and epistemological aspects of religion. These interpret religion as transcendence. A second group is composed of sociological studies that focus upon the nature of order, defining religion in terms of its capacity to confer order, primarily social order, upon life as a whole. In the third group belong psychological studies that focus upon religion as spontaneity.[27] While each type of discussion includes reference to all three dimensions of religion—for example, the discussions of religion as transcendence include reference to its ordering capacities and to its spontaneous character—these three types of discussion of religion are for the most part unrelated to each other, which is a central problem in religious scholarship. Much of the meaning and appeal of Erikson's psychology lies in the fact that his psychology articulates all three types or genres of religious thought, and in so doing, unites through psychology what remains divided by these genres.

Quite possibly the most fundamental division in contemporary religious thought lies between those who view religion as a sui generis phenomenon given to men from beyond their existing knowledge about themselves and their world, and those who view it as a projection of some infrastructure, either sociological or developmental, which is then said to be experienced "as if" it existed beyond history and consciousness. "Transcendence" is no doubt the most time-honored term in contemporary religious thought and represents the first view. It is certainly the most visible term that traditional religion has bequeathed to the world of modern religious thought.

Transcendence takes its most typical form as the reality of a God whose existence is believed to lie beyond the realm of finite conscious self-awareness. Most representative of this tradition are the writings of such figures as Paul Tillich, Martin Buber, Reinhold Niebuhr, and Rudolph Bultmann.[28] Each in his own way attempted to establish an anaylsis of the human self in relation to orders of reality that are immanental—that is, accessible to human reason—and then in relation to an order of reality that transcends what is immanental. Put another way, these writers are theological existentialists, and the order of reality they seek to describe is "existential." Erikson's work articulates this tradition, for it speaks of religion as transcendence, and it displays, at certain points, an existentialist turn all its own.

Erikson's likeness to this tradition can easily be illustrated by juxtaposing it to a portion of the work of Paul Tillich, the existentialist theologian who, more than any other, has attempted to relate the view of religion as transcendence to depth psychology. One of Tillich's most well-read books is also his most psychological—*The Courage To Be*. Toward the end of the book Tillich attempts to explain his understanding of the transcendence of God. He refers to two views of God, calling one "the God of theological theism" and the other "the God above God," arguing that the first is in effect a false god, one that has to give way, under the impact of his analysis, to the second. Tillich writes:

> The God of theological theism is a being beside others. . . . He is seen as a self which has a world, as a cause which is separated from its effect. . . . He is a being, not being itself. . . . As such we are objects for him as subjects. . . . God as a subject makes me into an object which is nothing more than an object. . . . God appears as the invincible tyrant . . . equated with the recent tyrants who with the help of terror try to transform everything into a mere object. . . . This is the God Nietzsche said had to be killed.[29]

Theological theism, as Tillich describes it, embodies a concept of God identical to the ruthless, authoritarian, patriarchal father-god so heavily criticized by Freud. For this reason this image of God is a projection of the Oedipal conflict. Or, to put the matter in more technical, psychological language, this God is a "super-ego" God. Therefore Tillich in effect, tells us that the God of theological theism, the God-image rooted in the superego of man, must be transcended or overcome. The God of theological theism must give way to the God above God—that is, to a God whose reality transcends the projections of the superego.[30]

Erikson's psychology articulates this analysis of transcendence, which is both theological and implicitly psychological. He would agree with the position set forth in this discussion of Tillich—namely, that the superego of man, as a source of imagery for the God of theological theism, must be transcended. However, Erikson introduces into his psychological system the equivalent of the transcendence of the superego in the form of the stage of identity. For identity is defined as a stage of growth that lies beyond the formation of the superego. The formation of the superego is the Freudian description of the structural formation of the person, but for Erikson development must, so to speak, pass beyond the phase of the superego. Identity is therefore Erikson's word for transcendence, although he does not, of course, indicate that this is the case.

So it is no surprise to find Erikson speaking of religion as a "super-I," (an "I" that transcends the superego) nor is it incorrect to ascribe to such references an existentialist meaning. Identity does indeed "transcend" the superego and theological theism. Therefore the concept of identity, although it is defined as a psychological concept, does have a religious aspect. Little wonder, too, that Erikson should turn his psychological perspective upon Martin Luther, the theological inspiration for the view of religion as transcendence that Tillich proposes. It makes good sense that Erikson should "see" identity in Luther's life, for that life displays a successful struggle against the cruel moralism of the superego.

The existentialist approach is by no means the only or primary way in which contemporary thought seeks to conceptualize religion. A second orientation speaks of religion in terms of its ordering functions and is associated with the rise of the social sciences and with their prestige. Like the theological view, this approach views religious reality as a reality beyond finite, human consciousness. But it does not engage the truth claims of this reality. Instead, it brackets this question by asserting that religion is a projection of immanental social forces arising from the matrix of social and historical interaction. And in lieu of a discussion of the transcendental character of religion, it seeks instead to analyze the structure of religion in terms of its order-conferring capacities. In this view religion is both a means whereby men bond themselves together into social community and a symbolic system by which they endow these bonds with meaning and plausibility.

Quite properly, then, this second view of religion is associated with the sociology of religion and social anthropology.[31] While there are many differences between their respective approaches, I take the work of social scientists like Clifford Geertz, Victor Turner and Peter Berger to be representative of this genre of discussion. Geertz speaks of religion as a system of sacred symbols that have the function of synthesizing "ethos" and "world-view."[32] *Ethos* refers to the style and mood of everyday life that men in a similar culture share, and *world view* refers to "their most comprehensive ideas of order." Religion projects a system of images composing a cosmic order that unites ethos and world view by rendering the ideas of order emotionally convincing.

Geertz is primarily concerned with the social cohesiveness of a culture, whereas Turner is concerned not only with solidarity—what he calls "structure"—but with the way in which people from time to time break away from massive cohesiveness and form communities characterized by immediacy and spontaneity—what he calls "liminality" and "communitas."[33] Turner is concerned with the fact "that there is a generic bond between men" and with the "related sentiment of 'human kindness.'" This bond is a product of men in their wholeness. It is also a product of the tension between structure and liminality, and this tension "generates myths, symbols, rituals, philosophical systems, and works of art."

Of these three social scientists, Berger is the one whose work best illustrates the primacy of order as the definitive characteristic of religion. Religion is always an interpretation of reality, and for Berger the reality of the everyday, work-a-day world of the "here and now" is the paramount reality of life. This reality is experienced as massive and inexorable. It forces the individual to give his attention entirely and wholly to it. However, the reality of everyday life is paradoxical: on the one hand, it has its origins in a projection of a social infrastructure, and on the other hand, it is experienced as entirely compelling and objective. It provides roles, values, and norms for members of society. That is to say, it acquires the appearance of being sui generis, detached from its origins in social projection, and for this reason constitutes the most fundamental source of order. This "objective reality" therefore also serves to structure and order subjective reality—the world of psychological inwardness, of personal identity—through the double process of primary and secondary socialization. Religion occupies a crucial place in the formation of both the objective and subjective aspects of social reality. Religion consists of a symbolic universe that orders everyday reality, giving it objective form and subjective plausibility. In this way, religion functions to order the objective and subjective reality of everyday life.[34]

Erikson relates religion as transcendence to the epigenetic stage of integrity, through belief in a "super-I" and through the stage of identity that transcends the superego. But these discussions hardly exhaust his analyses of religion. He also speaks of religion as order, through his understanding of religion as ideology, and this view closely resembles Berger's understanding of religion as a symbolic universe. By making facts amenable to ideas, ideology relates the "facts" of everyday life to the "ideas" of a symbolic universe. Like ideology, a symbolic universe creates a world image that underlies scientific and political thought. And, of course, both ideology and the order created by a symbolic universe structure personal identity.

Erikson's concept of religion as actuality bears a striking resemblance to Turner's concept of liminality as "existential communitas," for both stress the immediacy and directness —Erikson through "activation," Turner through "spontaneity"—of social interrelations that undercut the conventional orderings of established social structures. And Erikson would agree with Geertz that an essential function of religion as ideology consists in its creating certitude and emotional plausibility in the mind of its adherents. In all this, religion bonds people together and then endows this sociality with an overarching sense of order.

Transcendence and order are no doubt major concepts through which contemporary thought has sought to conceptualize and explain the nature of religion, and Erikson's thought clearly articulates both at crucial points. A third way of talking about religion, or genre of religious thought, speaks of religion as spontaneity. In this case the focus is not upon the epistemological and ontological aspects of a realm of existence transcending human history, nor is it upon roles, values, and norms that are mediated through the social order. Instead, religion is understood primarily in terms of affectivity and emotion expressing the spontaneous immediacy of personal consciousness. Religion is a highly experiential range of significant feeling states encompassing many major moods of life: feelings of joy, peace, and devotion; of guilt, loyalty, and obligation; of mystery, wonder, and surrender. Insofar as it is true that religion as transcendence is associated with the discipline of theology, and religion as order with sociology, it is probably correct to say that religion as spontaneity is linked with the psychology of religion.

Psychologists' theories of religion differ because their psychologies are different. But the works of many of the originative and formative psychologists on religion show considerable unanimity when they are considered in terms of the dimension of spontaneity. William James was concerned with what he called the inner experiences of individual great-souled men. His psychological framework sought to capture such illusive facets of spontaneity as: immediate luminousness, immediate assurance, the habitual center of personal energy, the hot place of a man's consciousness, the sense of something wrong, the ineffable.[35] While Freud's negative epistemology of religion linked it with such vicissitudes of desire as guilt and loss of self-regard, he also spoke of "the ultimate source of religious sentiments" as an "oceanic feeling," a "primary ego feeling of something limitless, unbounded, a feeling of oneness."[36]

Jung emphasized the factor of spontaneity in religion perhaps more strongly than any other psychologist. According to him, religion was exactly this: a spontaneous or natural emergence of transpersonal, archetypal material producing powerful affects of far-ranging consequence for the aims of all mental development. Theological discussions of Jung have emphasized the archetypal nature of religion, because they are themselves oriented toward religion as transcendence.[37] But Jung also spoke of the centrality of libido and the flow of energy in his psychological analysis of religion.[38] More recently, Abraham Maslow has defined religion as the basic, inner core of all experience, the full coming into awareness of the expressive powers of the self. Religion is a "peak experience," a private, ecstatic revelation, detached from institutions and theology.[39] The suggestion that in all these instances religion is associated with spontaniety does not exclude the presence of transcendence or order. But it does mean that spontaneity is the dominant mode by which religion is defined, and that if elements of transcendence and order do appear in these psychological discussions of religion, they do so as objectifications and organizations of the spontaneous in religious experience.

It is testimony to the breadth and inclusiveness of Erikson's work that a discussion of religion could dwell so long on such nonpsychological factors as transcendence and order, before necessarily turning to the more evidently psychological process of spontaneity. Erikson does, like other psychologists, speak of religion in this way. Religion is comprised not only of integrity (transcendence), or of ideology (order), but also of trust, hope, and faith. In fact, of these three epigenetic references to religion, the view of religion as grounded in trust and hope is primary. Erikson underscores again and again the view that, whatever else it is, religion is, at its best, a sense of basic trust—by which he means the spontaneous and immediate sense of givenness and worthwhileness of life. And both nostalgia and actualism contain elements of spontaneity.

Despite the enormous differences in conceptual system and historical background between Erikson and James, the former would approve of the latter's emphasis upon a personal sense of "immediate assurance" as a fruit of religion. For James the capacity to trust is the result of a conversion experience, whereas for Erikson it is the first acquisition of life, and, if released through a conversion experience, then that experience is a working through of the cruelty of the moralistic superego. Jung's discussion of libido and energy must not be taken in a mechanistic sense, for Jung joined these to notions of "value" and "will," and thereby to the process of finding meaning. But while the thrust of the individuation process is a coming to terms with the meaning of one's own life, it must be emphasized that the problem of self-regard or self-esteem is central to successful growth. Jung's references to "inflation," for example, can be taken as references to a sense of "false esteem" or "false trust," and the archetype of the self, which guides the individuation process is, like basic trust, essential for the growth process at its inception. Erikson would surely disagree with Maslow's insistence that religious experience occurs apart from institutions and ideology, but the experience of self-actualization, which is so fundamental to religious experience, and which derives from an inner core of personal being preceding socialization, has a strong element of esteem, and, in this, contains parallels to the concept of basic trust.

Transcendence, order, and spontaneity represent three orientations within contemporary thought, each of which attempts to understand the nature of religion in a particular way. They are distinct and self-defining, which is to say that those who support a particular orientation find in it sufficient reason not to explore either of the other two. If anything, adherents to one orientation usually interpret the other in terms of their prior commitments.[40] Consequently, these are not discussed in any unified or integrated fashion. On the contrary, they constitute elements in an intellectually pluralized situation. Erikson's work, however, extends into all three dimensions or ways of speaking about religion. Because the life cycle is from the beginning recognized as a simple whole, and because the three dimensions all interlock with different phases of the life cycle, these dimensions are unified through Erikson's work. For this reason his writings will appeal most to people who are exposed to more than one of these orientations to religion (such as those with an interdisciplinary approach to religion) and will be least attractive to those firmly anchored in only one orientation (for example, theologians and classic psychoanalysts).

The psychoanalytic study of religion has been paradoxical, in that it has combined great interest in religion with intense criticism of it. In a superficial sense Erikson follows this pattern: he belongs to the Freudian tradition, and it is not a coincidence that his two major historical studies have been on religious figures. However, in his hands the critical, negative thrust of psychoanalysis has become appreciative and positive.

The way in which Erikson has reduced the conflict between classic psychoanalysis and religion can be seen by reviewing his treatment of Protestantism at two key points, those of identity and ideology. Erikson has created a psychological point of view that, while it begins with a Freudian base, not only interprets the Protestant tradition, but also includes an element of that same tradition that he interprets. Thus, the concept of identity is not only a developmental transformation of the Freudian concept of the superego; it also bears an important resemblance to the Protestant conception of self-transcendence. In this, Erikson's approach to religion consists of a double movement of reduction and affirmation. He reduces Protestantism by interpreting its developmental infrastructure. But then he affiirms an aspect of Protestantism that, if purified by this interpretive analysis, persists in the form of an identity-inducing process. It is probably more correct to say that the concept of identity is a psychological construct used to interpret religion, but that it also contains some residual, religious coloration.

This double movement also holds true for the related Eriksonian concept of ideology. On the one hand, Erikson reductively interprets Luther's theology as ideology. Luther would not accept the view—nor do Lutherans or Protestants accept the view—that theology is "really" ideology. On the other hand, Erikson also affirms theology, for ideology is said to be a necessary ingredient in the formation of a stable identity. While it can be argued that incorporating an aspect of religion into a psychological system only complicates further the critical task of specifying the components of a psychological interpretation of religion, this analysis does explain how Erikson succeeds in transforming the psychoanalytic criticism of religion into a "higher" and "positive" interpretation of it.

CONCLUSION: THE PERSISTENCE OF THE PROBLEM OF PROJECTION IN ERIKSON'S THOUGHT

While it is correct at one level—at the level of content—to group contemporary thought on religion into three orientations, these can in fact be reduced to two—at the level of presuppositions. The most fundamental division in contemporary thought about religion lies between the view of religion as a sui generis phenomenon given to men from beyond their existing knowledge and the view of religion as the projection of some infrastructure. From this more fundamental, presuppositional point of view religion as order and religion as spontaneity—that is, the sociological and psychological approaches to religion—are both based upon the assumption of projection, whereas the view of religion as transcendence completely disavows the projective hypothesis.

This hypothesis stipulates that religious phenomena are experienced by the believer "as if" they were completely real and completely independent of him, although from the interpreter's point of view their meaning lies as much in their origin as in their experiential convincingness. The projective argument was articulated most cogently by Feuerbach and Marx, and later by Freud. It receives a powerful contemporary restatement in the writings of Berger and Luckmann. The above discussions of Erikson's psychology have for the most part dwelt upon his innovative transformation of Freud, and have neglected the extent to which, despite its innovations, it remains within the epistemological confines of the psychoanalytic tradition.

Erikson speaks of religion as transcendence, and in doing so he joins the theologians in emphasizing the sui generis nature of religious reality. And his discussions of ideology also emphasize its sui generis nature and are remarkably free from sociological reductionism. But beneath these trends lies a more fundamental commitment to the view of religion as projection:

> Man's creation of all-caring gods is not only an expression of his persisting infantile need for being taken care of, but also a projection onto a super-human agency of an ego-ideal.[41]

> Religions offer the adolescent . . . rites and rituals of confirmation as a member of a totem, clan or a faith, a nation or a class, which henceforth is to be his super-family.[42]

> If I assume that it is the smiling face and the guiding voice of infantile parent images which religion projects onto the benevolent sky, I have no apologies to render to an age which thinks of painting the moon red. Peace comes from the inner space.[43]

It should be noted that, in viewing religion as a projection of a developmental infrastructure, Erikson is assigning to it a positive, not a negative significance. To put the matter bluntly, religion is a "good projection." But this valuation of religion does not cancel out its fundamentally projective character, nor does it obviate the problems that ensue whenever the projective view is employed. For Erikson only stipulates its positive nature.

In this omission, Erikson jeopardizes his entire psychological theory of religion. All that he says—in terms of transcendence and integrity and in terms of order and ideology—rests upon the projective hypothesis. The view of religion as transcendence is an expression of the question of whether the projection is real and true. Erikson stipulates that this is so, but offers no discussion or evidence. The view of religion as order is the question of the nature of the structure of the projection. Erikson offers ideology as an answer, but tells us only that ideology is developmentally necessary and leaves open such questions as what in an ideology is convincing and plausible and whether some ideologies are truer than others, or, if truth is not the criterion, then whether some ideologies are better than others. These questions of transcendence and order are related to the problem of spontaneity, the problem of the origin of the projection—how it was created. Erikson does little more than identify its epigenetic rootage, stipulating its moral rightness and epistemological validity.

The problem of projection is the most fundamental problem in the classic social scientific approaches to religion. As such, it is a key question in modernity's attempt to come to terms with the possibility of retrieving religious meaning from the past for the contemporary world. It is a problem that receives little or no attention in the psychological sciences. The persistence of this problem in Erikson's psychology signifies a fundamental indebtedness to these modalities of thought.

NOTES

1. Freud's theory of development is referred to throughout his writings and at many specific points as well. One of the best fundamental elucidations of it is found in Sigmund Freud, *A General Introduction to Psychoanalysis*, trans. Joan Rivière (New York: Washington Square Press, 1952). Erikson's theory of epigenesis is well stated in Erik H. Erikson, *Childhood and Society*, 2d ed. (New York: W. W. Norton & Co., 1963), chap. 7, entitled "Eight Ages of Man;" a longer elaboration of it occurs in idem, *Identity and the Life Cycle: Selected Papers*, Psychological Issues, vol. 1, no. 1 (New York: International Universities Press, 1959), chap. 2, entitled "Growth and Crises of the Healthy Personality." This second source also contains a discussion of the relation of Freud's and Erikson's psychologies by David Rapaport, entitled "A Historical Survey of Psychoanalytic Ego Psychology." A later version of the epigenetic theory appears as chap. 3 of Erik H. Erikson, *Identity: Youth and Crisis* (New York: W. W. Norton & Co., 1968).

2. This point is brought out with special clarity in Sigmund Freud, *The Ego and the Id*, ed. James Strachey, trans. Joan Rivière (New York: W. W. Norton & Co., 1960).

3. Freud's theory of the family can be found in Sigmund Freud, *Group Psychology and the Analysis of the Ego*, trans. James Strachey (New York: Bantam Books, 1960); and in idem, *Civilization and Its Discontents*, trans. Joan Rivière (New York: Doubleday Anchor, 1958).

4. This viewpoint of Freud's is expressed in Sigmund Freud, "A Philos-

ophy of Life," in *New Introductory Lectures on Psychoanalysis*, trans. W. J. H. Sprott (New York: W. W. Norton & Co., 1933).

5. Sigmund Freud, "Obsessive Acts and Religious Practices," *Collected Papers of Sigmund Freud*, ed. Ernest Jones, trans. Joan Rivière, 5 vols. (New York: Basic Books, 1959), 2: 25–35.

6. Sigmund Freud, *Totem and Taboo*, trans. James Strachey (New York: W. W. Norton & Co., 1950).

7. Sigmund Freud, *The Future of an Illusion*, ed. James Strachey, trans. W. D. Robson-Scott (New York: Doubleday Anchor, 1957).

8. Sigmund Freud, *Moses and Monotheism*, trans. Katherine Jones (New York: Vintage Books, 1955).

9. See Freud, *Civilization and Its Discontents*.

10. See Freud, *Totem and Taboo*.

11. References for these allusions to religion are found in the third section of this paper, entitled Erikson's Understanding of Religion.

12. See, for example, Erikson's discussion of "negative conscience" in Luther's life. In it Erikson identifies a morbid sense of sin with an excessively dominant superego. Erik H. Erikson, *Young Man Luther: A Study in Psychoanalysis and History* (New York: W. W. Norton & Co., 1958), pp. 214–16.

13. See the distinction between morality, associated with the superego, and virtue, associated with the ego, in Erik H. Erikson, "Human Strength and the Cycle of Generations," in *Insight and Responsibility* (New York: W. W. Norton and Co., 1964), esp. pp. 149–50.

14. Erikson remarks: "When religion loses its actual power of presence, then, it would seem, an age must find other forms of joint reverence for life which derive vitality from a shared world image." Erikson. *Identity: Youth and Crisis*, p. 106. See also Erikson, *Identity and the Life Cycle*, p. 65.

15. For a strong criticism of Freud, arguing that his psychology is excessively individualistic, see Philip Rieff, *Freud: The Mind of the Moralist* (New York: Viking Press, 1959). For a discussion of psychoanalysis as congenial to social and historical analysis, see Fred Weinstein and Gerald M. Platt, *Psychoanalytic Sociology* (Baltimore: Johns Hopkins University Press, 1973).

16. See Freud, *Group Psychology*, p. 71, where Freud writes: "There must therefore be a possibility of transforming group psychology into individual psychology."

17. Erikson, see esp. *Identity and the Life Cycle*, p. 65; idem, *Childhood and Society*, p. 250; and idem, *Identity: Youth and Crisis*, p. 83.

18. Erikson, *Young Man Luther*, p. 22. For further discussion of the meaning of ideology for Erikson, see Erikson, *Identity and the Life Cycle*, pp. 142, 157.

19. Erik H. Erikson, "Autobiographic Notes on the Identity Crisis," *Daedalus* 99, no. 4 (Fall 1970): 757–8. See also idem, *Identity: Youth and Crisis*, p. 220.

20. The following discussion is drawn from Erikson, "Psychological Reality and Historical Actuality," in *Insight and Responsibility*, pp. 162–66.

21. Erikson briefly summarizes Hartmann's views and criticizes them for being "Cartesian." Erikson, *Insight and Responsibility*, p. 163.

22. Ibid., pp. 164–65.

23. Erik Erikson, *Gandhi's Truth: On the Origins of Militant Nonviolence* (New York: W. W. Norton & Co., 1969). This discussion of religious actuality is drawn from pp. 396–400.

24. Ibid., p. 39.

25. Erikson's references to nostalgia are reminiscent of Freud's discussions of "longing" in Sigmund Freud, *The Problem of Anxiety*, trans. Henry A. Bunker (New York: W. W. Norton & Co., 1936).

26. Erikson, *Young Man Luther*, pp. 263–64.

27. For a more detailed discussion of these three categories as a way of analyzing contemporary thought on religion, see Peter Homans, "The Persistence of Religion and its Effects upon Psychology," *Man, Religion and Freedom*, ed. Robert Choquette (Ottawa: University of Ottawa Press, 1974).

28. For a review of this genre of theological thought, see John B. Cobb, Jr., *Living Options in Protestant Theology* (Philadelphia: Westminster Press, 1962). For a recent and more critical theological discussion of this style of thinking, see David Tracy, *Blessed Rage for Order* (New York: Seabury Press, 1975), pp. 27–30.

29. Paul Tillich, *The Courage to Be* (New Haven: Yale University Press, 1952), pp. 184–85.

30. For a thorough analysis of the implicit psychological meaning of Tillich's theological thought and a criticism of his thought from a psychological point of view, see Peter Homans, *Theology After Freud: An Interpretive Inquiry* (Indianapolis: Bobbs-Merrill, 1970), pp. 79–90.

31. For a discussion of some of the basic materials in sociology that take this point of view, see Robert A. Nisbet, *The Socilolgical Tradition* (New York: Basic Books, 1966), chap. 6, entitled "The Sacred." For a discussion of existentialist theology from the point of view of the sociology of knowledge, and therefore from the point of view of the projective argument, see Peter Berger, "A Sociological View of the Secularization of Theology," *Journal for the Scientific Study of Religion* 6, no. 1 (Spring 1967): 3–16. For a theologically oriented discussion of the projective argument, see John Bowker, *The Sense of God: Sociological, Anthropological, and Psychological Approaches to the Origin of the Sense of God* (Oxford: Clarendon Press, 1973).

32. Clifford Geertz, "Religion as a Cultural System," in *The Interpretation of Cultures* (New York: Basic Books, 1973), pp. 87–125.

33. Victor W. Turner, "Liminality and Communitas," in *The Ritual Process: Structure and Anti-Structure* (Chicago: Aldine Publishing Company, 1969), pp. 94–130.

34. Peter L. Berger and Thomas Luckmann, *The Social Construction of Reality* (New York: Doubleday & Co., 1967).

35. William James, *The Varieties of Religious Experience* (New York: Modern Library, n.d.).

36. Freud, *Civilization and Its Discontents*, esp. pp. 1–6.

37. A rich theological literature exists on Jung, all of it ahistorical and a-sociological. See, for example, Victor White, *God and the Unconscious* (London: Harvill Press, 1952). For a critical review of this literature that

takes a more psychobiographical point of view, see Peter Homans, "Psychology and Hermeneutics: Jung's Contribution," *Zygon: Journal of Religion and Science* 4, no. 4 (December 1969): 333–55.

38. The best discussion of Jung's theory of religion in the light of his analytical psychology remains C. G. Jung, *Two Essays on Analytical Psychology*, trans. R. F. Hull (New York: Meridian Books, 1956). For references to energy and libido see pp. 72–73.

39. Abraham H. Maslow, *Religions, Values, and Peak Experiences* (Columbus: Ohio State University Press, 1964).

40. Thus, for example, Tillich interprets Freud and Marx; Turner interprets Buber, and, by implication, religious existentialism; Berger interprets neo-orthodox theology and psychoanalysis; James interprets the over-beliefs of theology; Jung interprets not only Catholicism and Protestantism, but also psychoanalysis; Maslow interprets theologies, church-related experiences, behaviorism, and parts of Freudianism.

41. Erikson, "Human Strength and the Cycle of Generations," in *Insight and Responsibility*, p. 132.

42. Ibid., p. 125.

43. Erikson, *Young Man Luther*, pp. 265–66.

7

Erikson and the Search for a Normative Image of Man

DON BROWNING

It is frequently overlooked that Erikson's psychology contains a normative image of man—an image of what man *should* be like in the context of Western technological society. Elsewhere I have referred to this image with the phrase *generative man*.[1] In this essay I will set forth Erikson's image of man and attempt to clarify its significance by discussing it in the context of other important social scientific efforts to determine who Americans *are* becoming and who they *should* become.

Modern Western societies are undergoing rapid social change. This condition of social unsettledness partially explains the difficulty of finding answers to either of two questions: (1) What kind of people are we becoming? and (2) What kind of people should we become? Certainly, the first of these two questions has received the most attention in recent years. The prestige of the social sciences has created a climate that favors the investigation of empirical questions. However, Erikson's psychology is somewhat distinctive in that in it he tries to answer both of these questions. For this reason, his work encompasses the attitudes of both the descriptive scientist and the constructive ethicist. Erikson has much to say about the kinds of character types modern societies have produced; he also has much to say about the kinds of character types we must become in order to survive the challenges of modernity.

Much of Erikson's writings constitute a contribution to recent social scientific efforts to discern the modal personality or basic character type that is emerging in American society. When Erikson is writing as a social scientist, his work has similarities to that of Erich Fromm, David Riesman, Philip Rieff, and Robert Lifton. When Erikson is discussing such concepts as *identity diffusion* and *totalism*, he is attempting to describe certain basic trends in the American character (especially that of its youth) in a way very similar in intent to Fromm's concept of the *marketing personality*, Riesman's concept of *other-directedness*, Rieff's concept of *psychological man*, and Lifton's concept of *Protean man*. When Erikson begins developing his normative image of man (his concept of *generative man*) his work clearly takes on the marks of a moral psychology. Here his work can be profitably compared and contrasted to such diverse traditions as William James's concept of the *strenuous life*, Norman Brown's concept of *Dionysian man*, and Erich Fromm's idea of *productive man*. At this level, his writings assume an ethical and even religious tone. He does not merely attempt to answer the question, Who is the good man? He also offers the outlines for a supporting ideology or *Weltanschauung* that hovers on the borderline between philosophy and religion.

WHAT'S HAPPENING TO AMERICANS?

A good deal of research into the American character has taken as its point of reference the hypothesis put forth by Max Weber in his famous *Protestant Ethic and the Spirit of Capitalism.*[2] Weber argued that Luther's doctrine of vocation and Calvin's doctrine of predestination combined to exert a powerful influence on the character structure of people living in Protestant, especially Calvinistic, countries. These two concepts help produce a person highly dedicated to his secular profession or calling (Beruf).[3] At the same time, these concepts produce a person who comes to interpret a lifetime of worldly success as a sign that God had elected him for salvation.[4] This combination of ideas motivated individuals in Protestant countries to rationalize and systematize their energies into a lifetime of highly methodical and ascetic economic activity in an effort to create wealth—not for the sake of enjoyment but for its value as a sign of salvation. Therefore, the Protestant ethic hypothesis is really a hypothesis about the Protestant personality type. It points toward an ideal Protestant man who was motivated by guilt and anxiety over his salvation to lead a highly disciplined, methodical, and ascetic life in an effort to gain wealth that he in turn would not permit hmself to enjoy. Because of the number of Calvinistic sects in the United States, Weber believed that this country constituted a clear exemplification of the attitude of worldly asceticism and the personality type that embodied the Protestant ethic.

Much of the recent research into the question of the American character has argued that the Protestant character type is for all practcal purposes dead. This is certainly the import of the work of Erich Fromm. Fromm synthesized Weber's Protestant ethic hypothesis with Freud's psychosexual theory of characterology. Fromm's concept of the *hoarding personality* is roughly analogous to Weber's characterization of the prototypical Protestant man. Fromm argued, however, that under the impact of corporate capitalism, the hoardng personality has been replaced by the *marketing personality*.[5] Modern man has now succumbed to the demands of the corporation and to the abstract principles of production, management, and marketability: he thinks of himself as merchandise to be bought and sold to the highest corporate bidder. He tailors his personalty to fit the needs of the corporate marketplace. He has, according to Fromm, become estranged from his own center of productive power. He sees himself as a commodity to be consumed (bought and sold), and understands his primary goal in life to be the consumption of other objects such as "sights, food, drinks, cigarettes, people, lectures, books, movies—all are consumed, swallowed."[6]

A similar thesis was developed by Davd Riesman in *The Lonely Crowd*.[7] Inspired to a considerable extent by the work of Fromm, Riesman developed a typology of social character that introduced his now-famous distinction among the tradition-directed man, the inner-directed man, and the other-directed man. His concept of the inner-directed man is roughly analogous to Weber's image of the Protestant man and Fromm's concept of the hoarding personality; his concept of the other-directed person is quite similar to Fromm's portrait of the marketing personality. Riesman, like Fromm, believes that there has been a shift from the inner-directed, disciplined, and ascetic character type spawned by the Protestant ethic to an other-directed type who finds his direction not from himself or from tradition but from his contemporaries, his peer groups, the mass media, and the marketplace.[8] Riesman sees emerging a new kind of individual with a "mobile sensibility" to the myriad of clues from his external social environment and with no firm sense of his own internal self-direction.

Erikson's writings on the concepts of identity, identity-confusion, and totalism take on heightened significance when placed in the context of this tradition of inquiry. Fromm was primarily concerned to show the effects of changing patterns of work (especially the shift from family capitalism to corporate capitalsm) on the Amercan character. Riesman broadened his inquiry and concentrated on the generalized effects of the shift from a production-oriented society to a consumption-oriented society. In addition to vocational patterns, he analyzed the general impact of this shift on friendship patterns, mass media, and politics in an effort to determine how they mediated this change to the phenomenon of social character. Erikson broadened his inquiry even further. Erikson was not concerned to investigate the effects on character and identity of specific patterns of social change in the realms of vocation, personal relations, and communication media. Rather, Erikson became preoccupied with the effects of change itself. He was concerned to study the characterological effects of change resulting from a variety of factors, but most specifically that change produced by a cultural vision that believed that uncontrolled laissez-faire economic and technologcal expansion would somehow bring about the good life. Therefore, Erikson was an early student of the phenomenon that we have recently learned to call "future shock."[9] However, the importance of his contribution lies not only in his identification of the phenomenon, but also in his development of a vocabulary and conceptuality that has broadened the explanatory powers of psychoanalysis to take account of this developing social and psychological reality. Furthermore, he developed within the context of psychoanalytic theory a concept of man that suggests a systematic ground for coping with the deleterious effects of rapid and continuous social change.

ERIKSON'S BASIC CONCEPTS

Before recounting Erikson's understanding of certain trends affecting the American character, I shall set forth some basic concepts that characterize all of his thinking. These concepts are present in one form or another throughout his writings—from the very earliest to the most recent.

First, it should be noted that Erikson's psychology is characterized by a double language. There is the organic language and metaphor of evolutionary biology and there is the language of freedom and existential meaning. This double language is not unique to the psychoanalytic psychology of Erikson. As Paul Ricoeur points out in *Freud and Philosophy*, and as Herbert Fingarette also states in *The Self in Transformation,* it can be found in the psychology of Freud himself.[10] It is clear, however, that Erikson sees man as free; yet at the same time, he sees this freedom operating in the context of certain broad regularities that characterize the adaptive struggle and the evolutionary process throughout the animal kingdom.

Second, Erikson sees his brand of psychoanalysis as a clinical discipline. But as a clinical discipline, it has a significant affinity with ethology—the study of animals in their natural setting. Of course, in this case, the animal that Erikson the clinician is studying is the human animal. This is why part of the vocabulary that Erikson uses to order his clinical observations about humans would also be applicable to a considerable extent to any creature in the animal kngdom. Note his use of the words *adaptation, ecological integrity, generativity, speciation, pseudospeciation,* and *average expectable environment.* These are terms that he gets directly or indirectly from the fields of evolutionary biology and the related field of ethology. Not only is there precedent for this kind of procedure in Freud and his renowned disciple Heinz Hartmann, but Erikson himself has been directly influenced by the writings of ethologist Konrad Lorenz, evolutionary theorists Sir Julian Huxley and C. H. Waddington, and biologist C. H. Stockard.

It is in the context of this general tendency of Erikson's to theorize about man with concepts that are applicable to the broader field of primate evolution that we can understand the specific meaning of some of Erikson's most important psychological concepts. For instance, the concept of the ego has a significant evolutionary-biological meaning for Erikson. It refers to the partially conscious and partially unconscious central organizing agency in man that strives to regulate the relationship between an individual and his environment.[11] Its task is to renew a sense of active mastery and wholeness between a person and his world when this relationship becomes disturbed. The ego performs this miracle of restoration through a process of playful and imaginative variation of actions and roles (the human counterpart to adaptation through trial and error at the animal level). Erikson interprets the phenomenon of play very much the way William James handled the idea of *will.* For James, *will* was the point at the human level at which the evolutionary process of random variation takes on the character of genuine freedom to entertain alternative courses of action.[12] Erikson develops much the same idea in connection with his concept of play; it is the ego's capacity for playfully envisioning new possibilities and synthesizing these possibilities with existing environmental conditions that enables man to gain a renewed sense of mastery and wholeness with his world.[13] The ego is the central organizing agency that assures the adaptation, survival, and continuity of both the individual and the race.

The ego has an epigenesis. Here Erikson extends his evolutionary and adaptive point of view on the ego by utilizing a concept borrowed from C. H. Stockard. The concept of epigenesis when applied to ego development means that the different functions of the ego develop from a "*ground plan*, and that out of this ground plan the *parts* arise, each part having its *time* of special ascendancy, until all parts have arisen to form a *functioning whole*."[14] As we will see later in this essay, Erikson believes that the various functions of the ego have their critical time of ascendancy; in order for a function to emerge at its proper time, it must be activated and supported by the proper environment—what Erikson sometimes calls (following Heinz Hartmann) an "average expectable environment."

In utilizing the epigenetic principle, Erikson is bringing together fragments of two philosophical worlds. He brings together an Aristotelian essentialism and a more modern evolutionary and adaptive point of view. The epigenetic principle suggests that man has certain potential (the "ground plan") and that in order to be healthy or strong (the two are synonymous for Erikson), this potential must be activated. This point of view is basically Aristotelian and essentialistic. On the other hand, in order for man to be healthy and strong, man must adapt to the contingencies of his environment. Erikson brings these two philosophical worlds together by suggesting that from the standpoint of the developing individual, his adaptive capacities are limited by the schedule of preexisting potentials that he brings to the demands of his environment. Man is not infinitely plastic. There must be a mutuality between man and his environment if creative adaptation is to occur. Obviously, Erikson's synthesis of these two philosophical worlds is not systematically worked out. Erikson's evolutionary-adaptive point of view is limited and sometimes dominated by the Aristotelianism of his epigenetic principle. With this combination, he cannot explain (in fact he simply ignores) how new epigenetic potential emerges in the course of man's evolutionary history. My point is, however, that this combination of philosophical worlds gives Erikson's evolutionary-adaptive point of view a conservative cast. Because of the structure of man's potential, there are certain psychological and social environments to which man individually and collectively cannot adapt. There are certain psychological and social environments that will undermine man's "health," his "strength," his "virtue," and his "spirit."[15] To Erikson *adaptation* means that man must not only adjust to the environment, but that the environment must become adjusted to fit the epigenetic potential in man. Life is always a matter of "mutual regulation and mutual activation" between man and his social and psychological world.

Finally, we must discuss Erikson's crucial concept of identity. The ego, as the central organizing agency of the human organism, is also reflexive. This means that it can gain a representation of itself and a representation of its successive identificatons with other people and their responses and appraisals. Erikson admits that his concept of identity has affinity with the interactional school of thought—that is, Mead's *self-concept* and Sullivan's *self-system*.[16] But Erikson, even more than these two thinkers, sees identity formation as a product of a true interaction between the individual and his social world. Identity is never merely something that parents give to their children or that past generations give to the present generation. Erikson defines identity as an "accrued confidence that one's ability to maintain inner sameness and continuity . . . is matched by the sameness and continuity of one's meaning for others."[17] This means that identity is a match between a child's own unique ways of maintaining continuity and sameness and those external identity-bestowing recognitions and perceptions of the community that surrounds him. It is important to note, however, that although identity is not totally dependent upon community response, it is greatly influenced by it. Further, Erikson's idea of identity suggests that some communities are so heterogeneous, disorganized, and rapidly changing that they cannot provide their children with the consistency of support and recognition necessary for the development of a viable identity. It is clear that Erikson believes that this is to considerable extent the case today with American society and with most of the Western world.

SOCIAL CHANGE, IDENTITY CONFUSION, AND TOTALISM

Erikson's psychology is a long commentary on the psychological effects of various kinds of rapid social change. Erikson studied several different types of change. Since Erikson himself was an immigrant, it is not surprising to learn that he was concerned with the psychological effects of immigration. Class mobility—upward and downward—has been another concern. The effects of what sociologists call *structural differentiation* (the process in advanced societies whereby primary and secondary institutions become increasingly more autonomous from one another) was a subject of interest to Erikson. Industrial and technologically induced change were also studied. And of course, Erikson was intensely concerned with the change brought about by human development itself, especially the transitions connected with adolescence, youth, and young adulthood.

In addition, Erikson was interested in the ideological and cultural sources of change. Erikson belived that the interplay between our Protestant heritage and the limitless space of the American frontier was an especially important source for our ideologies of change.

Erikson tends to see the United States as a country where change has been the very essence of its national experience. To this extent, America is the prototype of modernity. Modernization entails change and Americans not only experienced change, but they also came to believe in it; it was a part of their faith to believe that change was always for the good.

Erikson has argued that there is an ideological dichotomy emerging in American life, especially among the country's youth. It exists between what Erikson calls the "technological youth," who are dedicated to a vision of unlimited technological expansion, and the new "humanist" youth, who are concerned with all those who have been left out and left behind by the modern world.[18] Erikson believes that both of these groups are playing out aspects of an inherited tendency in the historic American identity. This is the tendency to stay "tentative" and to keep one's options open.[19] Both types of identity are products of the American social and cultural reality where change has been the primary experience and the primary value. Both the technological and the humanist youth are afraid of containment and limitation of either time, space, or material resources. For this reason, Erikson suspects that neither the technologist nor the humanist have the characterological strength to either understand or control the various ways in which ideologies of change undermine the possibility of healthy identities and injure the integrity of the cycle of the generations. Erikson's answer to the present situation is to develop a new character type (a type that I have come to call *generative man*) and to ground this character type on a new ideological resource—a resource that is nothing other than a philosophy of the evolutionary-adaptive cycle of the generations.

The key terms in Erikson's description of the American identity are *tentativeness, asceticism, identity confusion,* and *totalism.* The first two terms describe tendencies in the American character that were influenced respectively by the experience of the American frontier and certain Protestant (especially Calvinistic) strains in American religious life. A certain degree of identity confusion (rootlessness) and a capacity for sporadic fits of totalism are more recent manifestations of these earlier influences.

It is partially because Erikson himself was an immigrant that he is so sensitive to the importance of this experience for the American identity. All Americans (with the exception of the Indians) are immigrants or the sons and daughters of immigrants. All American families sometime in their past have suffered the dislocation of leaving old localities, identities, and fidelities and of comng to a new land where, both by necessity and by choice, they have had to forge new definitions of themselves. Erikson has had the experience of lost identity with a double measure. His Danish mother remarried a German Jewish pediatrician when Erikson was only three.[20] They withheld for years from the young Erik the knowledge that the Jewish doctor Homburger was not his real father. It is somewhat ironic that Erikson, the man so responsible for naming and describing the identity crisis, has had more than a little difficulty discovering his own. And it is of further interest to note that this same man, after a period of aimless wandering and a belated education as a lay analyst in Vienna, later immigrated to the United States, where the problem of identity seems to be everyone's problem.

America's immigrants came to its shores because of the unlimited space of its frontier. This experience of inexhaustible space engendered, according to Erikson, a series of dichotomies in the identity of these early Americans. Quite early in our history the new American learned to base his "final ego identity on some tentative combination of dynamic polarities such as migratory and sedentary, individualistic and standardized, competitive and co-operative, pious and freethinking, responsible and cynical, etc."[21] Erikson's thinking corresponds more with the work of Seymour Lipset, who stresses the continuity of the American character than it does with the thought of either Fromm or Riesman, who are constantly emphasizing its discontinuity.[22] Erikson believes that the varieties of American identity have played out one or more extremes of a polarity of characteristics, every expression of which assumes its opposite.

There is, however, a characteristic that synthesizes the various dichotomous elements. Erikson argues that the individual American generally feels secure in his identity "as long as he can preserve a certain element of deliberate *tentativeness* of autonomous choice."[23] It has always been the case, and to some extent still is, that the average American must feel that "the next step is up to him" and that whether he is "staying or going," settling or moving on, the decision is his and his options are basically open.

In emphasizing the influence of spatial configurations on the American identity, Erikson is simply applying to this special situation a method of investigation that he has also applied in his studies of identity formation in the Sioux,[24] the Yurok,[25] and the Russian.[26] In applying this approach to the American identity, Erikson's work shows an affinity with the emphasis upon spatial factors in historical and literary traditions of Frederick Jackson Turner, Sidney Mead, and R. W. B. Lewis.[27] What is unique, however, about Erikson's contribution is his introduction of the concept of *spatial configurations* into psychoanalytic conceptualization for illuminating the subtleties of the American identity.

But there is another element that Erikson has highlighted in the early American identity. This has to do with the *ascetic* element—the so-called Protestant factor that gave many Americans their capacity for initiative and discipline. Erikson gives more formal attention to Lutheranism than he does to Calvinism. Erikson sees the life and thought of Luther as depositing two important characterological tendencies that gradually found their way into American life. The first is a heightened sense of initiative and the second is an intense need to conform to the masters of the public realm. The heightened sense of initiative is a consequence of the way that the concept of justification by faith enabled Luther—and possibly his followers—to overcome his bad conscience and to recapture that deeper capacity for activity and initiative first granted by a mother's recognition.[28] The need to conform is a result of Luther's doctrine of vocation (Beruf), which led many Lutherans to believe that it was their sacred obligation to serve God by following the directions of secular authorities.[29]

Erikson nowhere presents a systematic discussion of the characterological consequences of the Calvinistic wing of the Protestant Reformation. In this, he varies considerably from other commentators such as Weber, Fromm, and Riesman. He simply assumes that the Calvinistic emphasis upon predestinaton helped intensify the twofold components of Protestant ascetism—an *initiative* that is throttled and directed toward dutiful *conformity*.

Hence, Erikson does indeed invoke the hypothesis of Protestant ascetism when he attempts to explain how the

American commitment to unrestricted mobility in the spaciousness of the American frontier gradually came to be directed toward a dutiful yet energetic conformity to the needs of America's expanding mercantile and industrial order. Erikson draws the following portrait. Erikson believes that, in a world of free mobility where people could always "move on," it was the early mothers of America who most often attempted to restrict the more exploratory tendencies of their adventurous husbands and sons. Generally desiring to remain settled herself, she would with a mother's intuitions raise her sons to flourish in the outside world—a world of open space and limitless possibilities. To educate her son for mobility and opportunity, she invoked the resources of her Protestant heritage—its doctrines of asceticism, disciplined work, and worldly profit as a sign of God's favor. When her son went out into the world, the mother knew he could be trusted, for she had indeed starved out of him his more sensual and rebellious tendencies, leaving him only with the desire to move, but to do so safely.

At a later time, when the frontier began to close, the son, if he could not move in space, could then exercise his mobility in the business and organizational world. To this extent, American business became the substitute for the American frontier. In this context, the mother's ascetic Puritanism began to resonate with the routinization of the machine. Hence, according to Erikson, this method of child rearing was effective in producng a type of person who had, simultaneously, a great deal of initiative and a high need to conform. This combination of initiative and conformity made him a superior "little boss."[31] Erikson acknowledges that these little bosses possessed certain virtues, but, on the whole, their contribution to their own children is deficient. As Erikson writes, "They present to the emancipated generations, to the generations with tentative identities, the ideal of an autocracy of irresponsibility."[32] Without a set of fundamental values, these little bosses place functioning, mobility, and appearances above all, and these are, according to Erikson, flimsy resources indeed upon which to build an identity for today's world.

So far we have been investigating how the two cultural resources of the vision of the frontier and Protestantism helped form in the American character its tentativeness and, later on, its urge toward conformity. These two qualities made Americans the great promoters of and adapters to the accelerated rate of social change in the twentieth century. Erikson, like Weber, tends to give priority to ideal or cultural factors as causes of social change. But he also emphasizes social factors. This vision of a better world through limitless technology and scientific expansion produces a variety of social systemic changes. These, in turn, have consequences for individual identity. Erikson gives the designation of *identity confusion* to the characterological consequences of such social systemic factors as technology, urbanization, increased structural differentiation, and mass media. Identity confusion (sometimes called *identity diffusion*) has both mild and extreme manifestations. In its milder forms, Erikson often refers to it as "rootlessness"; in its more extreme or pathological forms, Erikson refers to it as "aggravated," "malignant," or "acute" identity confusion.[33] Although it has its pathological forms, it is clear that Erikson believes that, on the whole, identity confusion in our day is a part of normal psychology.

Identity confusion refers to an inability of the ego to actively synthesize the various aspects of one's experience and self-image. It suggests a "split" in one's self- and role-definitions and a loss of center.[34] Identity confusion often takes an aggravated form in adolescents and young adults. Erikson believes that Biff in Arthur Miller's *Death of a Salesman* expresses this condition well when he says, "I just can't take hold, Mom, I can't take hold of some kind of a life."

Identity confusion is a special problem of youth. The simultaneous activation of their sexuality, demands for vocational decision, and opportunities for interpersonal intimacy and commitment, present young people with new experiences requiring synthesis into their identities.

But the full meaning of identity confusion can be understood only when one understands precisely the function and purpose of identity. From the broadest possible perspective, identity serves the purpose of defining one's relationship to the cycle of the generations. Identity gives definition to the great variety of biological, social, and cultural components that establish a person's place in the context of those who go before him and those who will come after him. In one place, Erikson lists some of these components that must be synthesized in order for a viable identity to emerge. He writes:

> From a genetic point of view, then, the process of identity formation emerges as an evolving configuration—a configuration which is gradually established by successve ego syntheses and resyntheses throughout childhood; it is a configuration gradually integrating *constitutional givens, idiosyncratic libidinal needs, favored capacities, significant identifications, effective defenses, successful sublimations, and consistent roles.*[35]

Any experience that inhibits the development of any of these components or that places upon them an ambiguous, contradictory, or poorly assimilated definition, will serve to undermine identity consolidation and help to create identity confusion.

Identity confusion in its mild forms is, to Erikson, an increasingly widespread characteristic of people at any age in the United States. It is, as I said earlier, a special problem of young people in American society. Especially is this true since tentativeness and conformity are America's characterological inheritances. I will list below several of the specific ways that our social system seems to induce identity confusion (especially among youth) and undermine the strength of the cycle of the generation. I can only mention a few of the many ways in which Erikson believes that identity confusion comes about.

Vocation is one important aspect of identity. Vocational self-definition is increasingly more difficult to achieve in American society.[36] In contrast to more primitive societies that offer a limited number of vocational possibilities, a rapidly expanding and changing technological society offers a plethora of vocational opportunities. The task of experimenting with the various possibilities and making a final choice, especially during a period of awakened sexual capacity in increased demands for interpersonal intimacy and commitment, presents many young people with a job of identity synthesis that is either beyond their ability, or that, if accomplished, is done incompletely and tenuously.

Erikson also believes that, along with this increase in vocational options, in America's highly differentiated and specialized society, young people are more isolated from the vocational sphere. They are less a meaningful part of the occupational pursuits of their fathers and mothers and more a separate subculture unto themselves. This means that patterns of interaction between youth and the adult world designed to incorporate and confirm youth into valid adult roles are seriously weakened and nearly absent. With these patterns of transmission and inclusion weakened, youth has a greater task of identity synthesis to accomplish, often under greater pressure and with fewer results.[37]

The identity confusion resulting from vocational pluralism and generational distance is further aggravated by the rate of technologically induced social change and by the general social and financial mobility that characterizes American society. The constant introduction of new knowledge and new techniques for doing things tends to undermine that sense of familiarity with the world that is fundamental to active identity synthesis. Technological change and social and financial mobility tend to erode the identity gains of lost or forgotten traditions; people can become confused in their self-definition by striving to become something new, while either forgetting or repudiating what they once were.[38]

Mass communications have effects on the ego's capacity to synthesize identity. Although, as Marshall McLuhan has suggested, mass communications (especially television) can offer modern man a more universal identity and a more immediate sense of participation in the affairs of the world,[39] Erikson calls attention to the possibility that they flood the ego with a kaleidoscope of undigested images. These ephemeral images can threaten unstable identities with attractive yet unsubstantial possibilities for identity experimentation.

Although Erikson believes that identity confusion does take on pathological manifestations in certain instances of acute adolescent identity crisis, on the whole the phenomenon about which he is speaking falls within the category of normal behavior in American society. The symptoms of identity confusion are vague and difficult to discern. It is clear that Erikson finds the most revealing signs of identity confusion in the loss of vitality in the ethics of care that must permeate the cycle of the generations—a loss that has manifested itself in broken marriages, abandoned children, and a general decline in the sense of fidelity between the young and the old.

RESOURCES FOR IDENTITY: GENERATIVE MAN

As I indicated earlier in this essay, Erikson not only asks the question, What kind of people are we becoming? He also asks and attempts to answer the question, What kind of people should we become? His thought has both descriptive and normative dimensions to it.

When seen as a whole, Erikson's thought has distinctively Weberian overtones; he strongly emphasizes the importance of ideal factors (cultural visions and ideologies) for the formation of identity. Erikson believes that people—especially adolescents—need commanding ideals and ideas by which to live in order to build an identity. Erikson frequently uses the word *ideology* to refer to the cluster of ideas, visions, and images from which a people gain their common identity. Erikson defines *ideology* as "'a way of life,' or what Germans call a *Weltanschauung*, a world-view which is consonant with existing theory, available knowledge, and common sense, and yet is significantly more: a utopian outlook, a cosmic mood, or a doctrinal logic, all shared as self-evident beyond any need for demonstration."[40] The importance of this and other definitions of *ideology* that Erikson offers is the way in which they combine an emphasis on a) current states of scientific knowledge, "existing theory, available knowledge," and

b) "common sense," or what he refers to in other passages as the "past" or "cultural traditions." By *existing theory* and *available states of knowledge*, it is clear that Erikson has in mind that body of knowledge associated with the adaptive-evolutionary point of view in biology and psychology. Throughout Erikson's writings, one can tell that for him this is the most commanding intellectual and scientific perspective in the modern world. The ideology that Erikson is proposing as a resource for the modern identity is one that will constitute a dialectic between adaptive-evolutionary perspectives on man and various cultural traditions that are regnant in contemporary society. In effect, this means that Erikson believes that the modern identity must be built on ideology derived from both understanding and evaluating each man's cultural tradition from the perspective of its adaptive-evolutionary significance.

We can best comprehend the intricacies of Erikson's thought on the resources for modern man's identity in the brief space remaining if we state in outline form the major structure of his vision.

(1) Identity must be grounded on the schedule of developmental emergences that characterize the cycle of the generations. As is well known, Erikson has an elaborate system for describing the major stages of human development. Over the years, he has discussed these stages from several different perspectives. He has discussed his famous eight stages of man from the perspective of the instinctual or epigenetic potentials involved, their characteristic psychosocial modalities and nuclear conflicts,[41] the accrued virtues or strengths that follow the successful resolution of these conflicts,[42] the major social institutions that correlate with the tasks of each stage, the moral significance of each stage,[43] and, finally, the pattern of social ritual that must be present for each stage to be successfully consolidated.[44] Throughout Erikson's entire set of writings is the implicit idea that it is the structure of these developments themselves—understood from the perspective of what they contribute to the evolutionary strength of the interlocking cycle of the generations—that must provide the foundation for the basic identity of modern man.

This is sometimes difficult to see in Erikson. He is constantly analyzing how certain cultural and social factors provide the ideological source for a people's identity. He is constantly looking at such cultural phenomena as the theology of the Protestant Reformation, the early American vision of an inexhaustible frontier, and the ideologies surrounding industrialization and technology in an effort to assess their relative strengths and weaknesses as sources for the formation of identity. In the process, Erikson is implicitly suggesting that in a time of cultural pluralism and ideological conflict, the structure of man's epigenetic development will itself constitute the chief source for modern man's identity.

(2) The ideological potential of man's epigenetic schedule of development can be best seen when these developments are viewed from the perspective of the adult stage of *generativity* and the accompanying virtue of *care*. Assuming some familiarity with Erikson's developmental stages on the part of the reader, a brief listing of the stages, nuclear conflicts, and virtues will be sufficient background for a more detailed discussion of generativity and care. For each of the eight stages of life, Erikson believes that there is a basic psychosocial crisis or *nuclear conflict*. For infancy, there is the conflict between trust and mistrust; for early childhood, the conflict between autonomy and shame (doubt); for the play age, there is the crisis of initiative versus guilt; for the school age (latency), there is the conflict of industry versus inferiority; for adolescence, the conflict of identity versus identity confusion; for young adulthood, the crisis of intimacy versus isolation; for adulthood, the conflict of generativity versus self-absorption; and for the mature age, the crisis of integrity versus disgust and despair.[45]

If the nuclear conflicts of each stage have a favorable resolution, an ego strength, or *virtue*, will emerge. Erikson uses the word *virtue* to refer to that "active" and "spirited" quality that is the very essence of what psychologists call *ego strength*.[46] A virtue is always a matter of synthesis; it is the result of a favorable synthesis out of the positive and negative dimensions of life's developmental crises and nuclear conflicts. These active syntheses, if successful, leave deposits that constitute adaptive strengths not only for the individual in question but for the larger cycle of the generations of which he is a part. The list of virtues in the order of the eight stages of life to which they correspond are as follows: hope, will, purpose, competence, fidelity, love, care, and wisdom.

Before we make some additional remarks about the central adult stage of generativity and the virtue of care, a few more clarifications are in order. First, insofar as man's epigenetic development is rooted in a ground plan that prescribes an optimal time of emergence for each stage and virtue, it is possible to say that Erikson has, in fact, reversed the logic of the traditional psychoanalytic theory of development. In traditional psychoanalytic theory, the beginning of development determines the later stages; in fact, later stages of development are sublimations of the earliest stages. Not so for Erikson. As he sees it, later stages of development have equal primordiality with early stages. For instance, there are biological foundations to the stages of generativity and care that are just as fundamental as the biological foundations of the earlier stage of trust and hope or of autonomy and will. In fact, according to the logic of Erikson's epigenetic principle, the *telos* of the early stages of development is actually determined by the later stages. This means that, since generativity and care are the central stage and virtue, respectively, of adulthood, that, seen from a normative perspective, all the earlier stages and virtues partially receive their meaning from what they contribute to the later stage of generativity and to the virtue of care. Seen from this perspective, Erikson's thought, as was mentioned earlier, is Aristotelian through and through; the meaning and goal of man is determined not by the beginning but by the end. The end of man is *care*, and care as a virtue is a result of both a biological need and an act, that is, an intended synthesis.

(3) Erikson sees generativity and care as a fundamental need of man that, as all needs, can be activated or frustrated by one's average expectable environment. Erikson defines generativity as "primarily the concern in establishing and

guiding the next generation."[47] Erikson cautions us throughout his writing not to identify generativity with the literal biological act of procreation, although, of course, in a general sense it must include this. But Erikson's point is, however, that stronger than the need to literally procreate is the more fundamental need to contribute through one's deeds to the establishment and guidance of the next generation. Some people are generative without being procreative.

The virtue that emerges when generativity is dominant over stagnation and self-absorption is *care*. "Care is the widening concern for what has been generated by love, necessity, or accident; it overcomes the ambivalence adhering to irreversible obligation."[48] Although such a definition has idealistic overtones, it is important to realize that it is neither philosophy nor religion, but rather ethology, upon which Erikson is grounding his concept. Man has a biological need to care. In one place he writes: "Evolution has made man a teaching as well as a learning animal, for dependency and maturity are reciprocal: mature man *needs to be needed*, and maturity is guided by the nature of that which must be cared for."[49] In another place, he writes: "Care is a quality essential for psychosocial evolution, for we are the teaching species. Animals, too, instinctively encourage in their young what is ready for release. . . . All of this is necessary to complete in man the analogy to the basic, ethological situation between parent animal and young animal. . . . Once we have grasped this interlocking of the human life stages, we understand that adult man is so constituted as to need to be needed."[50]

It is because Erikson views man from the perspective of the broader framework of ethology and evolutionary biology that he can feel justified in saying such things as "man *needs* to teach" and that man has a "teaching passion." This is not an unusual idea from the perspective of such outstanding scientists as Theodosius Dobzhansky. Dobzhansky himself believes that man has encoded within his gene structure a deep and unconscious need to generate and maintain the cycle of the generations.[51] What Erikson has contributed is the additional idea that this impulse is also the grounds for broader acts of cultural generativity and care. For true generativity to exist, this teaching and caring passion must extend to whatever "man generates and leaves behind, creates and produces (or helps to produce)."[52]

Although generativity and care have behind them, according to Erikson, their own instinctive and biological energies and structures, it must not be thought that these qualities of the adult stage of life are a product of automatic biological unfolding. On the contrary, Erikson sees their emergence as, in part, a matter of synthesis on the part of the central organizing agency called the ego. Erikson sees man's instinctive structures as pluralistic and highly plastic. Although this is similar to Freud's early position, his later thought tended to narrow man's instinctual life to the two broad categories of sex and destruction. Erikson is more like William James in his theory of the instincts.[53] He believes that man is rich in instinctive structures and tendencies; the epigenetic developmentals all have instinctive foundations. But in man, instinctive tendencies are unstable and plastic and need to be activated, guided, and consolidated by the external environment and induced by one's own capacity for decision and choice. Generativity is the result of an active synthesis and hierarchical ordering of a large number of life experiences and instinctive tendencies. Even if generativity and care are the end and goal of biological development, in man these modes of existence must be chosen and stabilized with ideological reinforcement.

(4) The full meaning of generativity and care as the center of identity for adults can only be understood when these qualities are seen in relationship to the other epigenetic potentials. For example, the content of generativity and care is partially supplied by the other developmentals. This is what Erikson means when he says that "maturity is guided by the nature of that which must be cared for." This quotation points to the interlocking character of Erikson's understanding of the cycle of the generations. Care does not know how to care until it determines the needs (for Erikson this means the developmental needs) of that which is cared for. Hence the structure of human development constitutes the ethical guidelines for adult generativity. Erikson is telling us that developmental psychology, broadly

conceived, must supply modern man with substantive guidelines for his ethics. Developmental psychology provides the content of that grand and elusive word—*love.* Loving or caring for another person should be guided by the objective requirements of his schedule of development. Love or care strives to provide the average expectable environment necessary for the activation of the other's developmental potential. Of course, to say this does not necessitate arguing that Erikson's characterization of man's developmental stages is correct or that it is beyond refinement. The point being made is more abstract; I am simply arguing that Erikson has provided both ethics and characterology with a novel concept by saying that the structure of human development itself constitutes a fundamental guideline for mature adult action.

But both Erikson and psychoanalysis, in general, tend to hold one's capacity to know oneself and one's capacity to know others in dialectical relationship. And this gets to the heart of Erikson's contributions to characterology and identity. In order for a person to be able to sense subjectively the developmental need of the other, he must to a considerable extent have rightly ordered and be somewhat aware of his own schedule of development. For example, mature generativity and care must be supported at the most primitive levels by an archaic sense of *basic trust* and *hope* achieved sometime during the first months of life. Furthermore, for adult generativity and care to have the ability for independent action, they must be grounded on deep-seated capacities for *autonomy* and *initiative* and their accompanying virtues of *will* and *purpose.*[54] The point is, however, that adult generativity and care are built upon an extensive and hierarchically organized foundation of ego strengths that have been organized into successively higher levels of the personality. Because the generative man can experience his own childhood capacity for trust and hope, he can act to encourage it in the other—perhaps his own or another's child. Because he can experience and accept his own earliest strivings for autonomy and initiative without being overcome by inevitable accompaniments of shame and guilt, he can so act as to activate these qualities in others.

(5) Erikson's concepts of generativity and care state in evolutionary-biological and developmental terms an ideology that has certain similarities to the Judeo-Christian and early Reformation idea that the purpose or calling (Beruf) of life is to serve mankind or, in Eriksonian terms, the cycle of the generations. Erikson's concept of generativity resurrects a basically ascetic vision of the meaning of life. The image of generative man implicit in Erikson's writings shifts the ideological commitments of psychoanalysis away from the Stoic concept of the goal of life as prudent hedonism à la Freud and Philip Rieff or the idea of life as Dionysian ecstasy à la Norman Brown or Wilhelm Reich. Although Erikson's image of generative man introduces back into psychoanalysis a basically ascetic view of life, it has none of the dualistic elements of earlier Gnostic and Manichean images of man or the more repressive and highly inhibitory views of man connected with the Protestant ethic. There is no dualism in Erikson because there is no sense in which the body and its needs are devalued; in fact, more than is even the case with orthodox Freudianism, the body and its schedule of developmentals are seen as positive resources for creative adaptation. In addition, Erikson's asceticism is different from that of the Protestant ethic. The Protestant man inhibited immediate pleasures and satisfactions for the sake of a lifetime of rationalized productivity. Generative man, although he hierarchically orders his various needs and satisfactions under his basic project of care, sees all of his basic needs and biological developmentals as contributing to his adult capacity for generativity and care. In addition, generativity and care are themselves biologically grounded and, when activated, grant man a basic kind of intrinsic satisfaction.

Yet, in spite of all of this celebration of the body in Erikson, his view of man is basically ascetic. Even though care has its own instinctive grounding, man is instinctually confused and for generativity to reign supreme in the adult person, it must be environmentally activated and individually chosen and confirmed. What Erikson in one place says about Gandhi's concept of Satyagraha fits equally as well with his philosophy of generative man—it is a "cure" for man's "instinctual complexity."[55]

And finally, Erikson's vision of generative man must never be given an overly pietistic and individualistic reading. Generativity and care are not practiced exclusively for Erikson in one-to-one or face-to-face situations. Erikson speaks of a "generalized generativity of institutions."[56] Institutions must be ordered so as to activate and confirm the individual and collective ego strengths (virtues) of a people. In order for man to fulfill his generative needs, he must expend a great deal of his energy toward the ordering of the public institutional world so that the developmental integrity of the entire cycle of the generations can be maintained and enhanced.

Erikson's reinterpretation of psychoanalysis has put it well within what Max Weber so adequately characterized as the Western tradition of *inner worldly asceticism*. There is throughout his writings an emphasis upon the maintenance and enrichment of life (the cycle of the generations) in this world through an ascetic activeness of the ego. In addition, through his interpretations of Luther and the Judeo-Christian elements in Gandhi's philosophy, he has given us something of a synthesis between his reconstructed psychoanalysis and selected elements in the Western religious tradition. This illustrates the way he has unobtrusively attempted to evolve a usable ideology for Western man by dialectically relating his evolutionary biology and developmental psychology to selected aspects of our cultural traditions. Erikson never suggests that evolutionary theory or developmental psychology alone are sufficient for the reconstruction of Western identity. Rather, he proposes—although never explicitly—that our ideologies be based on a reinterpretation of our religious and cultural traditions, in light of the emerging disciplines of evolutionary theory and developmental psychology exemplified by his brand of psychoanalysis.

If inner worldly asceticism is an accurate characterization of the central thrust of Erikson's psychology, it stands in considerable contrast to certain other major trends in contemporary psychology. As I have already indicated, it differs from the hedonic Stoicism of Freud and Philip Rieff and the Dionysian romanticism of Norman Brown and his followers. Brown's vision of psychoanalysis, as well as the instinctual utopianism of a good portion of the human potential movement (à la Carl Rogers, Fritz Perls, and William Schutz), can be accurately characterized in Weberian terms as contemporary forms of inner worldly mysticism. Brown and the human potential movement differ from Erikson in their common emphasis upon the free and unstressful harmony between man and his social and natural environment once the restraining influence of social institutions are removed. On the other hand, Erikson's emphasis upon generativity and care as a partial result of an active synthesis by the ego puts him close to the ascetic emphasis implicit in many schools of existentialism. There is in Erikson, as there is in Kierkegaard and Sartre, an emphasis upon the importance of decision and risk. But Erikson differs from all existentialists because of his emphasis upon life's developmental structures and regularities, in the context of which decisions must be made and by which, to a considerable extent, decisions must be guided.

Finally, Erikson's asceticism has much in common, I believe, with William James's almost forgotten ideal of the *strenuous life*. The strenuous life is, for James, basically a life of engaged concern. It is the opposite of the attitude of "I don't care."[57] John Wild has been successful, I believe, in demonstrating the existential overtones in James's concept.[58] Both James and Erikson differ, however, from the asceticism of the traditional Protestant ethic and its inhibition of vital enjoyments. Although James believes that reason and perception must guide what he sometimes calls the "passional" nature of man, he shares with Erikson a positive appreciation of its role in the strenuous life. In one place he writes that "the capacity for the strenuous mood probably lies slumbering in every man, but it has more difficulty in some than in others in waking up."[59] In another place he writes that "the capacity for the strenuous mood lies . . . deep down among our natural human possibilities."[60] But regardless of the natural tendencies toward it that James believes to exist in man, the strenuous life must be awakened by challenging circumstances and great cultural ideals. And finally, it must be chosen. Both James and Erikson are too much aware of the ambiguous and unpredictable aspects of life and history to give much support to the idea that through simple relaxation or the spontaneous unfolding of life's potentials that men will automatically harmonize with each other and with their environments. Both generativity and the strenuous mood are, finally, results of synthesis, an active pulling together by the self of one's varied impulses and experiences into a structured sense of care and concern for the world and its future. This is their positive vision of what man should be in order to live with the increasingly more fragmentary, changing, and disparate aspects of modernity. More specifically in the case of Erikson, generativity, guided by the developmental structure of the cycle of the generations, is the measure and norm by which modernity's transactions should be both evaluated and, in some cases, refused. Generativity is Erikson's antidote to the confusion of rapid social change.

NOTES

1. See Don Browning, *Generative Man* (Philadelphia: Westminster Press, 1973), and idem, "Generative Man and the Future of Sexuality," *Criterion* (Winter 1971): 17–22.

2. Max Weber, *The Protestant Ethic and The Spirit of Capitalism* (New York: Charles Scribner's Sons, 1958).

3. Ibid., pp. 79–92.

4. Ibid., pp. 98–127.

5. Erich Fromm, *Man For Himself* (New York: Rinehart & Co., 1947), pp. 62–82.

6. Erich Fromm, *The Sane Society* (New York: Rinehart & Co., 1953), p. 166.

7. David Riesman, *The Lonely Crowd* (New Haven: Yale University Press, 1961).
8. Ibid., pp. 22–23.
9. Alvin Toffler, *Future Shock* (New York: Bantam Books, 1971).
10. Paul Ricoeur, *Freud and Philosophy* (New Haven: Yale University Press, 1970); Herbert Fingarette. *The Self in Transformation* (New York; Harper & Row, 1963).
11. Erik H. Erikson, *Identity: Youth and Crisis* (New York: W. W. Norton & Co., 1968), p. 211.
12. William James, *The Will to Believe* (New York: Dover Publications, 1956), pp. 1–31, 111–44, and Philip Wiener, *Evolution and the Founders of Pragmatism* (Cambridge: Harvard University Press, 1949), p. 104.
13. Erikson develops his thought on the relation of play and the ego in several places. See Erik H. Erikson, *Childhood and Society* (New York: W. W. Norton & Co., 1963), pp. 209-38, and idem, "Play And Actuality," in *Play and Development*, ed. Maria W. Piers (New York: W. W. Norton & Co., 1972), pp. 127–68.
14. Erik H. Erikson, *Identity and the Life Cycle: Selected Papers* Psychological Issues, vol. 1, no. 1 (New York: International Universities Press, 1959) p. 52.
15. All of these concepts are roughly equivalent for Erikson. See his discussion of the developmental stages and the concept of virtue in Erik H. Erikson, *Insight and Responsibility* (New York: W. W. Norton & Co., 1964), pp. 111–57.
16. Erikson, *Identity and the Life Cycle,* p. 147.
17. Ibid., p. 89.
18. Erikson, *Identity: Youth and Crisis,* p. 36.
19. Erikson, *Childhood and Society,* p. 286.
20. Erik H. Erikson, "Autobiographic Notes on the Identity Crisis," *Daedalus* 99, no. 4 (Fall 1970): 742; see also Robert Coles, *Erik Erikson: The Growth of His Work* (Boston: Little, Brown and Co., 1970), p. 13.
21. Erikson, *Childhood and Society,* p. 286.
22. Seymour Lipset, *The First New Nation* (New York: Doubleday & Co., 1967), pp. 115–58.
23. Erikson, *Childhood and Society,* p. 286. Emphasis added.
24. Ibid., pp. 114–65.
25. Ibid., pp. 166–86.
26. Ibid., pp. 359–402.
27. Frederick Jackson Turner, *The Frontier in American History* (New York: H. Holt & Co., 1920); Sidney Mead, *The Lively Experiment* (New York: Harper & Row, 1963); and R. W. B. Lewis, *The American Adam* (Chicago: University of Chicago Press, 1955).
28. Erik H. Erikson, *Young Man Luther: A Study in Psychoanalysis and History* (New York: W. W. Norton & Co., 1962), p. 208.
29. Ibid., pp. 238–39. It might be pointed out that Erikson's interpretation of the Protestant Reformation varies significantly from other recent psychoanalytic interpretations, namely, Fromm's and Norman Brown's.
30. Erikson, *Childhood and Society,* pp. 291–97.

31. Ibid., p. 322.

32. Ibid.

33. Erikson, *Identity and the Life Cycle*, p. 122; see also idem, *Identity: Youth and Crisis*, p. 212.

34. See the following discussions of identity confusion: Erikson, *Identity and the Life Cycle*, pp. 88-95, 122-47, and idem, *Identity: Youth and Crisis*, p. 212.

35. Erikson, *Identity and the Life Cycle*, p. 116.

36. Erikson, *Identity: Youth and Crisis*, p. 132.

37. Ibid., p. 235; see also Erik H. Erikson, "Ontogeny of Ritualization," *Psychoanalysis: A General Psychology*, ed. R. M. Lowenstein (New York: International Universities Press, 1966), p. 612.

38. Erikson, "Autobiographic Notes," p. 743.

39. Marshall McLuhan, *Understanding Media: The Extensions of Man* (New York: McGraw-Hill, 1964).

40. Erikson, *Young Man Luther*, p. 41.

41. For a diagram of the instinctual, psychosocial, and institutional components of each stage, see Erikson, *Identity and the Life Cycle*, p. 166.

42. Erikson, *Insight and Responsibility*, pp. 111-57.

43. Erik H. Erikson, "Reflections on the Dissent of Contemporary Youth," *Daedalus* (Winter 1970): 155-74.

44. Erikson, "Ontogeny of Ritualization," pp. 601-21.

45. Erikson, *Childhood and Society*, pp. 247-74, and idem, *Identity: Youth and Crisis*, pp. 91-141.

46. Erikson, *Insight and Responsibility*, p. 113.

47. Erikson, *Identity: Youth and Crisis*, p. 138.

48. Erikson, *Insight and Responsibility*, p. 131.

49. Erikson, *Identity: Youth and Crisis*, p. 138. Emphasis added.

50. Erikson, *Insight and Responsibility*, p. 131.

51. Theodosius Dobzhansky, *The Biology of Ultimate Concern* (New York: New American Library, 1967), pp. 87-88.

52. Erikson, *Insight and Responsibility*, p. 131.

53. William James, *Psychology: The Briefer Course* (New York: Harper Torchbooks, 1961), pp. 258-81.

54. For a fuller exemplification of the way in which the earlier developmentals are related to mature adulthood, see Browning, *Generative Man*, pp. 179-97.

55. Erikson, *Gandhi's Truth: On the Origins of Militant Nonviolence* (New York: W. W. Norton & Co., 1969), p. 418.

56. Erikson, "Ontogeny of Ritualization," p. 619.

57. James, *The Will to Believe*, p. 212.

58. John Wild, *The Radical Empiricism of William James* (New York: Doubleday & Co., 1970).

59. James, *The Will to Believe*, p. 211.

60. Ibid., p. 213.

Notes on Contributors

ARJUN APPADURAI teaches at the University of Pennsylvania, where he is assistant professor of Anthropology and South Asian Studies. He received his doctorate from the Committee on Social Thought at the University of Chicago and was previously a Visiting Scholar at the Center for the Study of World Religions at Harvard University. His special field of interest is the anthropology of religion and, more specifically, involves the study of South Indian religious institutions.

HEINRICH BORNKAMM is well known, both in European and in English-speaking scholarly circles, for his many books on the Reformation and on Luther. He held professorships at several German universities and since 1948 served as professor of Church History at the University of Heidelberg. Three of his books have been translated into English: *Luther's World of Thought*, *The Heart of the Reformation Faith*, and *Luther's Doctrine of the Two Kingdoms in the Context of His Theology*. Professor Bornkamm died in January 1977.

DON BROWNING is professor of Religion and Psychological Studies at the Divinity School of the University of Chicago. He is the author of *Atonement and Psychotherapy*, *Generative Man: Psychoanalytic Perspectives*, *The Moral Context of Pastoral Care*, and a forthcoming volume entitled *Pluralism and Personality: William James and Some Contemporary Cultures of Psychology*.

DONALD CAPPS holds advanced degrees from Yale University (B.D., S.T.M.) and the University of Chicago (Ph.D.) and is currently associate professor of Pastoral Care and Psychology of Religion at the Graduate Seminary, Phillips University, Oklahoma. He is coeditor of *The Religious Personality*, *Psychology of Religion: A Guide to Information Sources*, *The Biographical Process: Studies in the History and Psychology of Religion*, and *Encounter with Erikson: Historical Interpretation and Religious Biography*.

MARK U. EDWARDS, JR., is the author of *Luther and the False Brethren*, coeditor and cotranslator of Bernd Moeller, *Imperial Cities and the Reformation*, and a regular contributor to the *Literaturbericht* of the *Archiv für Reformationsgeschichte*. Currently an assistant professor of History at Wellesley College, he received his doctorate in history from Stanford University and spent three years as a Junior Fellow in the University of Michigan Society of Fellows.

PETER HOMANS is associate professor of Religion and Psychological Studies at the University of Chicago. He received his A.B. from Princeton University and his Ph.D. from the University of Chicago. He served as editor and contributor to *The Dialogue between Theology and Psychology* and is the author of *Theology after Freud: An Interpretive Inquiry*. He has also published articles on the psychology of popular culture and on the sociology of psychology.

WAUD H. KRACKE is associate professor of Anthropology at the University of Illinois at Chicago Circle. He received his doctorate in anthropology from the University of Chicago, and is a graduate of the research training program of the Chicago Institute for Psychoanalysis. He is the author of a forthcoming book, *Force and Persuasion: Psychological and Social Dimensions of Leadership in an Amazonian Society*, based on his field research with a group of Brazilian Indians. His other writings include a forthcoming psychoanalytic study of the dreams of these Indians, as well as various articles on their social structure.